Fashion Accessories

JOHN PEACOCK

Fashion Accessories

THE COMPLETE 20TH CENTURY SOURCEBOOK

WITH 2000 FULL-COLOUR ILLUSTRATIONS

Thames & Hudson

For Jamie Camplin

First published in the United Kingdom in 2000 by
Thames & Hudson Ltd, 181A High Holborn,
London WC1V 7QX

British Library Cataloguing-in-Publication Data
A catalogue record for this book is available
from the British Library

ISBN 0-500-51027-X

Printed in Hong Kong by H & Y Printing Limited

Contents

Introduction

Fashion Accessories illustrates the evolution of women's and men's accessories during the twentieth century. It focuses on fashionable items, that is to say, styles adopted by the majority which are sufficiently distinctive, despite individual differences, to be recognizable as belonging to a particular time.

The collection is divided into seven periods. Each begins with 'the complete look', a page showing stylishly dressed figures with complementing accessories for the opening year of the period. This is followed by pages focusing on the accessories themselves. Two pages then show the whole period 'at a glance', and the section ends with a page devoted again to 'the complete look', but this time showing a group of accessorized figures from across the entire period.

Following the main illustrations in each section are eight pages of schematic drawings accompanied by detailed descriptions of every accessory. At the end of the book, eight pages of line drawings illustrate the main accessories 'at a glance' and demonstrate the evolution and major development trends from 1900 to 1999.

Fashion Accessories covers both women's and men's items, but it will become clear that developments and changes in women's fashion were far more numerous and more major than those in menswear, which therefore requires fewer examples.

Certain accessories appear consistently throughout the century, shoes being the most obvious example. Others come and go: parasols turn up only in the early years; umbrellas feature strongly in the early 1950s, women's boots from the mid-1950s and men's shoulder bags from the 1970s. A date is given for each accessory, except for early in the century, when many styles, especially in menswear, carried over from the late nineteenth century and continued for some years with little alteration.

For the first half of the twentieth century, hats were a staple of the well-dressed woman's wardrobe. This period saw a huge range of shapes, colours, fabrics, textures and trimmings. Hats of 1900 were decorated with feathers, bird's wings, fruit, flowers and ribbons. The cloche of the 1920s was followed in the thirties by wider-brimmed hats. During World War II in France and the UK, headwear was made from anything that came to hand – plaited silk neckties, old felt trilbies, even paper – and turbans were worn for both day and evening. The 1950s saw tiny half-hats covered in silk flower petals or *ombré* feathers. Coloured plastic straw hats and large butchers'-boy caps were popular in the 1960s. By the 1970s hat styles were usually restricted to large, unstructured straw or felt fedoras or knitted, pull-on hats.

Handbags have a relatively recent history: the framed leather bag did not appear until the second half of the nineteenth century. Bags have most often been made from leather, snakeskin, lizardskin and the like, but more exotic materials have also been used, among them embroidered velvet, bead-embroidered silk, linked silver chains and leather-look plastic. Since bags do not need to fit any part of the body, they have come in all shapes and sizes: small silk bags embroidered with pearls and beads in the 1920s; wafer-thin embossed leather clutch bags in the 1930s; outsized coloured plastic leather-look patent bags in the 1960s and in recent years shoulder bags and backpacks for both men and women.

Gloves enjoyed their hour of glory in the twenties and thirties, made from leather, felt, silk or cloth, or crocheted in silk or cotton. Pretty, frilled cuffs eventually grew into flared gauntlet cuffs and by the late thirties reached halfway up the arm. In the fifties see-through nylon gloves with ruched and buttoned decoration were popular, as, in the eighties, were fine leather 'driving gloves' with openwork decoration.

Scarves, stoles and shawls of every variety, including fox furs, curled feather boas, 1940s scarf squares worn as turbans and 1970s long unisex knitted wool scarves can all be found here, as can jewelry – one of fashion's essential accessories – which occupies one page in each section.

Styles in women's footwear appear and reappear: boots from the early part of the century have been constantly reinvented; the pointed bar-strap shoes of the 1920s made a comeback in the 1950s with stiletto heels; and the platform soles of the late thirties and forties were reintroduced in exaggerated form in the 1970s.

Men's shoes, on the contrary, have altered little over the past one hundred years: the leather lace-up shoe of 1900, with toecap and brogue detail, is almost indistinguishable from any classic style of today. But certain changes have occurred: step-in shoes appeared in the 1940s, crepe soles and combined heels were adopted by some young men in the 1950s, pointed toes aped those of women in the late 1950s, the 1960s brought in elastic-sided chelsea boots with high, shaped, stacked heels and pointed toes reminiscent of those worn at the beginning of the century, and since the 1970s lace-up, topstitched, white canvas sports shoes with ridged rubber soles have become universally popular.

At the beginning of the century men's hats included a number of styles: the top hat, homburg, trilby, bowler and boater. These shapes would remain much the same for many years, with minor alterations. Since the 1960s, however, men, like women, have worn hats less and less, today reserving the top hat for weddings and covering their heads only for certain sports. For those men who do wear hats, the baseball cap has become the most common style.

The essential accessory for the well-dressed man is the necktie, still the chief means of enlivening that twentieth-century male uniform – the suit. The tie exists in an enormous range of fabrics, colours, patterns and textures, and fashion dictates the size of the knot and the width of the body.

Fashion history has recorded the names of many of those responsible for the most innovative accessory designs of the twentieth century: we know that Salvatore Ferragamo created the first wedge sole, Nathan Clark the first desert boot, 'Coco' Chanel the first quilted bag with gilt chain, and so on. These and other international designers and companies can all be found in the directory at the end of this book.

I have drawn chiefly from British, North American, French and Italian sources. These include contemporary magazines, periodical journals, brochures and catalogues, museum collections, original photographs and my own costume collection. A bibliography lists books that have been useful in compiling this survey and which may prove helpful to others.

1900

1900

1901

1901

1902

1903

1903

1904

1904

1905

1905

1906

1906

1906

1907

1907

1908

1908

1909

1909

1909

1910

1910

1911

1912

1912

1913

1900

1908

1905

1900–10

1901

1913

1913

1912

1913

1900–10

1909

1913

1902

1901

1900

1912

1913

Women's Bags and Purses 1900–1913

1900

1900

1901

1902

1902

1902

1903

1903

1903

1904

1905

1905

1905

1906

1907

1908

1910

1911

1911

1913

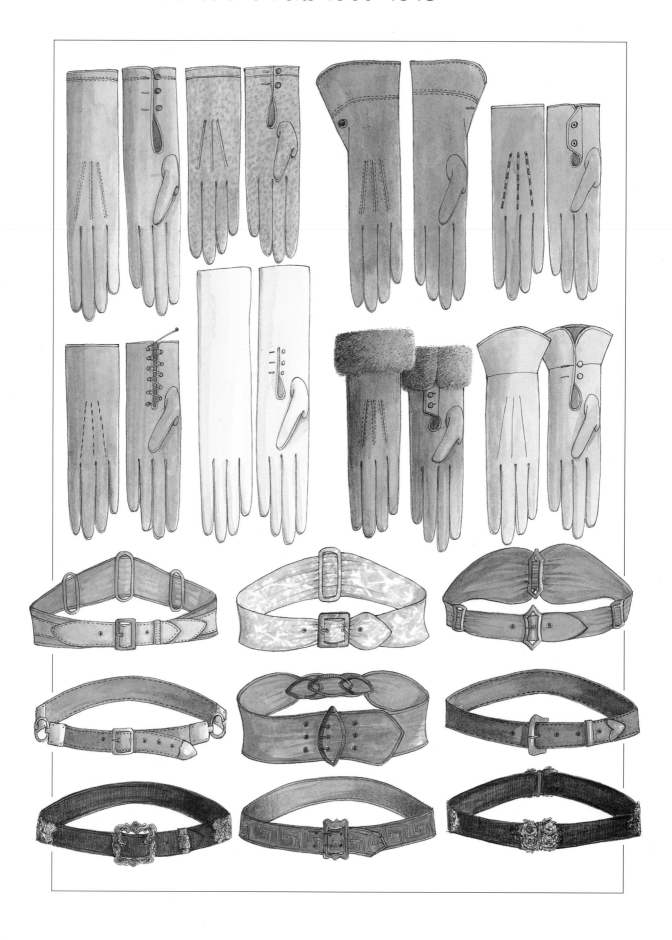

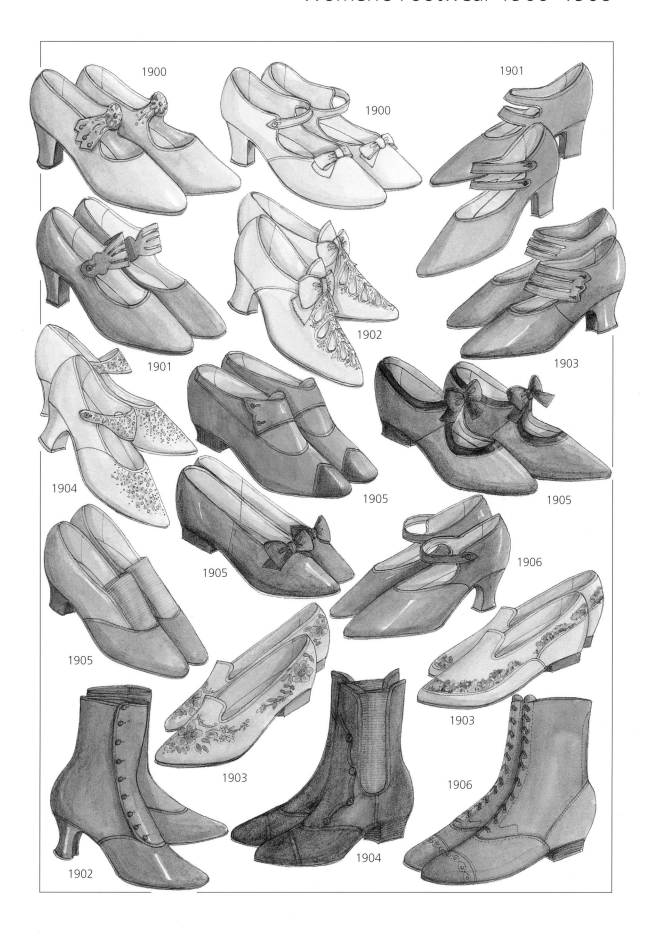

Women's Footwear 1907–1913

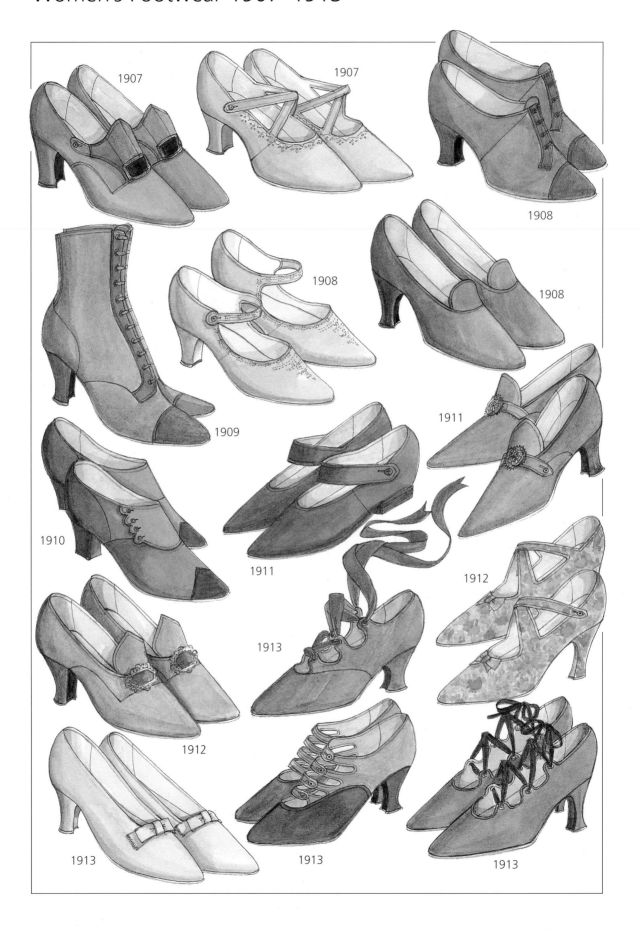

1907

1907

1908

1908

1908

1909

1910

1911

1911

1911

1912

1912

1913

1913

1913

1913

1913

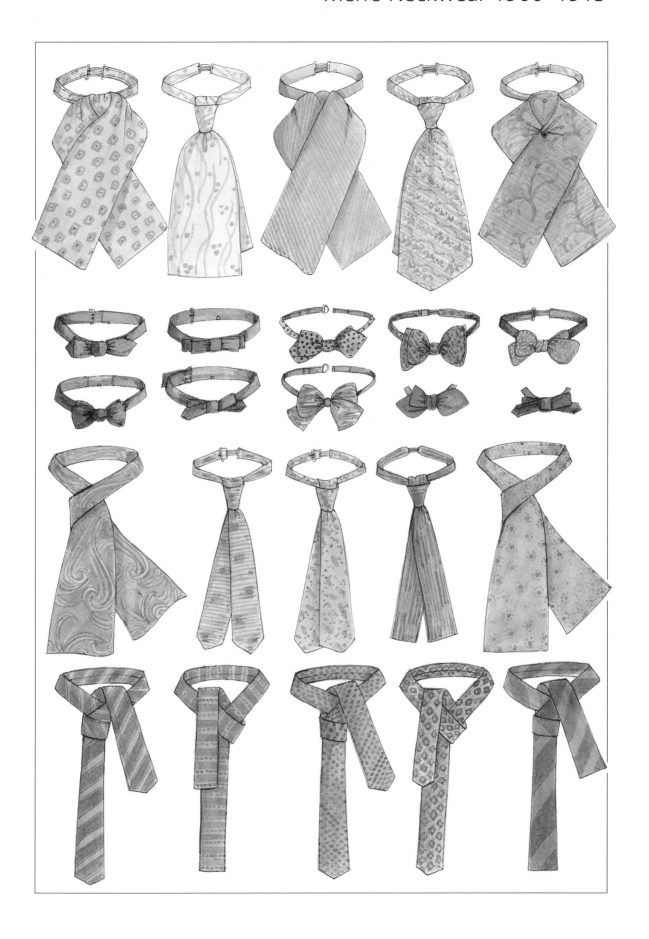

1900

1900

1909

1910

1913

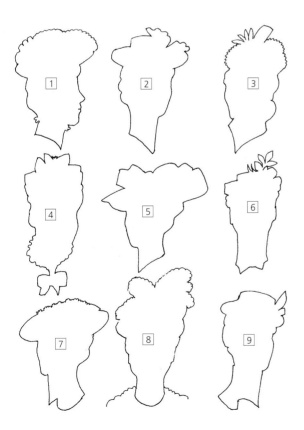

The Complete Look 1900

1 Lilac spotted silk afternoon dress, open jacket-effect bodice, bloused above deep waistband; full-length inset sleeves, gathered at elbow-level, tight to wrist; open flared overskirt; underskirt with train, lace and satin trimmings; silk-chiffon bloused underbodice with high stand collar. Natural-straw hat, upswept split brim, silk edging, trimmed with large cloth flowers under brim at one side and with coloured ostrich plumes over crown. Pearl drop earrings; matching three-strand necklace. Grey kid gloves. Patterned parasol, long stick with bird's-head handle. Grey leather boots, pointed toes, topstitched edges and detail. 2 Fitted single-breasted black wool coat, three-button fastening, high lapels, stitched cuffs. Single-breasted cloth waistcoat. Striped trousers. White shirt; spotted silk ascot scarf; pearl stick-pin. Grey silk top hat. Black leather boots, grey cloth uppers, side-front button fastenings. 3 Single-breasted brown wool-tweed jacket, four-button fastening, high lapels, flap pockets, narrow sleeves, button trim. Checked wool trousers. White shirt; three-colour striped silk necktie. Brown bowler hat, hard crown, curled brim. Kid gloves. Brown leather lace-up ankle-boots, pointed toes, stitched edges. 4 Green corded-silk dress, fitted bodice cut in pointed panels matching heads of three-quarter-length sleeves, black lace underbodice matching undersleeves gathered into deep self-fabric cuffs, shaped hip-yoke and wide flared front panel of ground-length skirt, back train. Brimless silk toque, trimmed with two-colour pleated rosettes, chiffon ruffles and drapery, cloth flowers on side-front and on top and a single coloured ostrich plume. Gold brooch worn on centre-front at base of high stand collar. Black leather gloves. Black silk bag, long ribbon handle, silver-gilt frame and clasp. Black silk umbrella, black flocked-velvet-chiffon bands, long ebony stick, silver handle. Black kid boots, buttoned sides, pointed toes.

Women's Hats 1900–1904

1 1900. Black straw hat, upswept brim set at an angle on a wide stiffened band concealed under large cloth flowers, crown covered with coloured ostrich plumes, loops and twists of silk ribbon and ruffles of chiffon. 2 1900. White cotton-canvas hat worn tilted forward on stiffened band, wide flat brim, wired edge bound in striped cotton, matching band of flat-topped crown and self-fabric ruffle decoration on side-front. 3 1901. Black woven-horsehair lace toque, decorated with pleated silk rosettes and fans, silk flowers, ribbon loops and tiny quills. 4 1901. Black woven-horsehair braid toque, openwork lace edges, blue paper flowers with yellow centres decorating self-fabric feather-shaped trim on front. 5 1902. Fine straw hat, tiny white silk flowers under wide undulating wired brim, concealing stiffened band, large silk bow trim covering shallow crown, matching colour of straw binding at edge of brim. 6 1903. Small grey straw boater, narrow straight flat brim and shallow flat-topped crown covered and draped in spotted veiling, side-top of crown trimmed with two large silk roses and velvet foliage. 7 1903. Velvet hat, wired brim bound in lilac and edged with fine red ribbon, worn tilted forward, stiffened band hidden by cloth violets and leaves, matching decoration on shallow crown and inner brim. 8 1904. Natural-straw hat, upswept brim filled with coloured curled ostrich plumes, side-front trimmed with large contrast-colour velvet bow, matching narrow ribbons, brooch at base. 9 1904. Blue straw boater, hard brim, pointed edge, shallow crown, flat top, silk-ribbon trim, off-centre loops and pointed ends.

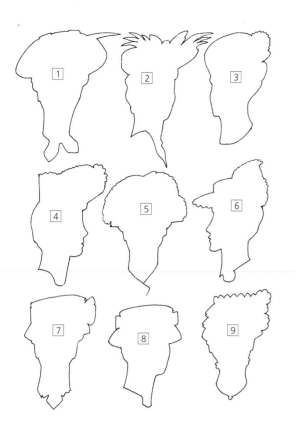

Women's Hats 1905–1908

1 1905. Natural-straw hat, wide brim swept up at back, worn tilted forward, flat crown pleated over swathes of coloured silk-taffeta, matching rosettes and trim, single brown quill. 2 1905. Green woven-horsehair-ribbon tricorne hat, upswept brim, shallow crown swathed in red silk, topped with outspread birds' wings. 3 1906. Hat of woven-horsehair ribbons, deep upswept brim, worn tilted forward, shallow crown swathed in silk-chiffon, large pleated black silk rosette on side-back, centre and lower edge trimmed with matching chiffon. 4 1906. Fancy-weave natural-straw hat, upswept fluted brim trimmed with dark natural-straw fringe, brim split and overlapped at one side, top of crown set at angle, trimmed with swathes of green silk and three large silk roses. 5 1906. Black straw hat, deep bell-shaped brim, grey silk-chiffon hatband, wide crown covered with coloured ostrich plumes. 6 1907. Fancy-weave natural-straw hat, flat brim, scalloped edge, swept up at back, worn tilted forward, stiffened band covered with curled ostrich plumes, flat-topped crown swathed in fine silk-velvet. 7 1907. Natural-straw hat, deep wide crown, domed top, green draped silk-chiffon band, side ruffles, narrow turned-down brim. 8 1908. Brown natural-straw hat, deep wide crown, domed top, pleated brown silk-ribbon band spotted in brown velvet, narrow turned-down brim, wired edge. 9 1908. Natural-straw hat, bell-shaped brim, shallow crown covered with two gathered tiers of scallop-edged lace, secured by narrow contrast-colour velvet ribbon, trimmed with three large velvet camellias at side-front.

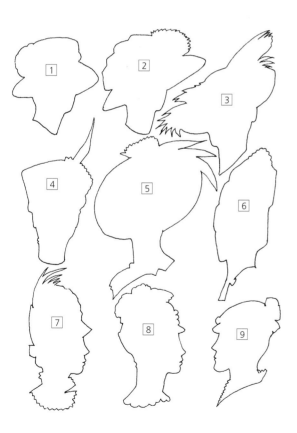

Women's Hats 1909–1913

1 1909. Brown natural-straw mushroom-shaped hat, wide turned-down brim, high domed crown, contrast-colour pleated-silk band, matching large ruffled rosette at side, large silver hatpins at each side centre-front. 2 1909. Outsized black straw hat, large wide crown swathed in green silk-taffeta, off-centre large black ostrich-feather pompon, wide brim, wired edge. 3 1909. Natural-straw hat, worn at an angle, wide brim, wired edge, turned up at one side, bird-of-paradise wings set in front of low domed crown, secured by knot of black silk. 4 1910. Smooth brown fur toque, high domed crown, sash of contrast-colour silk across middle, three-colour pleated petersham-ribbon motif on side-front, single quill. 5 1910. Natural-straw hat, outsized wired brim, swept up at one side, black edging, two-colour ostrich-feather pompons and quills. 6 1911. Brimless red velvet hat, high unstructured crown, self-fabric pointed tab with white pleated silk edge at one side, flared embroidered lace band, frilled edge. 7 1912. Black woven-horsehair hat, worn tilted back away from face, narrow wired brim turned up at back, high crown swathed in black silk-taffeta, whole bird-of-paradise as trim at one side. 8 1912. Small natural-straw hat, narrow wired brim turned up at back, low domed crown, hatband composed of three rows of self-straw coils, back trimmed with curled ostrich plumes. 9 1913. Small natural-straw hat, angled to one side, narrow upswept wired brim, wide shallow crown edged with cloth flowers and leaves, large ruffle of silk at back.

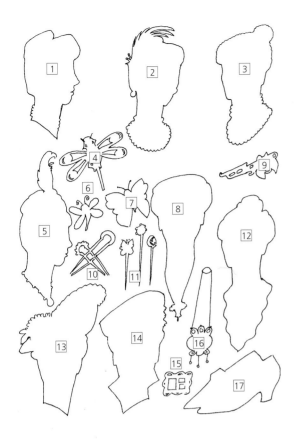

Jewelry 1900–1913

1 1900. Silver-gilt and white paste jeweled haircomb. White paste pendant earrings set with large imitation topazes. Deep choker necklace, panels of imitation pearls separated by silver-gilt rods, front panel of engraved silver set with white paste stones. 2 1908. Silver hairbrooch set with pearls, red bird-of-paradise plumes. Large imitation-pearl drop earrings, edged with white paste stones. Strings of imitation pearls in various sizes. 3 1905. Imitation-pearl choker, silver-gilt spines set with white paste stones, imitation-amethyst pendants. Two rows of graded pearls. 4 1900–10. Silver dragonfly brooch, set with coloured-glass stones. 5 1913. Silver-gilt tiara set with imitation diamonds and pearls, blue ostrich plume, crescent-shaped hairbrooch and haircomb. Gold locket on pearl and gold chain. 6 1913. Enamelled gold dragonfly brooch. 7 1913. Silver-gilt butterfly brooch decorated with translucent coloured enamels. 8 1912. Silver-gilt hairbrooches set with imitation emeralds. Silver-gilt pendant flower basket, set with multi-coloured glass stones, suspended from fine chain. 9 1901. Bee and flower design enamelled brooch. 10 1913. Silver-gilt hairpins decorated with imitation pearls and imitation gems. 11 1900–10. Butterfly, flower, and crescent-and-star design hatpins, in silver-gilt, gold and silver. 12 1909. Fine twisted wire and coloured-glass pendant necklace. 13 1901. Black woven-horsehair hat trimmed with yellow cloth flowers and ostrich plumes, wide black taffeta-ribbon band and bow pinned with two oblong silver buckles set with white paste stones. 14 1900. Felt hat, upswept brim, black velvet edging, front trimmed with four black quills, engraved silver-gilt buttons and brooch. 15 1912. Bronze belt buckle, leaf design. 16 1902. Peacock design pendant in silver and gold, decorated with pearls in varying sizes, fine chain, clasp fastening. 17 1913. Black patent-leather shoes, pointed tongues trimmed with silver buckles set with red and white paste stones.

Women's Bags and Purses 1900–1913

1 1900. Leather bag, engraved silver frame and clasp, silk handle, bow knot. 2 1900. Brown leather bag, square frame, brass clasp and fittings, self-leather handle. 3 1901. Pleated black silk evening bag, engraved silver frame and clasp, self-fabric handle. 4 1902. Cream silk evening bag gathered onto carved ivory frame, clasp, self-fabric handle, bow knot. 5 1902. Small cream leather bag, metal frame, clasp, leather handle. 6 1902. Large leather travelling bag, brass fittings, double locks and clasp, short reinforced handle. 7 1903. Pink satin bag gathered onto silver frame, clasp, self-fabric handle, bow knot. 8 1903. Calfskin bag, metal frame, silver trim, clasp, rouleau handles. 9 1904. Linked silver chain purse, silver ball pendants on hem, clasp, long chain handle with finger ring. 10 1905. Black silk evening bag patterned with large velvet spots, gathered onto silver frame, clasp, satin handle, bow knot. 11 1905. Leather bag, metal frame, silver fittings, long self-leather handle. 12 1905. Slim leather bag, metal frame, silver fittings, double self-leather handles, contrast-colour silk lining. 13 1906. Small leather purse, silver frame, flap-and-button fastening, double cord handle, tassel trim. 14 1907. Calfskin bag, metal frame, silver clasp and trim, long yellow and grey cord handles, tassel trim. 15 1908. Ostrich-leather bag, metal frame, brass clasp fastening and trim, double rouleau handles. 16 1911. Brown leather purse, hand-painted design, flap-and-button fastening, two long leather thong handles. 17 1911. Brown felt purse, two-tone embroidery, flap-and-button fastening, long two-colour cord handles. 18 1913. Brown leather bag, silver frame, clasp and fittings, double handles, purse set onto front, flap-and-stud fastening. 19 1910. Red velvet purse, flap-and-gold-stud fastening, gold wire embroidery, matching long handle, tassels and fringes.

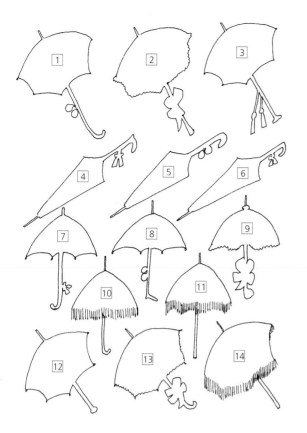

Umbrellas and Parasols 1900–1913

1 Pink silk umbrella edged in scalloped contrast-colour silk, edges finished with coloured chainstitch embroidery, long stick, bent handle, pink silk cord and pompon trim. 2 Black silk parasol, three-tier lace and chiffon edging, chiffon lining, long ebony stick, silver handle, silk-ribbon trim. 3 Blue silk parasol covered in fine black lace, trimmed with narrow black velvet ribbon, long ebony stick, silver handle, black silk cord and tassels. 4 Blue two-tone striped silk umbrella, stick and carved bent handle painted black, black silk cord and tassels. 5 White cloth umbrella, blue band with crenellated edge, painted spots, long stick painted white, ivory bird's-head handle, blue cord and pompons. 6 Black silk parasol, banded in lace, chainstitch embroidered edges, white painted stick, engraved bent handle, black silk cord and tassels. 7 Cream silk parasol, lace appliqué, embroidered edges, long stick, bent handle, cream silk cord and tassels. 8 Cream cloth umbrella with stripes in red and blue pattern, long cane stick and handle, red cords and pompons. 9 Peach-coloured silk parasol, appliqué lace trim, frilled chiffon edging, matching lining, long wooden stick, natural handle, peach satin ribbon. 10 Dark-brown silk parasol, appliqué black lace motifs, black embroidery, matching pointed flap edges and deep silk fringe, black ebony stick and bent handle. 11 Beige silk parasol, appliqué lace motifs, pointed flap edges, braided and embroidered edges, deep silk fringe, long straight stick painted cream. 12 Cloth umbrella, multi-coloured stripes, long stick, flat-topped silver handle. 13 Brown spotted silk parasol, banded and edged with ruched silk-chiffon, wooden stick, bent handle, brown silk bow. 14 Silk parasol, multicoloured pattern, silk fringe, straight wooden stick.

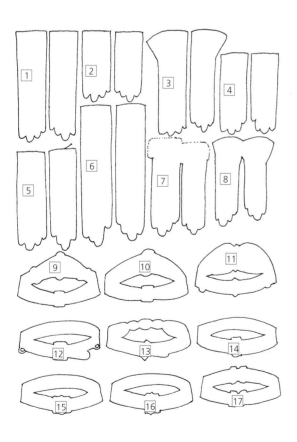

Women's Gloves and Belts 1900–1913

1 Long leather gloves, piped edges, contrast-colour handstitching, three-button fastening at back of wrist. 2 Short textured-leather gloves, piped edges, contrast-colour topstitching, two-button fastening at back of wrist. 3 Long suede gauntlet gloves, contrast-colour handstitching, single side-button fastening. 4 Short kid gloves, contrast-colour topstitching and embroidery, two-button strap fastening at back of wrist. 5 Short leather gloves, contrast-colour handstitching, hook-and-lace fastening at back of wrist. 6 Elbow-length kid gloves, three-button fastening at back of wrist. 7 Short leather gloves, topstitching, two-button strap fastening at back of wrist, fur cuffs. 8 Long leather gauntlet gloves, piped edges, topstitching, silk lining, two-button fastening at back of wrist. 9 Leather belt handstitched onto contrast-colour canvas, high back, oval supports covered in canvas, brass buckle and eyelets. 10 Blue and white patterned silk belt, deep back gathered through oval support covered in self-fabric, silver-gilt buckle and eyelets. 11 Olive-green leather belt, wide back gathered through bronze shaped support, matching side supports, buckle and eyelets. 12 Brown leather belt, handstitched edges, silver side rings and holding plates, matching small buckle, eyelets and belt tip. 13 Pink leather belt, deep front gathered through pointed lozenge-shaped buckle, three rows of eyelets, narrow back supports of same shape. 14 Leather belt, handstitched edges, brass half-buckle, bar and tip. 15 Black petersham-ribbon belt, engraved silver buckle, side plates and bar. 16 Blue leather belt, classical key pattern painted in green, self-leather lining, silver-gilt buckle and double row of eyelets. 17 Black petersham-ribbon belt, engraved silver clasp fastener, back and side hinges.

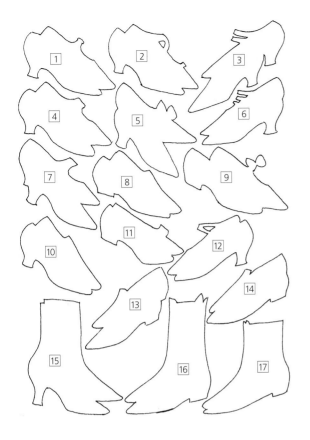

Women's Footwear 1900–1906

1 1900. Kid shoes, blunt toes, wide bar-straps, decorative openwork, three-button fastening, low heels. 2 1900. Cream kid shoes, blunt toes, self-bow trim, narrow bar-strap, low heels. 3 1901. Blue leather shoes, pointed toes, double bar-straps, low heels. 4 1901. Brown leather shoes, almond-shaped toes, wide bar-straps, decorative openwork, single-button fastening, low heels. 5 1902. Pink satin evening shoes, high vamps, pointed tongues, self-fabric bow trim, crystal bead embroidery around openwork fronts, pointed toes, low louis heels. 6 1903. Black patent-leather shoes, pointed toes, wide bar-straps cut into three, three-button fastening, red linings, low louis heels. 7 1904. Satin evening shoes, pointed toes, bar-straps, wide over insteps, bead embroidery, medium-high heels. 8 1905. Brown leather walking shoes, high vamps, wide straps, two-button fastening, pointed patent-leather toecaps and low heels. 9 1905. Black leather shoes, pointed toes, bar-straps, front fastening covered by patent-leather bow, matching trim and flat heels. 10 1905. Olive-green leather shoes, blunt toes, high vamps, elasticated front gusset, low heels. 11 1905. Black patent-leather shoes, pointed toes, black petersham-ribbon trim, flat heels. 12 1906. Olive-green leather shoes, pointed toes, bar-straps, medium-high louis heels. 13 1903. Velvet house slippers, pointed toes, low tabs, multi-coloured embroidered flowers and leaves, leather soles and flat heels. 14 1903. Cloth house slippers, pointed toes, low tabs, multicoloured embroidery, leather soles and flat heels. 15 1902. Grey leather button-boots, side-front fastening, pointed toes, red linings, high louis heels. 16 1904. Black leather boots, scalloped edge-to-button fastening, elasticated side gussets, pointed toecaps, low stacked heels. 17 1906. Leather lace-up boots, pointed toecaps, perforated detail, low stacked heels.

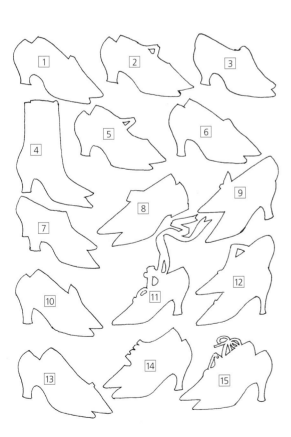

Women's Footwear 1907–1913

1 1907. Pink leather shoes, pointed toes, buckle trim, high black leather tongues, self-leather strap-and-button fastening, high heels. 2 1907. Satin evening shoes, pointed toes, gold and crystal bead embroidery, crossed bar-straps, medium-high louis heels. 3 1908. Brown leather oxfords, high vamps, pointed black patent-leather toecaps, lace-up bars and high louis heels. 4 1909. Leather boots, pointed black patent-leather toecaps, lace-up bars and high louis heels. 5 1908. Gold kid evening shoes, pointed toes, fine gold bead embroidery, matching bar-straps, medium-high heels. 6 1908. Plum-coloured leather shoes, pointed toes, high rounded tabs, high louis heels. 7 1910. Brown leather shoes, dark-brown leather pointed toecaps, matching heels, high vamps, scalloped four-button fastening. 8 1911. Green leather shoes, pointed toes, wide bar-straps, low stacked heels. 9 1911. Black leather shoes, pointed toes, high pointed tabs, bar-straps, button fastenings, engraved silver buckle trim, high louis heels. 10 1912. Black leather shoes, high vamps, high pointed tabs, silver buckle trim, pointed toes, high louis heels. 11 1913. Black kid tango shoe, red laced ribbon fastening around ankles, pointed toes, high louis heels. 12 1912. Patterned silk-brocade evening shoes, pointed toes, self-fabric bow trim, crossed bar-straps, high louis heels. 13 1913. Cream kid shoes, pointed toes, flat cream satin bow trim, high louis heels. 14 1913. Two-tone leather shoes, four bar-straps with centre-front fastenings, pointed toes, high louis heels. 15 1913. Black satin evening shoes, black scalloped sides laced through with ribbon fastening, pointed toes, high louis heels.

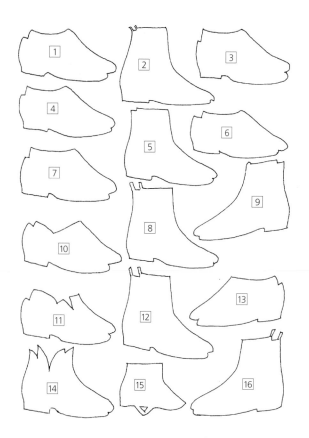

Men's Footwear 1900–1913

1 Leather lace-up shoes, blunt toes, apron fronts, brogued edges and detail, stacked heels. 2 Black leather boots, elasticated side gussets, pointed toecaps, brogued detail, low stacked heels. 3 Leather lace-up shoes, no toecaps, low stacked heels. 4 Canvas sports shoes, no toecaps, contrast-colour leather lacing bars, matching back of heels and textured-rubber soles. 5 Brown leather boots, laced through eyelets over insteps, hooks to finish, pointed toes, toecaps, low stacked heels. 6 Two-tone leather lace-up shoes, pointed toes, leather toecaps matching back of heels, lacing bar and trim, low stacked heels. 7 Leather shoes, blunt toes, no toecaps, double row of handstitching to edges and detail, low stacked heels. 8 Black leather boots, laced through eyelets over instep, hooks to finish, low stacked heels. 9 White leather sports boots, blunt toes, shaped toecaps to under strap-and-buckle fastening over instep, stacked heels. 10 Red leather house slippers, pointed toes, raised and stitched decoration, low wrapover sides, low stacked heels. 11 Olive-green cloth house slippers, pointed toes, low wrapover sides, square tabs, bound and embroidered edges, low stacked heels. 12 Leather boots, pointed toes, no toecaps, low stacked heels, grey cloth uppers, elasticated side panels, button opening on side-front instep. 13 Black glacé-kid evening shoes, pointed toes, no toecaps, ribbon laces, low stacked heels. 14 Black leather boots, blunt toes, no toecaps, short elasticated side gussets, low stacked heels. 15 Cloth spats, side-button fastening, strap-and-buckle fastening under foot. 16 Black leather boots, pointed toes, toecaps, side-front button fastening, low stacked heels.

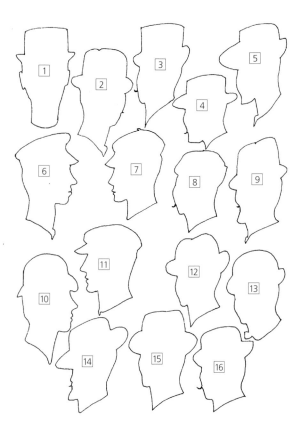

Men's Hats 1900–1913

1 Brown fur-felt hat, tall flat-topped hard crown, self-colour petersham-ribbon band, curled brim. 2 Felt homburg hat, soft creased crown, contrast-colour wide silk band and bow, narrow stiffened brim, turned-up edge. 3 Black silk top hat, medium-high crown, petersham-ribbon band and bow, curled brim. 4 Natural-straw boater, hard flat-topped crown and narrow brim, pale-blue petersham-ribbon band and bow. 5 Soft fur-felt hat, high crown, central crease, self-colour petersham-ribbon band, bow and binding of upswept brim. 6 Navy-blue beaver-cloth cap, small leather peak, gold braid and button trim. 7 Flecked wool-tweed cap, sectioned crown, button trim, small peak. 8 Checked wool cap, earflaps buttoned over crown, small peak. 9 Black felt homburg hat, tall crown, central crease, wide petersham-ribbon band and bow, stiffened brim, curled sides. 10 Black felt bowler hat, hard rounded crown, petersham-ribbon band and bow, matching edges of narrow curled brim. 11 Grey cloth cap, half band at back, small peak, topstitched edges. 12 Fur-felt homburg hat, soft crown, central crease, wide self-colour band and bow, hard brim curled at each side. 13 Brown felt bowler hat, hard rounded crown, narrow petersham-ribbon band and bow, matching binding of curled brim. 14 Natural-straw hat, tall crown, flat top, stitched crease, coloured petersham-ribbon band, tied bow, wide brim turned up at sides. 15 White straw hat, tall crown, central crease, black petersham-ribbon band and bow, wide brim turned up at sides, stitched edges. 16 White straw panama hat, shallow crown, pressed crease, blue petersham-ribbon band and bow, soft brim, turned up at back, stitched edges.

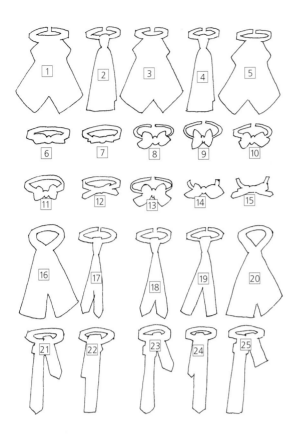

Men's Neckwear 1900–1913

1 Patterned silk ascot scarf, adjustable self-fabric band, elastic extension. 2 Patterned silk four-in-hand scarf, large knot, self-fabric band, buckle adjustment, elastic extension. 3 Ribbed ascot scarf, adjustable self-fabric band, elastic extension. 4 Patterned silk four-in-hand scarf, large knot, self-fabric band, buckle adjustment, elastic extension. 5 Patterned silk ascot scarf, button pin with dark stone, self-fabric band buckle adjustment, elastic extension. 6 Black silk evening bow-tie, self-fabric band, buckle adjustment. 7 Black silk evening bow-tie, self-fabric band, buckle adjustment. 8 Pink and black spotted silk bow-tie, elasticated neckband. 9 Blue patterned silk bow-tie, adjustable neckband. 10 Spotted silk bow-tie, elasticated neckband. 11 Black satin evening bow-tie, adjustable neckband. 12 Black grosgrain bow-tie, adjustable neckband. 13 Green patterned silk bow-tie, elasticated neckband. 14 Red silk bow-tie, stiffened undercollar attachment. 15 Black silk bow-tie, stiffened undercollar attachment. 16 Blue patterned silk cravat, swirling pattern. 17 Multicoloured patterned silk tied necktie, adjustable self-fabric neckband. 18 Yellow patterned silk tied necktie, large knot, adjustable self-fabric neckband. 19 Multicoloured patterned silk tied necktie, adjustable self-fabric neckband. 20 Lilac silk cravat, deep-lilac spot pattern. 21 Silk necktie, red and pink diagonal stripes. 22 Wool necktie, green patterned horizontal stripes. 23 Blue spotted silk necktie. 24 Patterned wool tie. 25 Silk necktie, lilac and blue diagonal stripes.

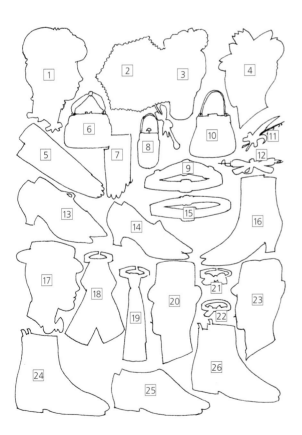

Accessories at a Glance 1900–1906

1 Natural-straw hat, trimmed with cloth flowers and foliage, and dyed ostrich plumes. 2 Pink silk parasol, lined and edged in silk-chiffon, long stick, pink ribbon bow, silver handle. 3 Blue straw brimless hat trimmed with grey ribbon and cloth violets. 4 Natural-straw hat, flat brim bound in red and green, matching self-straw bows, red and green quills. 5 Elbow-length white kid gloves, four-button fastening above wrist. 6 Green leather bag, silver-gilt frame, black ribbon handle. 7 Short brown leather gloves, two-button fastening. 8 Small fur bag, silver frame, jeweled clasp, leather handle. 9 Mauve striped silk belt, silver supports, buckle and eyelets. 10 Suede bag, engraved silver frame and clasp, rouleau handle. 11 Silver brooch set with imitation emeralds. 12 Yellow and red enamelled silver-gilt brooch. 13 Cream leather shoes, pointed toes, bar-straps, fine embroidery. 14 Brown suede shoes, pointed toes, high tabs, silver buckles, high louis heels. 15 Brown leather belt, silver buckle and trim. 16 Button-boots, light-brown leather uppers, brown leather apron fronts, pointed toes, louis heels. 17 Natural-straw boater, narrow brim, flat-topped crown, blue and red band. 18 Patterned silk ascot scarf, adjustable neckband. 19 Patterned silk four-in-hand, large knot, adjustable neckband. 20 Silk top hat, medium crown, black petersham-ribbon band, curled brim. 21 Red silk bow-tie, elasticated neckband. 22 Black silk bow-tie, elasticated neckband. 23 Grey felt homburg, tall crown, soft crease, black petersham-ribbon band, matching binding on curled brim. 24 Brown leather boots, laced through eyelets over instep, hooks to finish, square toes, no toecaps. 25 Brown leather lace-up shoes, brogued apron fronts and detail, low stacked heels. 26 Brown leather boots, elasticated sides, blunt toes, no toecaps, low stacked heels.

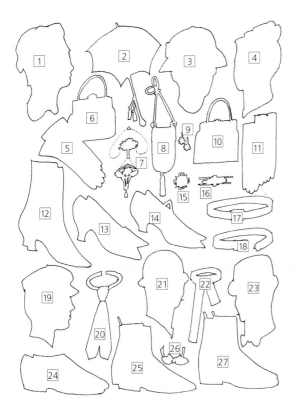

Accessories at a Glance 1907–1913

1 Brimless purple cloth hat, soft crown gathered onto wide self-fabric band, trimmed with velvet, lace and gold braid, pleated edging. 2 Lilac silk umbrella, striped border, pattern above. 3 Natural-straw hat, deep crown, draped chiffon band, bow trim, turned-down brim, cloth flower trim. 4 Brimless felt hat, softly pleated crown, red pompon trim. 5 Kid gloves, gauntlet sides, button fastening. 6 Black leather bag, silver frame and clasp, two rouleau handles. 7 Enamelled metal pendant, waterlilies and leaves, pearl drop, fine chain. 8 Pink cloth purse, buttoned flap embroidered with flowers, cord handles, tassel trim. 9 Gold and pearl drop earrings. 10 Green leather bag, silver-gilt frame and clasp, two rouleau handles. 11 Green kid gloves, handstitching, single-stud fastening. 12 Canvas boots, pointed toes, black leather toecaps, matching lacing bars and high heels. 13 Suede shoes, pointed toes, self-suede bow trim, louis heels. 14 Kid shoes, pointed toes, cross-straps, louis heels. 15 Engraved gold brooch, silver and gold wire loops, pearl trim. 16 Silver-gilt brooch set with imitation pearls and coloured stones. 17 Canvas belt, handstitched edges, brass buckle and double eyelets. 18 Blue petersham-ribbon belt, handstitched edges, silver buckle and clasp. 19 Tweed cap, sectioned crown, button trim, peak. 20 Patterned silk tied necktie, adjustable neckband. 21 Brown bowler hat, soft crown, hard brim, curled edge trimmed with petersham-ribbon to match band. 22 Knitted silk striped necktie. 23 Natural-straw panama hat, pleated crown, curled brim. 24 Leather lace-up shoes, pointed toecaps, stitched edges and details, low stacked heels. 25 Leather boots, pointed toes, no toecaps, canvas buttoned uppers, stacked heels. 26 Silk bow-tie, stiffened undercollar attachment. 27 Brown leather lace-up boots, pointed toecaps, handstitched detail, stacked heels.

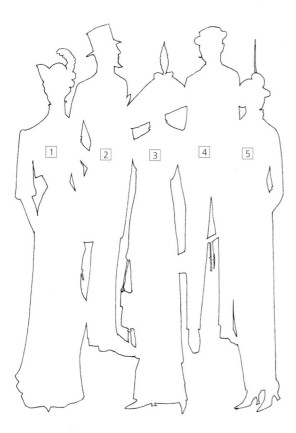

The Complete Look 1900–1913

1 1900. Patterned silk outfit: short bolero, velvet and lace braid trim, matching collar, tight lower sleeves and skirt panels, upper sleeves gathered at elbow-level, ruched plain silk waist sash; ground-length flared skirt, back train. Natural-straw tricorne hat, worn tilted forward on brow, tall draped crown trimmed with cloth roses and ostrich plume. Drop earrings, small brooch worn on stand collar of lace blouse. Kid gloves; matching bag, silver frame and clasp, rouleau handle. Silk umbrella. Leather boots, pointed toes. 2 1900. Single-breasted dark-grey wool tailcoat; matching waistcoat. Grey trousers. White shirt; purple silk four-in-hand necktie. Black silk top hat, curled brim. Grey gloves. Black leather elastic-sided boots. 3 1910. Cream patterned silk dress, V-shaped neckline, plain chiffon infill, lace edging matching hems of elbow-length sleeves, trim above high waist sash and above tucked hemline of narrow skirt. Large natural-straw hat, outsized wired brim, curled ostrich plume and bow trim. Single row of imitation pearls; matching earrings. Cream elbow-length kid gloves. Cream silk umbrella, banded in green, long stick, silver handle, tassel trim. Gold velvet purse, long cord handle, tassel trim. Cream kid shoes, bar-straps, pointed toes, louis heels. 4 1909. Single-breasted blue and grey striped jacket, four-button fastening, flap pockets. Single-breasted collarless waistcoat; matching trousers. White shirt, wing collar; patterned silk bow-tie. Straw boater, shallow flat-topped crown, striped band, hard flat brim. Brown leather lace-up boots. 5 1913. Flecked linen two-piece suit: single-breasted jacket, kimono-style sleeves gathered into deep velvet cuffs, matching covered buttons, collar and high waist-belt; narrow ankle-length skirt, centre-front unpressed box-pleat. Frilled blouse. Brown cloth hat, gathered crown, two self-fabric motifs on centre-front, long quill above, narrow brim. Kid gloves. Pink silk parasol, long stick, curved handle, pompon trim. Brown leather shoes, three bar-straps, pointed toes, louis heels.

Women's Hats 1914–1918

1914

1914

1914

1914

1914

1915

1915

1915

1915

1916

1917

1917

1917

1917

1918

1918

1918

1914

1915

1915

1915

1918

1919

1917

1919

1927

1922

1922

1922

1927

1921

1926

1923

1928

1914

1915

1918

1920

1926

1927

1923

1928

1927

1928

1924

1924

1924

1924

1925

1925

1925

1926

1925

1926

1926

1927

1926

1927

1927

1928

1928

1928

1928

1919

1919

1920

1920

1920

1920

1921

1922

1921

1922

1923

1923

1914

1915

1919

1920

1922

1928

1928

1927

1925

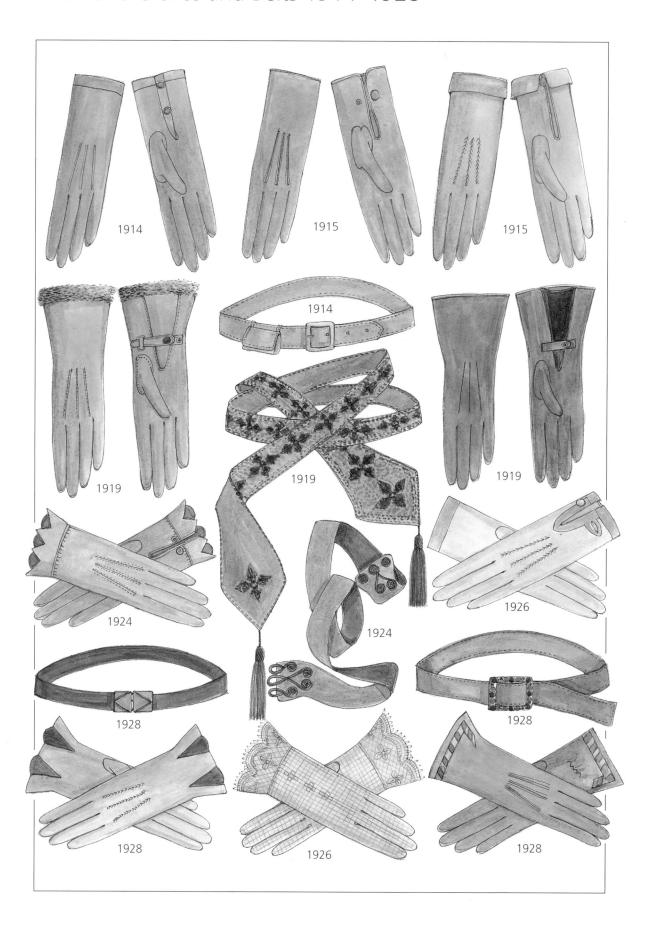

1914

1915

1915

1919

1914

1919

1919

1924

1919

1926

1928

1924

1928

1928

1926

1928

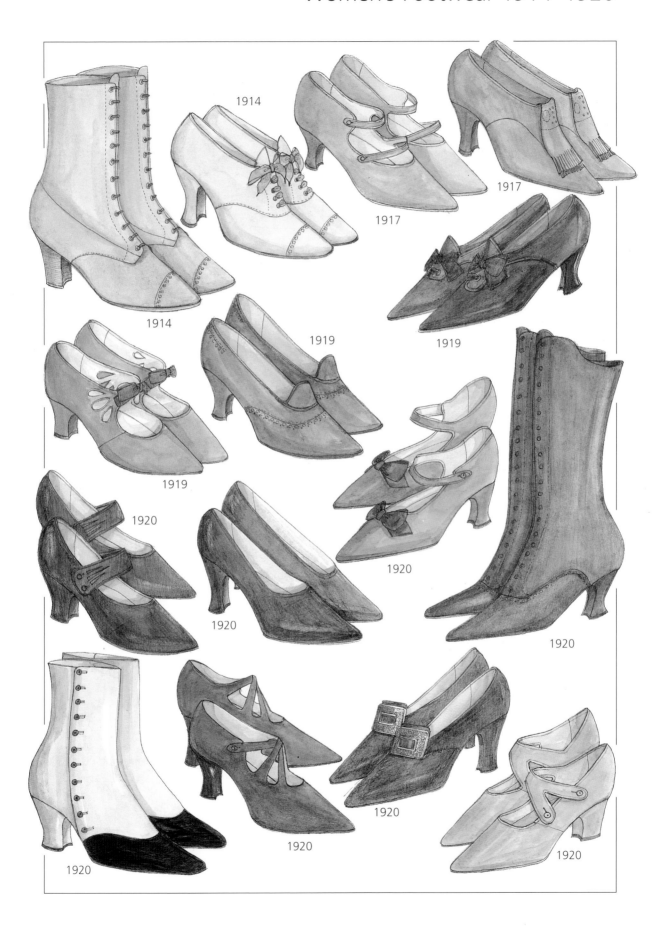

1914

1917

1917

1914

1919

1919

1919

1919

1920

1920

1920

1920

1920

1920

1920

1920

Women's Footwear 1921–1928

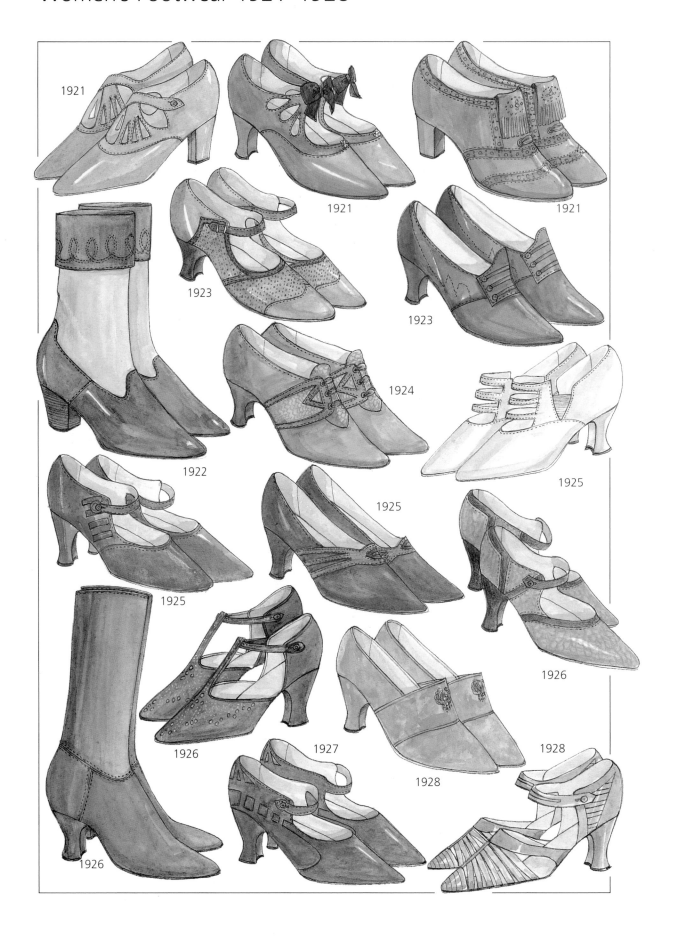

1921

1921

1921

1923

1923

1924

1922

1925

1925

1925

1926

1926

1927

1928

1928

1926

1914

1916

1923

1924

1928

The Complete Look 1914

[1] Wool two-piece suit: single-breasted fitted hip-length jacket, contrast-colour velvet belt under bust, matching collar, side panels, shaped cuffs of full-length inset sleeves and covered buttons; narrow ankle-length wrapover skirt, button detail at mid-calf. Natural-straw hat, upswept brim, black ostrich plumes. Leather gloves. Black cloth bag, amber frame, long self-fabric handle. Black leather lace-up boots, pointed toecaps. [2] Green-grey wool two-piece suit: single-breasted unfitted jacket, wide black velvet lapels, matching trim on ankle-length wrapover skirt and wide half-belt under unpressed box-pleats, diamond-shaped buttons. Black felt hat, upswept brim, cloth flower trim, grey binding and wings at one side. Gold chain earrings, large imitation-pearl balls. Black leather gloves. Black leather bag, silver-gilt chain, frame and clasp. Button-boots with pointed toes. [3] Flecked red linen two-piece suit: edge-to-edge bolero, three-quarter-length sleeves, fur cuffs matching collar; buttoned straps on front edges, sleeves and front of high-waisted narrow ankle-length skirt. White silk blouse, wing collar. Red felt hat, brown velvet turned-back brim trimmed with two long brown feathers. Cloth gloves. Leather bag, long cord handle. Leather shoes, pointed toes, round buckles. [4] Three-piece grey and brown striped wool suit: single-breasted jacket, three-button fastening, flap pockets; single-breasted waistcoat; narrow trousers. White shirt; red silk tie. Natural-straw boater, hard crown and brim, blue ribbon band. Brown leather gloves. Brown leather lace-up shoes, pointed toecaps. [5] Blue silk two-piece costume: high waisted top, low V-shaped neckline, white pleated silk edging, elbow-length dolman sleeves, black fur trim above hemlines, matching uneven hem of top; ankle-length skirt, side-front drapery. White lace blouse. Brimless black fur hat, feather trim at one side, brooch. White glass bead necklace. Long black kid gloves. Black cloth bag, gilt frame. Black leather shoes, pointed toes, round buckles.

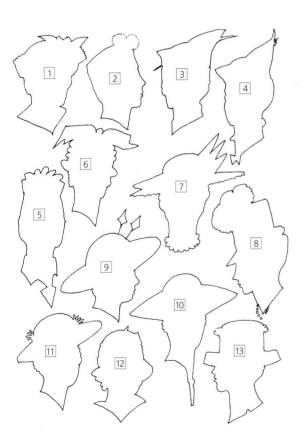

Women's Hats 1914–1918

[1] 1914. Dark-blue straw hat, deep upswept brim, pleated white organdie edging, high crown, black waxed ribbon-and-loop trim. [2] 1914. Brimless straw cloche, high crown, green velvet-ribbon and silk pompon trim. [3] 1914. Felt hat, high crown, uneven upswept brim, side-front wrapover, topstitched edges, long coloured quill. [4] 1914. Black straw hat, small crown, uneven tricorne-shaped upswept brim, velvet binding, feather on highest point, blue cloth posy of flowers at centre-front. [5] 1915. Dark-blue straw pillbox, flat top trimmed with black waxed-satin-ribbon loops, black silk pompon at centre-front. [6] 1915. Black straw hat worn at an angle, high crown covered in small pink cloth flowers, black waxed ribbon trim, patterned silk band, narrow brim. [7] 1915. Navy-blue polished-straw hat, wide brim, high crown, ribbon wings, knot trimmed with self-fabric buttons, gold embroidery. [8] 1916. Woven-straw top hat, tall crown, flat top, ostrich plume trim, wide purple silk band, narrow curled brim. [9] 1917. Natural-straw hat, wide shallow crown, twisted navy-blue petersham-ribbon band, matching bow trim, ostrich-feather pompon, long navy-blue shaved quills, wide brim, wired edge. [10] 1917. Natural-straw tricorne hat, tall crown, wide lilac silk-ribbon band, trimmed with purple satin berries and large green velvet leaves. [11] 1917. Dark-yellow natural-straw hat, wide shallow crown, white silk daisy-trimmed band, wide turned-up brim with wired edge. [12] 1918. Natural-straw cloche hat, high crown swathed in pale-blue panne-velvet, cross trim of wide navy-blue waxed-satin ribbon, narrow wired brim. [13] 1918. Black polished-straw hat, top edge of tall crown trimmed with black curled ostrich feathers, deep petersham-ribbon band, narrow brim, wired turned-up edge, short transparent silk veil.

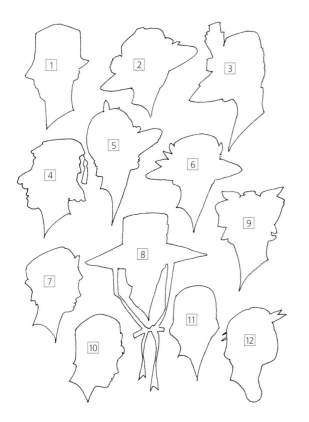

Women's Hats 1919–1923

[1] 1919. Natural-straw hat, blue velvet-ribbon band and bow trim high on close-fitting domed crown, narrow brim, turned down at front and up at back, hat worn low on brow. [2] 1919. Natural-straw hat, high wide crown, deep embroidered ribbon band, wide brim trimmed with velvet flowers, berries and foliage. [3] 1920. Black polished-straw hat, high domed crown, pleated black velvet band, matching large wired bow and fan trim on centre-front, asymmetric brim. [4] 1920. Turquoise panne-velvet hat, high crown draped over frame, tassel trim at back, diagonal pale-grey lace trim, matching short veil over narrow wired brim. [5] 1920. Grey felt scuttle-shaped hat, high domed crow, draped silk-chiffon band, wide front brim narrowing to back, side trim of orange silk roses and green velvet foliage. [6] 1920. Natural-straw hat, high crown, wide cream silk band, matching stylized asymmetric flowers with green stamens, wide turned-down brim, wired edge. [7] 1921. Brown straw brimless pull-on cloche hat, softly pleated domed crown, self-colour pleated petersham-ribbon fan-shaped motifs above base edge, imitation-pearl centres. [8] 1921. Blue and white patterned silk hat, high draped crown, flat top, red velvet-ribbon band, ends fall from back and tie at front, wide brim, wired edge, plain blue silk lining. [9] 1922. Deep-purple panne-velvet brimless hat, sectioned crown gathered under large self-fabric-covered button on top, outsized wired bow and ends trim back, hat worn low on brow. [10] 1922. Natural-straw pull-on cloche hat, high domed crown, multicoloured cloth flowers trim band above narrow turned-down wired brim, hat worn low on brow. [11] 1923. Close-fitting felt cloche hat, domed crown trimmed with cut-out flower and leaf shapes, narrow turned-down brim. [12] 1923. Suede cloche hat, close-fitting crown, wide brim turned back, secured by two green shaved quills, hat worn low on brow.

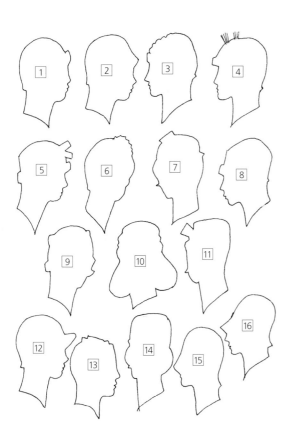

Women's Hats 1924–1928

[1] 1924. Blue felt cloche, small brim turned up at front, embroidered ribbon trim. [2] 1924. Natural-straw cloche, small turned-down brim, pink, green and yellow petersham-ribbon edging, matching band and pleated fan-shaped side trim. [3] 1924. Blue felt cloche, narrow brim split on sides, turned up at front and back, velvet flower trim on centre-front, velvet-ribbon band, matching flat bow and ends on back. [4] 1924. Natural-straw cloche, narrow brim turned up at front, edged in red, matching draped band, velvet flower and corn trim. [5] 1925. Orange varnished-straw hat, high crown, turned-up narrow brim, side pleat, brown petersham-ribbon trim. [6] 1925. Felt cloche, small brim turned up at front, pleated self-felt fan-shaped detail on centre-front, half-moon brooch trim. [7] 1925. Felt cloche, small turned-down brim, handstitched self-felt band and bow trim. [8] 1926. Green varnished-straw hat, domed crown trimmed with circles of striped velvet, matching edge of narrow upswept brim. [9] 1926. Red corded silk pull-on hat, unstructured sectioned crown, self-fabric bow trim, small brim turned down at front and up at back. [10] 1926. Green velvet hat, black satin-ribbon band, matching piped edges of wired turned-down brim and green satin leaf-shaped motifs on centre-front of tall draped crown, suede and leather flower trim. [11] 1927. Felt cloche, dented crown, wide machine-stitched brown satin band and trim, narrow brim turned up at front. [12] 1927. White waxed-straw hat, crown and narrow brim trimmed with blue silk, matching band. [13] 1927. Close-fitting brimless black felt cloche, trimmed with shaped bands of white felt. [14] 1928. Green knitted-silk hat, draped crown, small wired brim, black band. [15] 1928. Blue felt hat, domed crown, contrast-colour velvet band and bow, brim wide on sides, openwork edge. [16] 1928. Blue varnished-straw hat, domed crown, lilac ribbon trim, matching band and loops, turned-down brim, paler-blue edge.

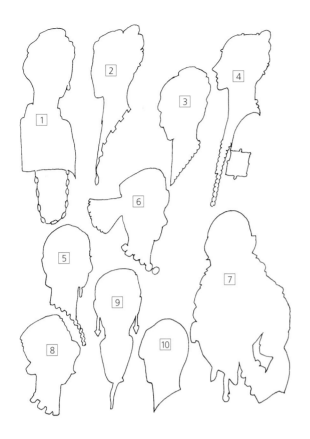

Jewelry 1914–1928

1 1914. Long amber bead and silver chain necklace; matching long drop earrings. 2 1915. Plastic hairslides/barrettes decorated with blue and white glass beads. Long silver-gilt drop earrings set with coloured-glass stones. Long fine silver chain necklace threaded with large and small blue glass beads, large blue glass pendant. 3 1918. Gold wire mesh tiara, worn flat against head, gold and pearl trim and edging, imitation-pearl necklace; matching drop earrings. 4 1920. Imitation-pearl bead hair decoration, gold disc above ears, set with large blue glass stone and edged with pearl beads, single pearl drop. Extra-long imitation-pearl necklace. Gold arm bangle, blue glass bead and pearl trim. 5 1923. Gold wire mesh tiara, set with black and white paste stones, flower design on centre-front and side above ears, worn low on brow. Black plastic drop earrings. Long necklace, half black and half gold glass beads separated by small imitation pearls. 6 1926. Black cloche hat, bird-of-paradise feather trim pinned by metal-gilt brooch set with imitation rubies. Short necklace of outsized red glass beads separated by tiny white glass beads. 7 1927. Short green, red and black plastic linked necklace, divided by bands of tiny imitation diamonds; matching hat clip, earrings and brooch. Large plastic wrist bangles worn over gauntlet gloves. 8 1927. Green felt cloche, narrow brim, crown draped in self-colour chiffon, stylized gold feather brooch trim. Short silver necklace, flat square black-glass beads separated by loops of silver. 9 1928. Long, silver and gold, arrow-shaped drop earrings, black-jet-pointed tips. Cobra necklace, flexible gold links, fastening under snake's head. 10 1928. Grey felt hat, asymmetric half-brim pinned back off centre-front with silver and imitation-diamond clip; matching long triangular-shaped drop earrings.

Women's Bags 1914–1928

1 1914. Small silk bag embroidered in cream and pale-blue beads, silver frame clasp and handle. 2 1915. Black snakeskin bag, engraved silver frame, matching clasp and chain handle. 3 1915. Lizardskin bag, ridged handle, matching clasp and frame, topstitched detail. 4 1915. Black and white grosgrain bag, silver frame, clasp with purple stone, fabric handle. 5 1917. Red silk bag embroidered in multicoloured glass beads, matching handle and scalloped fringed hem, tortoiseshell frame and fastening. 6 1918. Black velvet bag, black and gold woven-ribbon front panel, velvet-ribbon handle, ivory frame and fastening. 7 1919. Gold brocade bag, woven flower design, scalloped hem, pleated trim, black velvet base, black and gold striped ribbon handle, ivory frame and fastening. 8 1919. Black silk bag, beaded and sequin-embroidered pattern above bead-fringed scalloped hem, ivory frame, fastening and linked handle. 9 1921. Black velveteen bag, engraved silver frame, self-fabric rouleau handle. 10 1922. Multi-coloured floral design beaded bag, silver frame and fastening, beaded rouleau handle, scalloped bead-fringed hem. 11 1922. Blue silk bag, silver frame, clasp fastening, self-fabric ribbon handle. 12 1927. Leather clutch bag, flat handle, topstitched detail, plastic crossover frame, brass clip fastening. 13 1923. Circular silk bag, central panel embroidered with multicoloured flowers, black plastic frame, elephant clasp fastening, self-fabric ribbon handle. 14 1926. Multicoloured tapestry bag, silver frame set with coloured stones, clasp, long chain handle. 15 1927. Canvas clutch bag, curved wooden frame, two metal clip fasteners, appliqué felt flowers and leaves on front panel. 16 1928. Leather clutch bag, sunray panels piped in suede, matching laced sides, brass frame and fittings.

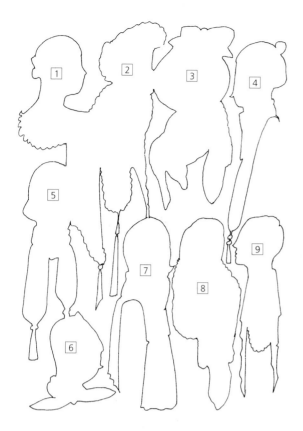

Women's Stoles and Scarves 1914–1928

1 1914. Long silk-chiffon stole, half-moon-shaped cape back, fine gold wire embroidery, two-colour marabou and ostrich-feather trim, matching asymmetric hems, asymmetric gold wire tassel trim. Tortoiseshell haircomb. 2 1915. Short grey and white curled ostrich feather and marabou ruffle, long black silk tassel trim. Brimless grey felt hat, topstitched detail, ostrich-feather trim. 3 1919. Dark-grey fox-fur stole. Black lacquered-straw hat, wide turned-back brim, large black silk-organdie bow trim. Long imitation pearls. 4 1920. Long green wool scarf, rounded ends trimmed with brown wool braid, matching long tassels. Pink velveteen beret flecked in red, wide crossover band, pintuck detail, brown silk pompon. 5 1922. Long blue wool scarf, multicoloured appliqué embroidery, pointed ends trimmed with long silk tassels. Matching blue cloche hat, turned-down brim, high crown trimmed with matching flower embroidery. 6 1927. Short black and white silk neckscarf, knotted at front. Black lacquered-straw cloche hat, narrow rolled-back white grosgrain brim, high rounded crown, matching threaded pointed tongue trim. 7 1925. Long scarf, central panel of brown fur, patterned panne-velvet ends. Brimless brown felt cloche hat, green appliqué felt trim. 8 1928. Brown fox-fur stole. Blue felt cloche hat, narrow turned-down brim, green and yellow pointed scalloped felt band. 9 1928. Long silk scarf, one half pink banded in blue, the other blue banded in pink. Long pink glass beads.

Women's Gloves and Belts 1914–1928

1 1914. Short blue leather gloves, black topstitching, double press-stud fastening. 2 1915. Short brown leather gloves, contrast topstitching, single press-stud fastening. 3 1915. Short beige cloth gloves, contrast topstitching, turned-down cuffs, loop-and-button fastening. 4 1919. Olive-green leather gauntlet gloves, contrast topstitching, fur lining and trim, strap-and-adjustable-press-stud fastening above large gusset. 5 1914. Canvas belt, contrast topstitching, small self-fabric purse, metal buckle and eyelets. 6 1919. Long fabric sash, multi-coloured glass bead design, green silk lining, beaded edge and single motif, tassel trim. 7 1919. Brown leather gauntlet gloves, black topstitching, strap-and-stud fastening over large brown suede gusset. 8 1924. Short yellow kid gloves, pointed scalloped cuffs, brown trim, lining and topstitching, single press-stud fastening. 9 1924. Gold-yellow cloth belt, braid loop-and-button fastening in brown, matching trim and silk lining. 10 1926. Short pale-grey kid gloves, black topstitching, wide pink binding, matching strap-and-covered-button fastening. 11 1928. Blue petersham-ribbon belt, orange and yellow plastic clasp fastening. 12 1928. Orange cloth belt, brown topstitching, silver buckle set with coloured glass, no spike or eyelets. 13 1928. Short kid gloves, contrast topstitching, small godets, no fastenings. 14 1926. Short crocheted cotton gloves, flared and scalloped cuffs, lace edges, flower motifs, threaded elastic through wrist seams. 15 1928. Short green cloth gloves, black topstitching, flared cuffs open on one side, narrow leather ribbon trim, painted gold and brown stripes.

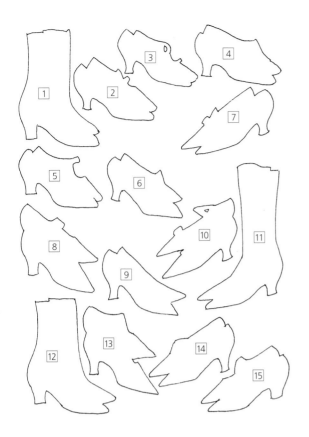

Women's Footwear 1914–1920

1 1914. Long leather lace-up boots, pointed toecaps, brogued detail, high stacked heels. 2 1914. Suede lace-up shoes, high vamps, ribbon laces, pointed toecaps, brogued detail, high louis heels. 3 1917. Pink satin shoes, two bar-straps, pointed toes, medium-high louis heels. 4 1917. Green leather shoes, high vamps, long fringed tongues, perforated decoration, pointed toes, high louis heels. 5 1919. Blue leather shoes, low vamps, pointed toes, petersham-ribbon bow-ties, openwork sides, medium-high heels. 6 1919. Brown leather shoes, high tongues, brogued seams, high louis heels. 7 1919. Black patent-leather shoes, petersham-ribbon bow-ties, pointed toes, high louis heels, red linings. 8 1920. Black leather shoes, wide bar-straps, openwork decoration, two-button fastening, pointed toes, medium-high heels. 9 1920. Black glacé-kid court shoes, pointed toes, high louis heels. 10 1920. Brown kid shoes, single bar-straps, pointed toes, brown satin bow trim, high louis heels. 11 1920. Long black leather lace-up boots, shaped tops, apron fronts, brogued detail, pointed toes, high louis heels. 12 1920. Black leather and white kid boots, side-button fastening, blunt toes, high heels. 13 1920. Dark-blue leather shoes, crossover straps, button fastening, pointed toes, high louis heels. 14 1920. Black glacé-kid shoes, high tongues, engraved metal buckles, pointed toes, high louis heels. 15 1920. Suede shoes, single bar-straps split into two, button fastening, pointed toes, low heels.

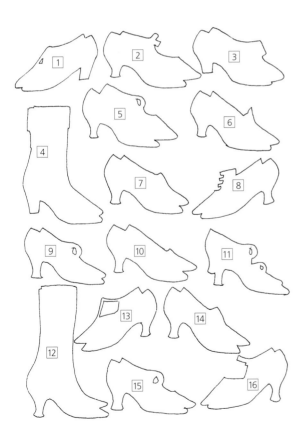

Women's Footwear 1921–1928

1 1921. Glacé-kid shoes, crossover straps, openwork detail, pointed toes, high heels. 2 1921. Blue glacé-kid shoes, openwork detail on bar-straps, centre fastening petersham-ribbon bow, pearl trim on low vamps, pointed toes, louis heels. 3 1921. Brown leather shoes, brogued detail, ribbon laces under fringed tongues, pointed toes, high heels. 4 1922. Black patent-leather boots, patent-leather turned-down cuffs, topstitched trim, pale-grey suede uppers, pointed toes, stacked heels. 5 1923. Beige suede bar-strap shoes, buckle fastenings, pointed toes, perforated and stitched detail, brown leather straps, louis heels and trim. 6 1923. Blue glacé-kid shoes, high tongues, suede button-and-strap trim, topstitched detail, pointed toes, louis heels. 7 1924. Brown suede lace-up shoes, high vamps, ribbon laces, yellow snakeskin tongues and strap trim, pointed toes, louis heels. 8 1925. White suede shoes, high tongues, cut-away detail forming straps, elasticated side gussets, pointed toes, louis heels. 9 1925. Green glacé-kid bar-strap shoes, dyed snakeskin inserts above and below button fastenings, pointed toes, louis heels. 10 1925. Brown leather shoes, shaped vamps and side panels trimmed in yellow suede, topstitched detail, pointed toes, louis heels. 11 1926. Yellow snakeskin bar-strap shoes, pointed toes, dark-brown leather louis heels and trim. 12 1926. Fitted black leather boots, topstitched seams, pointed toes, louis heels. 13 1926. Black satin T-strap evening shoes, bead embroidery on fronts and straps, pointed toes, louis heels. 14 1928. Gold brocade evening shoes, high vamps, brooch trim, pointed toes, louis heels. 15 1927. Bar-strap shoes, brown kid fronts, matching trim, pointed toes; louis heels and main body in contrast-colour suede. 16 1928. Silver kid bar-strap shoes, open strap fronts, pointed toecaps, cut-away sides, louis heels.

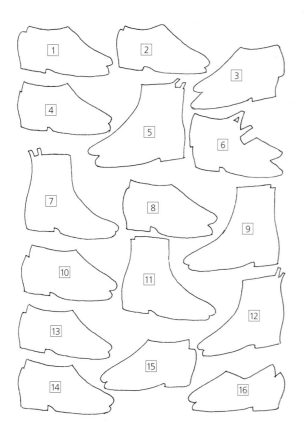

Men's Footwear 1914–1928

[1] Black leather lace-up shoes, brogued detail, ribbon laces, apron fronts, stacked heels. [2] Black leather lace-up shoes, brogued detail, blunt toes, toecaps, stacked heels. [3] Black leather lace-up shoes, brogued and topstitched detail, pointed toecaps, stacked heels. [4] Brown leather lace-up sports shoes, side vents, blunt toes, elongated toecaps, topstitched detail, rubber soles and heels made in one piece. [5] Brown leather boots, laced through eyelets over instep, hooked above, blunt toes, brogued detail on toecaps, stacked heels. [6] Grey rubber beach shoes, strap-and-buckle fastenings, cut-away sides, blunt toes, soles and heels made in one piece. [7] Black leather boots, laced through eyelets over instep, hooked above, pointed toecaps, stacked heels. [8] Two-tone leather lace-up shoes, topstitched detail, pointed toecaps, stacked heels. [9] Brown leather boots, laced through eyelets over instep, hooked above, pointed toecaps, brogued detail, stacked heels. [10] Leather lace-up shoes, pointed toes, winged toecaps, brogued and topstitched detail, stacked heels. [11] Brown leather boots, laced through eyelets over instep, hooked above, pointed toecaps, brogued and topstitched detail, stacked heels. [12] Black leather lace-up boots, pointed toecaps, brogued and topstitched detail, textured uppers, stacked heels. [13] Brown and white leather lace-up shoes, pointed toecaps and half-apron fronts, topstitched detail, stacked heels. [14] Blue and white leather lace-up shoes, pointed toes, mock-apron fronts, brogued and topstitched detail, stacked heels. [15] Brown suede lace-up shoes, pointed toecaps, brogued detail, stacked heels. [16] Red leather step-in slippers, pointed toes, cut-away sides, blue suede trim, stacked heels.

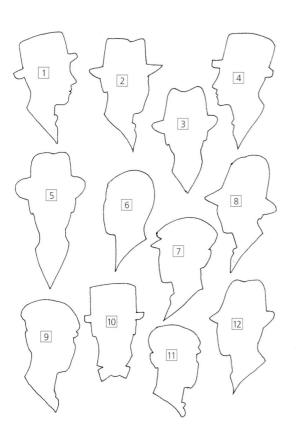

Men's Hats 1914–1928

[1] Fur-felt hat, soft crown, flat top, narrow self-colour silk-ribbon band, turned-up curled brim. [2] Black fur-felt trilby, high crown, central crease, wide petersham-ribbon band, wide stiffened brim turned up at either side. [3] Brown felt trilby, tall crown, deep central crease, wide petersham-ribbon band and flat bow, hard brim turned up at either side, petersham-ribbon binding. [4] Olive-green flecked wool-tweed hat, soft high wide crown, flat top, inset self-fabric band and bow, narrow curled brim. [5] Black fur-felt homburg hat, hard crown, central crease, wide silk-grosgrain band, brim turned up at sides, silk binding. [6] Blue rubber bathing hat, adjustable chinstrap. [7] Brown flecked wool-tweed cap, full crown cut in one piece, wide stiffened peak. [8] Olive-green fur-felt fedora, high crown, central crease, wide self-colour silk-ribbon band and flat bow, wide turned-down brim. [9] Green beaver-cloth cap, full crown cut into eight sections, topstitched decoration, ventilation holes above ears, small stiffened peak. [10] Black wool hat, wide crown, seamed flat top, wide petersham-ribbon band and bow, narrow turned-up brim, topstitched edge. [11] Brown wool cap, full crown cut in one piece, dart shaping, small stiffened peak. [12] Black fur-felt trilby, tall crown, central crease, petersham-ribbon band and bow, narrow turned-down brim.

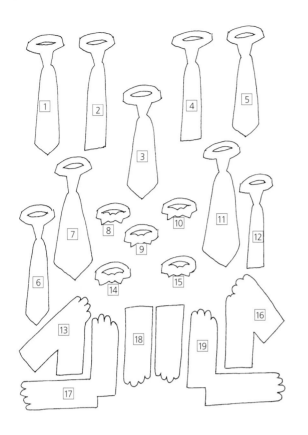

Men's Neckwear and Gloves 1914–1928

1 Lilac checked silk necktie, narrow body, pointed hems.
2 Red patterned wool necktie, narrow body, straight fringed hems. 3 Green patterned silk scarf-tie, wide body, open pointed hems. 4 Wool necktie, horizontal stripes, narrow body, straight fringed hems. 5 Blue patterned silk necktie, over-patterned with large spots, narrow body, pointed hems. 6 Grey checked artificial-silk necktie, narrow body, pointed hems. 7 Green patterned cotton scarf-tie, wide body, open pointed hems. 8 Brown patterned silk bow-tie, to be tied by wearer. 9 Grey striped silk bow-tie, to be tied by wearer. 10 Pink spotted silk bow-tie, to be tied by wearer. 11 Lavender patterned artificial-silk scarf-tie, wide body, open pointed hems. 12 Multicoloured horizontally striped knitted artificial-silk and cotton necktie, narrow body, straight hems. 13 Handstitched yellow-brown chamois-leather gloves, single-button fastening at back of wrist. 14 Green striped silk bow-tie, to be tied by wearer. 15 Brown patterned artificial-silk bow-tie, to be tied by wearer. 16 Handstitched brown textured-leather gloves, single-press-stud fastening at back of wrist. 17 Handstitched tan hogskin gloves, single-button fastening at back of wrist. 18 Handstitched leather gloves, two-button fastening at back of wrist. 19 Handstitched red-brown kid gloves, pintucked inserted panel, scalloped edge, single-button fastening at back of wrist.

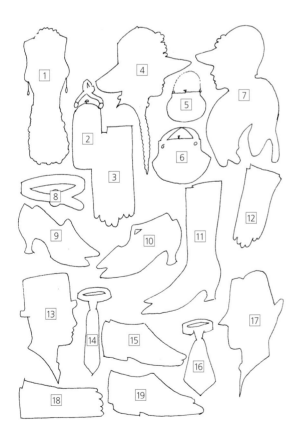

Accessories at a Glance 1914–1920

1 Black silk hat, self-fabric pleated rosette on centre-front. Red and white glass bead necklace; matching drop earrings. 2 Multicoloured beaded bag, long handle, tortoiseshell clasp and frame. 3 Grey kid gloves, three-button fastening at back of wrist. 4 Ruched pink silk-chiffon hat, wire frame, tall crown, flower trim, wide brim. Imitation-pearl necklaces. 5 Small multicoloured beaded bag, silver-gilt clasp, frame and fine chain handle. 6 Silk bag, large grey and black pattern, black velvet side gussets and ribbon handles, ivory clasp and frame. 7 Blue felt cloche hat, wide front brim, tall crown, draped chiffon band, trimmed with pink silk roses. Black fox-fur stole. Blue glass beads. 8 Multicoloured beaded belt, oval yellow plastic buckle, red silk lining. 9 Brown lace-up leather shoes, pointed toecaps, louis heels. 10 Green leather bar-strap shoes, openwork detail, pointed toes, louis heels. 11 Patent-leather boots, beige suede knee-high uppers, side-button fastening, pointed toes, louis heels. 12 Green textured-leather gloves, black topstitching, button fastening at back of wrist. 13 Pale-grey felt hat, tall crown, flat top, self-colour petersham-ribbon band, narrow curled brim. 14 Striped wool necktie, narrow body, pointed hems. 15 Brown leather lace-up shoes, pointed toecaps, brogued detail, stacked heels. 16 Blue striped silk scarf-tie, wide body, pointed hems. 17 Felt trilby, tall crown, centre crease, self-colour petersham-ribbon band and bow, wide brim. 18 Kid gloves, contrast topstitching, press-stud fastening at back of wrist. 19 Brown leather lace-up shoes, pointed toecaps, brogued detail, stacked heels.

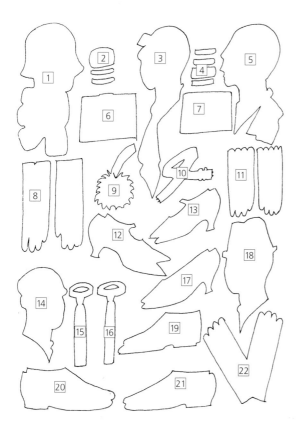

Accessories at a Glance 1921–1928

1 Tan felt cloche hat, domed crown, wide silk-ribbon band, turned-down brim. Fur scarf. 2 Wide plastic bangle, carved decoration; orange plastic bangle; wooden bangle. 3 Beige felt cloche hat, topstitched ribbon band threaded through oval buckle. Yellow silk scarf edged in brown and white. 4 Green plastic bangle; green carved wood bangle; pink, white and brown striped plastic bangle; carved bone bangle. 5 Blue felt cloche hat, topstitched cut-out detail on crown, matching band and bow, narrow shaped brim. Multicoloured patterned panne-velvet scarf, round lacquered-raffia brooch. 6 Brown leather clutch bag, strap-and-button trim, topstitched detail. 7 Silver leather clutch bag, flap decorated with stylized pink leather bow, matching trim. 8 Blue kid gloves, loop-and-button fastening at front, pink trim. 9 Tiny reticule covered in pink ostrich feathers, ribbon handle. 10 Green suede belt, hook-and-bar fastening, split yellow plastic disc trim. 11 Beige kid gloves, scalloped edges, button fastening at back of wrist. 12 Leather bar-strap shoes, cut-out sides, pointed toes, button trim, louis heels. 13 Leather bar-strap shoes, brogued pointed toecaps, contrast-colour suede trim, louis heels. 14 Olive-green wool-tweed peaked cap. 15 Blue checked silk necktie, narrow body, straight hems. 16 Red patterned silk necktie, narrow body, straight hems. 17 Brown leather shoes, low vamps, brogued detail, pointed toes, louis heels. 18 Grey felt homburg, tall crown, central crease, self-colour band and bow, curled brim. 19 Two-tone leather lace-up shoes, apron fronts, pointed toecaps, topstitched detail, stacked heels. 20 Two-tone leather lace-up shoes, pointed toecaps, stacked heels. 21 Leather lace-up shoes, pointed toecaps, brogued detail, stacked heels. 22 Handstitched beige leather gloves, two-button fastening at back of wrist.

The Complete Look 1914–1928

1 1914. Two-piece light-blue wool suit: hip-length single-breasted jacket, large buttons, full-length sleeves, three tiers from under elbow-level, fur-edged hems, matching trim on hipline and hem of ankle-length skirt between panels of knife-pleats, some handstitched detail. Brimless blue felt toque, black feather trim. Fox-fur stole. Short black kid gloves. Black silk bag, tortoiseshell clasp and frame, long handle. Leather boots, beige suede uppers, side-button fastenings, pointed toecaps. 2 1916. Mid-calf-length checked wool overcoat, double-breasted fastening, large collar, raglan sleeves, topstitched seams. Wool peaked cap. White collar-attached shirt; green striped wool necktie. Brown wool trousers, turn-ups. Yellow leather gloves. Leather boots, off-white suede uppers, side-button fastenings, pointed toecaps. 3 1923. Red artificial-silk unfitted dress, three-quarter-length cuffed sleeves, mid-calf-length skirt. Jet and silver chain hip-belt. Long black artificial-silk scarf. Long black jet beads; matching drop earrings. Green felt cloche hat, turned-back brim, black taffeta rosette at one side of crown. Short green kid gloves, pointed edges. Black leather clutch bag, buttoned flap, topstitching. Grey silk stockings. Black leather T-strap shoes, louis heels. 4 1924. Brown wool two-piece suit: double-breasted jacket, wide lapels, flap pockets; straight-cut trousers, turn-ups. White collar-attached shirt; striped silk necktie. Grey felt hat, tall crown, flat top, turned-up brim. Brown leather gloves. Two-tone leather lace-up shoes, apron fronts, stitched detail, stacked heels. 5 1928. Green wool-crepe dress, unfitted bodice, V-shaped neckline, stitched detail, matching hip basque on knee-length knife-pleated skirt, full-length sleeves, green suede belt, round buckle. Brimless felt cloche hat, topstitched side panel. Outsized black bead necklace; matching drop earrings. Black fox-fur stole. Short kid gloves. Various coloured bangles. Black leather clutch bag, pointed flap, stitched detail. Flesh-coloured silk stockings. Black leather shoes, button trim, pointed toes, louis heels.

Women's Hats 1929–1933

1929

1929

1929

1930

1930

1930

1930

1931

1931

1932

1932

1933

1933

1933

1934

1934

1934

1934

1935

1936

1936

1935

1936

1936

1937

1937

1938

1937

1938

1938

1939

1939

1939

1939

1940

1940

1940

1940

1941

1941

1941

1942

1941

1942

1942

1942

1931

1929

1942

1929

1935

1935

1940

1940

1937

1942

1942

Women's Bags and Purses 1929–1942

1929

1929

1930

1930

1931

1931

1930

1931

1932

1932

1931

1933

1932

1933

1933

1934

1934

1935

1935

1935

1936

1937

1935

1938

1938

1939

1941

1942

1940

1940

1942

1929

1931

1933

1934

1935

1937

1938

1936

1935

1940

1942

1929

1929

1935

1930

1929

1929

1932

1933

1935

1936

1929

1931

1935

1940

1938

1938

1939

1941

1941

1942

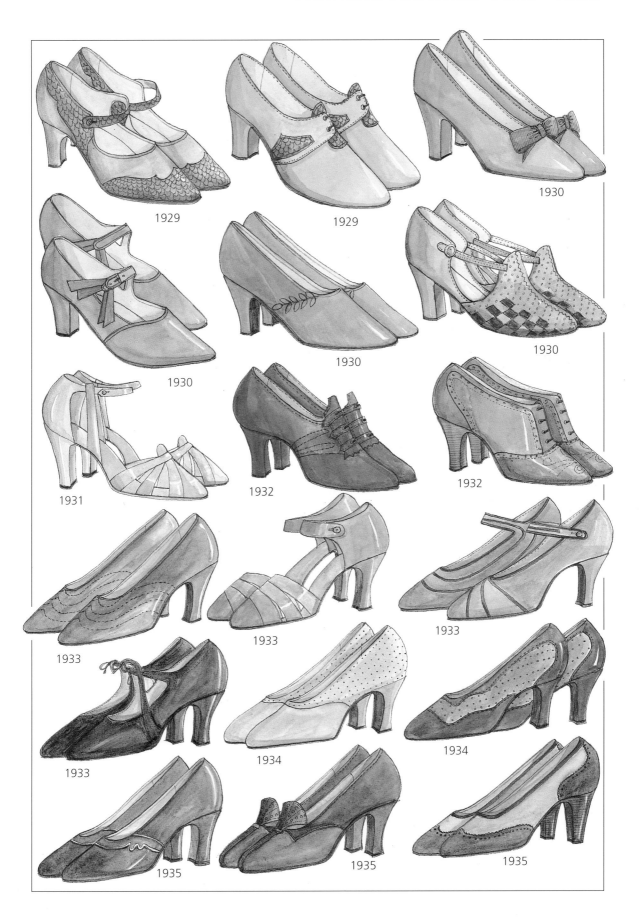

1929

1929

1930

1930

1930

1930

1931

1932

1932

1933

1933

1933

1933

1934

1934

1935

1935

1935

Women's Footwear 1936–1942

1936

1936

1936

1937

1937

1938

1938

1940

1940

1940

1941

1941

1941

1941

1942

1942

1942

1942

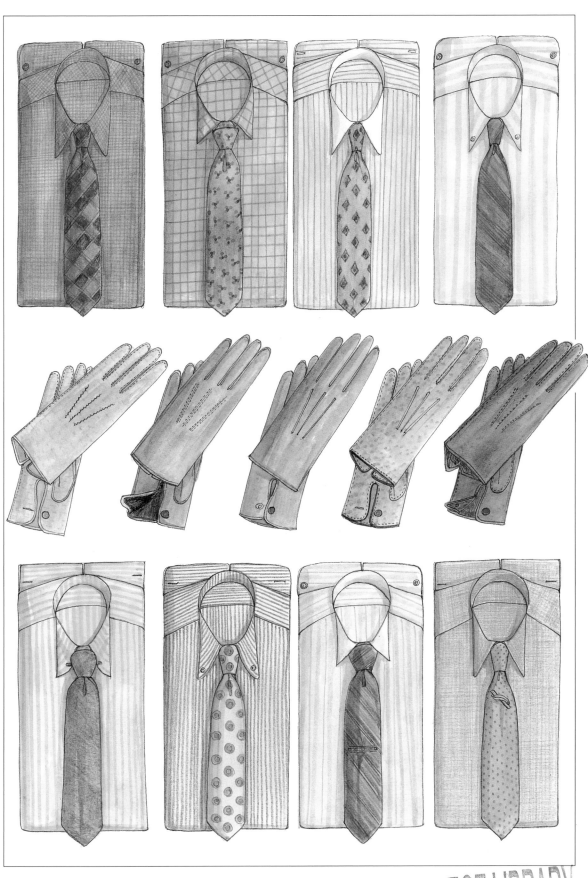

1929

1935

1937

1940

1942

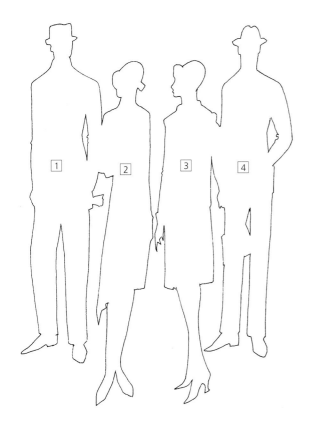

The Complete Look 1929

1 Grey three-piece wool suit: waisted single-breasted jacket, double-breasted lapels, flap pockets; double-breasted waistcoat, wide shawl collar, straight hem; narrow trousers, turn-ups. White shirt with collar attached, pin through pointed collar; dark-green silk necktie. Grey felt trilby, central crease, wide band, turned-up brim. Brown leather gloves. Brown leather lace-up shoes, pointed toecaps, stacked heels.
2 Green patterned silk-velvet dress, unfitted hip-length wrapover bodice, narrow roll collar, flesh-coloured silk infill, full-length inset sleeves, straight knee-length skirt, bias-cut waterfall side panel, green leather belt, diamond-shaped plastic buckle clasps. Brown straw cloche hat, wide petersham-ribbon band and bow trim, turned-down brim. Green glass beads. Brown leather clutch bag, orange plastic frame and clasp. Short green leather gloves, scalloped cuffs, cut-out detail. Two-tone leather bar-strap shoes, pointed toes, apron fronts.
3 Blue patterned silk dress, unfitted hip-length bodice, boat-shaped neckline, full-length inset sleeves, straight knee-length skirt, knife-pleats from shaped hip-yoke. Black silk-velvet scarf, bias-cut waterfall ends, silver brooch; matching earrings. Black straw cloche hat, wide satin band, brim turned up at front. Short black cloth gloves, pleated cuffs. Black leather clutch bag, silver fastening, blue leather trim. Black leather shoes, wide bar-straps, pointed toes, button trim, high louis heels.
4 Two-piece checked linen suit: single-breasted jacket, three-button fastening, patch pockets; straight-cut trousers, turn-ups. White cotton shirt, stiff collar; rust-red artificial-silk necktie. Felt trilby, central crease, black band, shaped brim. Black leather gloves. Two-tone leather lace-up shoes, apron fronts, pointed toes, stacked heels.

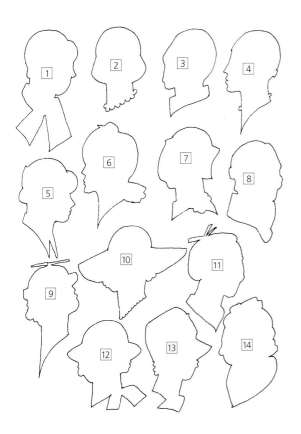

Women's Hats 1929–1933

1 1929. Blue felt cloche hat, moulded crown cut into four sections, topstitched self-fabric band, matching turned-up front brim. Striped silk-velvet scarf. 2 1929. Beige felt cloche hat, narrow and elongated brim turned up and split at centre-front, topstitched edge, wooden brooch-pin. Glass-bead necklace. 3 1929. Blue felt cloche hat, tall crown cut into sections, mock earflaps, self-felt motif.
4 1930. Evening cap, multicoloured glass-bead embroidery, scalloped edge, double earflaps, satin bow at back. Green glass and wire necklace. 5 1930. Navy-blue straw hat, open top crown infilled with ribbon-embroidered net, narrow brim, blue silk-ribbon trim.
6 1930. Pink felt hat, wide brim swept up at front, secured by brown silk-taffeta bow, back brim gathered under band of matching taffeta.
7 1930. Fawn felt hat, asymmetric cut, creased and pleated swept-back brim. Green suede flower brooch. 8 1931. Brimless persian-lamb hat, draped into self-fabric band at back, black velvet crown. Collar in matching persian lamb. 9 1931. Small beige felt hat, narrow turned-up brim, shallow crown, bow trim, matching band. 10 1932. Navy-blue straw hat, shallow crown, blue chiffon drapery, blue plastic bow trim, matching narrow band, wired brim edged with veil of embroidered silk-organdie. Graded imitation-pearl necklace. 11 1932. Pink velvet beret, woven design of dark-pink velvet ribbon, satin-ribbon trim on crown. 12 1933. Black silk hat, wide white silk-ribbon band, matching crossed bands over shallow crown, wired brim, white silk lining. 13 1933. Olive-green felt hat, tall crown, long crease caught under knotted petersham-ribbon band, turned-down brim, split at one side under knotted band. 14 1933. Black felt turban-style hat, crossover rolled brim, knotted at centre-front, asymmetric fan of pleats. Fur collar.

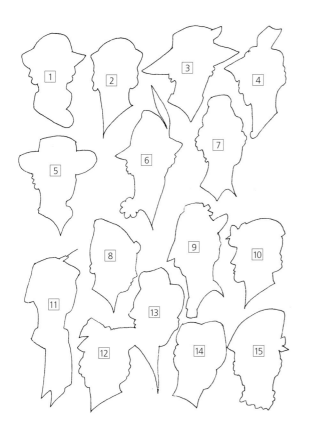

Women's Hats 1934–1938

1 1934. Light-brown felt hat, shallow crown, wide striped silk band with plain suede band across it, set at an angle and threaded through an oval ring, turned-down brim. Fur collar. 2 1934. Grey felt hat, narrow turned-up brim, close-fitting crown forming mock buttoned-down flap to one side of front. 3 1934. Brown straw hat, shallow crown, topstitched dark-brown silk band, matching knotted bow, wide brim. 4 1935. Brimless red velvet hat, tie detail, wired ends. 5 1935. Blue felt hat, small crown, flat top, wide twisted silk band, wide brim, wired edge. Neckscarf matching hatband. 6 1936. Dark-yellow felt hat, tapered crown ending in rounded point, narrow black leather band, green feather trim, wide brim, wired edge. Suede flower brooch. 7 1936. Brimless black felt hat, tapered crown, spiral fur trim. 8 1936. Brimless green felt skullcap, sectioned crown tapered to rounded point. 9 1936. Light-brown felt hat, tapered crown, waisted flat top, self-colour suede bow trim at one side, wide brim, wired edge. 10 1937. Brimless cream cloth hat, shallow crown topped with flat cap, lilac ribbon bow and trim. 11 1937. Brimless dark-yellow felt hat, flat crown set onto narrow topstitched band, matching flap securing decorative wood and metal pin. Brown patterned silk-velvet scarf. 12 1937. Red velvet cap, large peak, stylized bow-and-strap trim on shallow crown, handstitched edges and detail. 13 1938. Brown straw hat, shallow crown, self-straw loop, red edging, matching band-and-bow trim, narrow brim. 14 1938. Blue straw hat, shallow crown trimmed with velvet berries and leaves, narrow brim turned up and split at back, wired edge. 15 1938. Cream straw hat, deep brim swept up to cover shallow crown, black satin-ribbon trim at edge of one side of brim, black silk-ribbon bow lined in cream silk at opposite side by head.

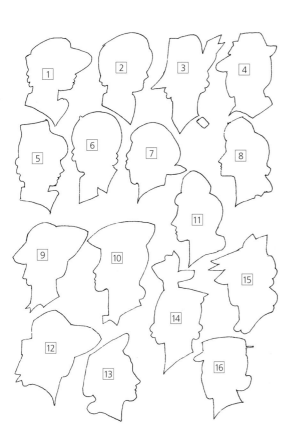

Women's Hats 1939–1942

1 1939. Brown felt hat, crumpled crown, dark-brown threaded petersham-ribbon band-and-bow trim on top, wide front brim turned up at back. 2 1939. Brown felt beret, one of four sections with handstitched trim. 3 1939. Black felt hat, wide pleated panne-velvet band, taffeta ends, wide brim, wired edge. 4 1939. Tan felt hat, brown leather band threaded through buckle part-way up tapered flat-topped crown, matching fringed tongue trim, wide front brim turned up at back. 5 1940. Pale-blue felt hat, shallow fitted crown, creased top, half-brim at front lined in brown felt, handstitched edges, matching threaded band, dark-blue felt buckle. 6 1940. Tan fur-felt beret, brown felt band-and-bow trim at front. 7 1940. Blue felt beret, machine topstitched decoration, matching band and bow trim. 8 1940. Tan felt hat, skullcap crown, moulded turned-back brim edged with pink felt. 9 1941. Brown straw hat, shallow crown, wide petersham-ribbon band, wide brim, wired edge, turned down at front and up at back. 10 1941. Fawn felt hat, crownless turned-up brim perched at an angle, secured by self-felt band around back of head. 11 1941. Pink felt hat, skullcap crown, stand-up bonnet brim at front. 12 1941. Dark-blue straw hat, small shallow flat-topped crown, wide black petersham-ribbon band, matching bow at back, wide turned-down brim, wired edge. 13 1942. Brown cloth beret, sectioned crown, wider at front, narrow band, hat worn on back of head. 14 1942. Olive-green taffeta turban, large loops and ends from ring covered in ruched self-fabric. 15 1942. Small green straw beret, wide band, self-straw loop and ends trim top of crown. 16 1942. Brimless blue felt hat, flat-topped crown, threaded feather trim, self-felt band around back of head.

Jewelry 1929–1942

1 1929. Cream and brown lace dress, low square neckline, large silk flowers at one side below shoulder, sleeveless bloused bodice above fitted hip-yoke, knee-length skirt, waterfall side panels dipping at either side. Rolled-gold necklace, set with paste and glass beads, centre pendant; matching long drop earrings. Multicoloured plastic and painted-wood bangles. Flesh-coloured silk stockings. Beige leather shoes, straps and pointed toes. 2 1931. Oblong silver brooch set with imitation diamonds. 3 1929. Cream and black plastic bow-brooch, imitation-diamond trim. 4 1942. Gold brooch in form of a bunch of flowers, set with rubies, emeralds and pearls. 5 1942. Pink wool dress, fitted bodice, V-shaped asymmetric neckline, padded shoulders, three-quarter-length sleeves, self-fabric belt, floor-length skirt, front panel gathered from under hip-yoke. Large paste brooch of flowers and leaves; matching clip earrings and hairslides/barrettes. Silver strap shoes. 6 1935. Silver and diamanté bracelet, snap fastening at side. 7 1935. Yellow bias-cut crepe dress, draped bodice, low neckline, twisted shoulder straps caught by diamanté clips, matching fastenings on self-fabric belt, floor-length skirt, slight back train. Long drop silver earrings set with white paste stones; matching wrist bracelet. 8 1940. Blue wool-crepe dress, fitted bodice, wrapover effect, drapery to side hip, high V-shaped neckline, padded shoulders, full-length fitted sleeves, ankle-length skirt. Necklace of imitation pearls bound in fine gold wire; matching large clip earrings and wrist bangles. Blue suede shoes. 9 1937. Diamanté dress or belt clips, square sapphire detail. 10 1940. Stylized gold bow-knot brooch. 11 1942. Flower-shaped brooch, 9-carat gold set with imitation emeralds, rubies and turquoise, surrounded by gold leaves and stems.

Women's Bags and Purses 1929–1942

1 1929. Clutch purse, shaped flap, vertical bands in contrast colours. 2 1929. Blue leather bag, topstitching, plastic frame and clasp. 3 1930. Black velvet evening bag, curved frame, long handle, silver trim. 4 1930. Beige leather bag, silver buckle and buttoned leather strap, matching frame and clasp, topstitching. 5 1930. Blue textured-leather bag, asymmetric flap, self-leather strap. 6 1931. Silk evening bag, side pleats, gold frame, pearl edging, matching clasp, chain handle. 7 1931. Leather bag, asymmetric flap, large press-stud. 8 1931. Leather bag, flap bound and trimmed in blue, concealed fastening. 9 1932. Green suede bag, metal frame and rigid handle made in one piece, jeweled clasp, topstitching. 10 1932. Leather bag, V-shaped contrast-colour inserts. 11 1934. Round bag, textured-leather sides and handle, suede front and back, zip fastening. 12 1933. Blue leather bag, metal frame and clasp, triangular-shaped motif at front. 13 1933. Leather bag, metal frame and double clasp, saddle design in topstitched contrasting colour. 14 1933. Blue leather bag, asymmetric set clasp, matching topstitching at opposite side. 15 1934. Half-moon-shaped leather bag, wide contrast binding, plastic clasp. 16 1935. Crocodile bag, topstitching, metal frame and clasp. 17 1935. Grosgrain evening purse, covered frame, silver clasp, diamanté trim. 18 1935. Leather bag, metal frame and clasp, flat handles, topstitching. 19 1936. Green leather bag, metal frame and clasp, flat handles. 20 1937. Leather bag, metal frame, silver trim and lock, rigid handle. 21 1938. Pleated silk evening bag, long handle, gold frame. 22 1938. Crocodile bag, metal frame, brass fittings, flat handles. 23 1939. White leather bag, blue covered frame and rouleau handles. 24 1940. Leather bag, wooden handles, topstitching. 25 1940. Suede bag, monogrammed central panel, zip fastening. 26 1941. Cloth bag, covered metal frame, plastic clasp, flat handles. 27 1942. Red cloth bag, covered metal frame, rouleau handle, plastic clasp. 28 1942. Suede and leather bag cut into panels, buttoned flap.

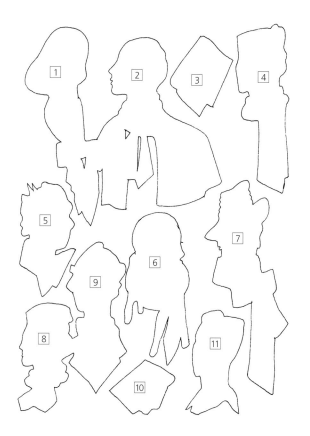

Women's Scarves and Capes 1929–1942

1 1929. Natural-straw cloche hat, domed crown, blue ribbon band, wide brim lined in spotted blue silk; matching long scarf tied into large bow. 2 1931. Gold lamé shoulder cape, black silk-velvet lining, tie neck. 3 1933. White silk scarf square, printed on one corner with wearer's name in dark blue, matching pink-edged border. 4 1934. Brimless tan velvet pillbox hat, piped through centre with yellow velvet, gold brooch of stylized leaves worn at one side. Long multicoloured patterned panne-velvet scarf, bordered on short edges and trimmed in plain orange. 5 1935. Beige felt hat, shallow creased crown, petersham-ribbon band, feather trim, brim turned up at sides. Short white ermine scarf, wrapped over at one side, secured by large button. 6 1937. Close-fitting brimless green felt hat, edged with double row of multicoloured feathers. Dyed stone-martin-fur scarf, fastening at one side under head. 7 1938. Blue felt hat, tall crown, horizontal pleats, asymmetric top, wide brim, wired edge. Grey squirrel scarf, wrapover, fastening under large self-fur bow. 8 1935. Brimless blue knitted-wool hat, edge patterned in green and blue, matching bow detail at one side and detail on short scarf above pointed ends. 9 1936. Green felt hat, shallow creased crown, ribbon band and bow, brown plastic brooch. Short multicoloured striped panne-velvet scarf. 10 1940. Wool scarf square, red and green pattern, brown border, fringed edges. 11 1942. Red-flecked pink wool scarf, plain red border, worn as a turban.

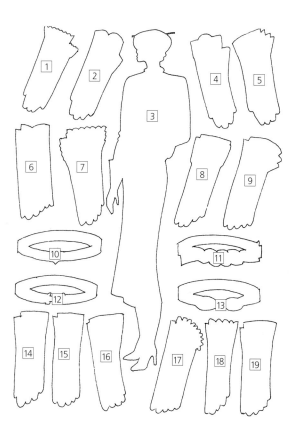

Women's Gloves and Belts 1929–1942

1 1929. Blue cloth gloves, pleated cuffs, single loop-and-button fastening. 2 1929. Kid gloves, shaped cuffs, embroidered trim. 3 1935. Green patterned wool dress, scarf neckline, raglan sleeves, padded shoulders, mid-calf-length skirt, wide tan leather belt, triangular shaped metal buckle. Brimless black felt hat, shaved quill trim. Tan leather bag, brass clasp fastening. Black felt gauntlet gloves, tan leather trim. Black leather shoes, tan trim, pointed toes, high heels. 4 1929. Cloth gloves, paler gathered inserts trim flared scalloped cuffs, dark topstitching. 5 1930. Kid gloves, asymmetric flared cuffs, button trim, dark topstitching. 6 1932. Blue textured-leather gloves, red trim. 7 1933. Knitted pink silk gloves, tiered scalloped gauntlet cuffs. 8 1935. Leather gloves, side gussets, contrast-colour leather trim and pipings. 9 1936. Black leather gauntlet gloves, topstitched cuffs, bone buttons. 10 1929. Brown leather belt, topstitched edges, brass buckle and eyelets. 11 1931. Beige suede belt, concealed fastening under beige and brown spotted twisted-silk trim. 12 1935. Blue suede belt, wide navy-blue leather bindings, topstitched detail, wide-spaced chrome clasp fastening. 13 1940. Navy-blue velvet belt, self-colour suede rouleau detail. 14 1938. Leather gloves, flared cuffs, gathered detail through plastic rings, leather backing, matching colour of topstitching. 15 1938. Cloth gloves, multicoloured embroidered detail. 16 1939. Leather gloves, unseamed gauntlet cuffs, side gussets, contrast-colour leather trim and bindings. 17 1941. Kid gloves, unseamed curved cuffs, edged with loops and triangles of self-kid, dark topstitching. 18 1941. Leather gloves, scallop-edged cuffs, perforated pattern, dark topstitching. 19 1942. Textured-leather gloves, tucked and topstitched gauntlet cuffs.

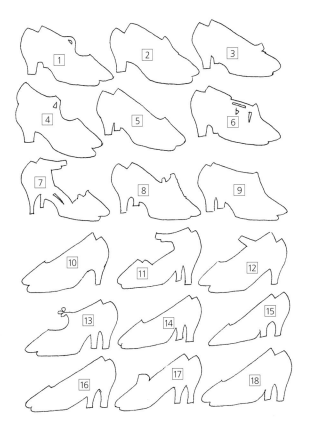

Women's Footwear 1929–1935

1 1929. Leather shoes, medium-high heels; bar-straps, apron fronts and side panels in dark snakeskin. 2 1929. Light-grey glacé-kid lace-up shoes, medium-high heels, tongues and shaped inset side panels in snakeskin. 3 1930. Light-brown leather shoes, medium-high heels, petersham-ribbon bow trim. 4 1930. Light-tan leather shoes, two-tone sunburst decoration at sides below buckled bar-straps, medium-high heels. 5 1930. Grey glacé-kid shoes, topstitched leaf design on side seams, medium-high heels. 6 1930. Suede shoes, medium-high heels, open sides linked above by narrow straps to high vamps, perforated self-suede fronts, threaded leather trim. 7 1931. Silver kid dance shoes, ankle-straps, open sides, low vamps, strap sides, solid toes, high heels. 8 1932. Green leather lace-up shoes, fastening through straps over decorative tongues, black topstitching, high heels. 9 1932. Brown leather lace-up shoes, high vamps, apron fronts, brogued detail, high stacked heels. 10 1933. Blue glacé-kid shoes, low vamps, topstitched detail, high heels. 11 1933. Gold satin dance shoes, wide ankle-straps, button fastening, open sides, low vamps, strap sides, solid toes, high heels. 12 1933. Beige suede shoes, high bar-straps, low vamps, fine brown leather bindings and trim, high heels. 13 1933. Black glacé-kid shoes, crossed bar-straps, laced fastenings, topstitched detail, high heels. 14 1934. Pale-grey suede shoes, low vamps, plain apron fronts, pinhole decoration on backs, high heels. 15 1934. Blue leather shoes, high heels, low vamps, panels of perforated beige suede at sides and front. 16 1935. Brown kid shoes, low vamps, fine pipings of white kid, high heels. 17 1935. Shoes with red suede uppers, perforated fan-shaped tongues and narrow centre-front panels, black glacé-kid fronts and high heels. 18 1935. Cream leather shoes, brown leather apron fronts, back heel decoration and bindings, high stacked heels.

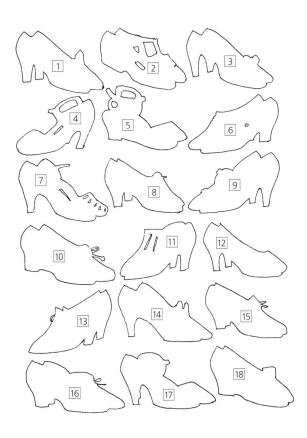

Women's Footwear 1936–1942

1 1936. Blue glacé-kid shoes, low vamps, attached tongues, topstitched detail, high heels. 2 1936. Brown leather T-strap shoes, open sides, split fronts, peep toes, flat heels. 3 1936. Blue leather shoes, low vamps, self-leather bow trim, scalloped red leather inset piping on side seams. 4 1937. Blue suede evening shoes, ankle-straps, cut-out detail, open sides, high gold leather heels, matching trim on strap fronts and peep toes, thin platform soles. 5 1937. Pink suede sling-back shoes, ankle-straps, open sides, low vamps, peep toes, high wedge heels, thin platform soles. 6 1938. Blue suede lace-up shoes, perforated panels, leather bindings and medium-high heels. 7 1938. Silver kid dance shoes, ankle-straps, open sides, strap fronts, high heels, platform soles. 8 1940. Tan suede lace-up shoes, brogued and perforated detail, ribbon laces, high heels. 9 1940. Red leather shoes, high vamps, elasticated sides, scalloped edges connected by black leather bow clips, topstitched detail, high heels. 10 1940. Brown leather lace-up shoes, green suede trim, perforated detail, leather laces, large tassel ends, high wedge heels. 11 1941. Cream suede T-strap shoes, shaped sides, decorative topstitching, high heels. 12 1941. Blue and violet two-tone leather shoes, serpentine seaming, low vamps, high heels. 13 1941. Brown leather lace-up shoes, snakeskin tongues, trim and high heels 14 1941. Black leather shoes, high vamps incorporating gathered bow detail above ruched fronts, topstitching, high heels. 15 1942. Tan leather shoes, high vamps, wide straps, side-laced fastening, platform soles, medium-high heels. 16 1942. Brown suede shoes, high vamps, shaped sides, handstitching, leather laces through self-suede straps, medium-high heels. 17 1942. Black suede shoes, ankle-straps, open sides, low vamps, peep toes, high red leather heels and platform soles. 18 1942. Brown leather shoes, high vamps, looped tongues, green snakeskin trim, wedge heels.

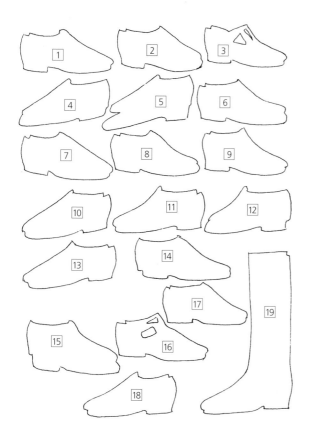

Men's Footwear 1929–1942

1 Brown leather lace-up shoes, pointed toecaps, topstitched edges and detail, stacked heels. 2 Olive-green leather lace-up shoes, apron fronts with piped seam, handstitched detail, rubber soles and heels. 3 Brown leather sandals, buckled T-strap, open sides, cut-out detail on fronts, rubber soles and heels. 4 Brown and cream leather lace-up shoes, raised seams, rubber soles and heels. 5 Leather lace-up shoes, white body, brogued detail and handstitching, blue leather pointed toecaps, matching tongues, facings and heel backs, brogued detail, stacked heels. 6 Tan and white leather lace-up shoes, brogued detail, pointed scalloped edges, blunt toes, stacked heels. 7 Brown sealskin lace-up shoes, raised seams, blunt toes, stacked heels. 8 Black leather lace-up shoes, blunt toecaps, brogued edges, matching tongues, stacked heels. 9 Olive-green and white leather lace-up shoes, raised seams, blunt toes, rubber soles and heels. 10 Black leather lace-up shoes, blunt apron fronts, brogued detail, pale-grey leather inset above, stacked heel. 11 Blue leather and white textured-leather lace-up shoes, pointed toecaps, brogued detail, handstitching, stacked heel. 12 Tan and white leather lace-up shoes, blunt toecaps, handstitching, rubber soles and heels. 13 Lace-up leather shoes, navy-blue heel backs, matching apron fronts, scalloped edges and handstitching, white leather uppers, perforated pattern, stacked heels. 14 Brown leather lace-up shoes, blunt toecaps, brogued detail, stacked heels. 15 Tan leather step-in shoes, high tongues under wide straps, blunt toes, handstitching, stacked heels. 16 Brown suede sandals, buckled T-strap fastenings, open sides, cut-out detail on fronts, rubber soles and heels. 17 Brown leather lace-up shoes, blunt toes, raised seams, stacked heels. 18 Black leather shoes, strap-and-buckle fastenings, handstitching, stacked heels. 19 Knee-high leather boots, dark-brown shoes with buckled straps, matching cuffs above cream legs.

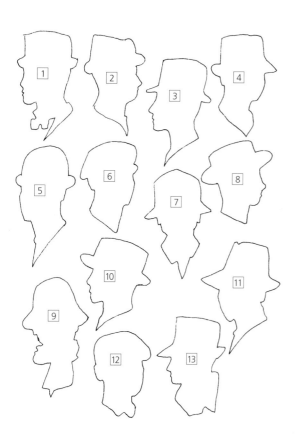

Men's Hats 1929–1942

1 Brown fur-felt hat, tall crown, creased on sides, narrow turned-up brim, brown petersham-ribbon binding, matching band. 2 Grey felt homburg, tall crown, centre crease, wide brim, curled edges, grey petersham-ribbon binding, matching wide brim. 3 Grey fur-felt hat, tall crown, long central crease, black petersham-ribbon band and bow, narrow brim swept up at sides. 4 Olive-green felt hat, tall crown, centre crease, wide olive-green petersham-ribbon band, wide brim. 5 Black hard bowler hat, tall rounded crown, narrow curled brim, black petersham-ribbon binding, matching band and bow. 6 Light-brown flecked wool-tweed cap, side sweep to seamed crown, wide stiffened peak. 7 Brown wool-tweed hat, tall unstructured crown, matching turned-down brim, self-fabric band and bow, topstitched edges. 8 Olive-green felt hat, deep crease around top of shallow crown, narrow olive-green leather band, straight brim, hat worn at an angle. 9 Brown wool-tweed hat, herringbone pattern, tall unstructured crown cut in four sections, inset self-fabric band and bow, wide unstructured brim, worn turned down. 10 Natural-straw boater, shallow crown with flat top, wide blue striped silk band and large bow, wide flat brim. 11 Blue fur-felt trilby, tall crown, centre crease, narrow petersham-ribbon band and bow, wide brim swept up at back, hat worn at an angle. 12 Light-brown wool cap, fitted crown overlaps shallow stiffened peak. 13 Black fur-felt trilby, tall crown angled to back, wide black petersham-ribbon band and bow, wide brim turned down at front and up at sides and back, hat worn at an angle.

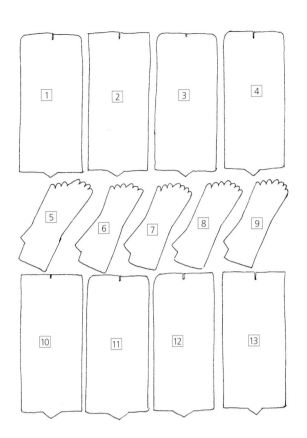

Men's Shirts, Ties and Gloves 1929–1942

[1] Brown checked brushed-cotton shirt, attached collar, long points, buttoned cuffs. Multicoloured checked silk tie. [2] Green checked brushed-cotton shirt, attached collar, short points, buttoned cuffs. Green patterned silk tie, windsor knot. [3] Blue, pink and grey striped cotton shirt, attached plain white collar, long points, linked cuffs. [4] Grey and white broad-striped cotton shirt, attached collar, long buttoned-down pointed collar, buttoned cuffs. Blue and green striped silk tie. [5] Handstitched pigskin gloves, single-button fastening at back of wrist. [6] Brown leather gloves, machine-stitched, single press-stud fastening at back of wrist, brown fur lining. [7] Olive-green leather gloves, machine-stitched, single press-stud fastening at back of wrist. [8] Handstitched textured-leather gloves, single-button fastening at back of wrist, edges piped in brown. [9] Handstitched brown kid gloves, single press-stud fastening at back of wrist, brown fur lining. [10] Brown and white striped cotton shirt, attached collar, long points, linked cuffs. Pink and brown broad-striped silk tie, gold pin between collar points and under double windsor knot. [11] Blue and white striped cotton shirt, attached collar, buttoned-down points, linked cuffs. Patterned yellow silk tie. [12] Grey and green striped cotton shirt, plain white attached collar, short points, buttoned cuffs. Brown and green striped silk tie, double windsor knot; gold bar-pin. [13] Blue textured-cotton shirt, attached collar, long points, linked cuffs. Pink spotted silk tie; gold bar-pin worn at an angle.

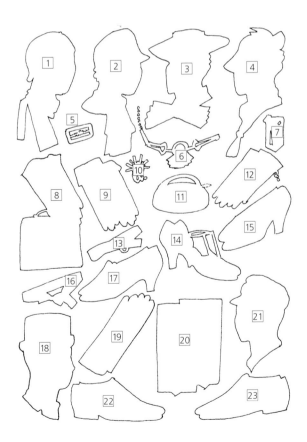

Accessories at a Glance 1929–1935

[1] Brimless fawn felt cloche, pleated self-felt bow trim. Green striped panne-velvet scarf. [2] Red felt hat, high crown creased from narrow band, half brim to front, blue felt flower trim. Blue patterned silk-taffeta scarf. [3] Blue straw hat, shallow crown, crease round top edge, petersham-ribbon band, wide brim. Blue spotted white organza scarf, pleated bow. [4] Olive-green felt hat, shallow crown, narrow band, turned-down brim, feather trim. Silk scarf, brooch pin. [5] Oblong silver brooch, set with pink stones. [6] Silver necklace, set with white paste stones. [7] Oblong metal brooch, set with black stones, black plastic ribbons. [8] Blue leather gloves, openwork detail on cuffs. Blue leather bag, grey textured-leather insert, scalloped edges, metal frame, small rouleau handle. [9] Leather gloves, handstitched cuffs caught under plain bar. [10] Gold brooch, set with blue stones. [11] Cream silk evening bag embroidered with beads and pearls, zip fastening. [12] Light-brown leather gloves, handstitched cuffs, tassel trim. [13] Pink ribbon belt, cream edging, round metal ring buckle. [14] Silver kid T-strap dance shoes, open sides, strap fronts, toecaps, high heels. [15] Blue leather shoes, perforated pattern and trim, high heels. [16] Blue leather belt, adjustable stud fastening under white bow. [17] Two-tone leather lace-up shoes, brogued detail, high heels. [18] Brown felt hat, flat top crown, turned-up brim, petersham-ribbon binding, matching band. [19] Handstitched light-brown leather gloves, button fastening at back of wrist. [20] Blue collar-attached cotton shirt, buttoned cuffs. Brown and blue silk tie. Green and white striped cotton collar-attached shirt, buttoned collar points and cuffs. Green patterned silk tie. [21] Olive-green tweed peaked cap. [22] Brown leather lace-up shoes, brogued detail, toecaps, stacked heels. [23] Cream leather lace-up shoes, brown trim, topstitching, rubber soles and heels.

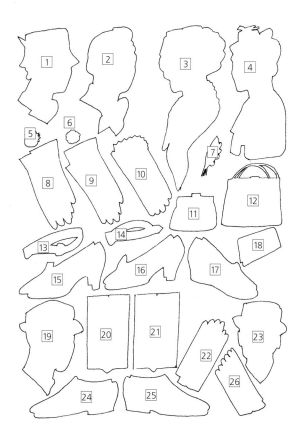

Accessories at a Glance 1936–1942

1 Brown felt hat, narrow band, feather trim, turned-down brim. Silk scarf. 2 Orange wool scarf worn as a turban. Green silk scarf square, brown and white edging. 3 Felt hat, gathered veil of spotted tulle. Fur scarf. 4 Small brown felt hat, tilted forward, shaped crown, flat top trimmed with ribbon bow, matching wide band and binding on turned-up brim, supporting band at back. Short fox-fur cape, petersham-ribbon ties. 5 Small gold brooch, set with imitation stones. 6 Gold brooch, set with imitation rubies. 7 Gold leaf-shaped brooch, set with blue stones. 8 Blue leather gloves, pink trim. 9 Tan textured-leather gloves, brown trim. 10 Beige leather gloves, pointed scalloped cuffs, button fastening. 11 Leather bag, appliqué pattern, metal frame, plastic clasp. 12 Brown snakeskin bag, metal frame and clasp, leather handles. 13 Red suede belt, covered buckle and bar. 14 Brown leather belt, metal buckles. 15 Brown leather shoes, high tongues, topstitching, high heels. 16 Red leather shoes, black leather bow detail, matching trim, heels and platform soles. 17 Cream suede shoes, turned-down tongues, tan leather trim, high wedge heels, platform soles. 18 Blue leather bag, handstitched trim, fastening on corners of full-length flap. 19 Brown felt hat, soft crown, narrow band, brim turned up at back. 20 Collar-attached brown striped cotton shirt, plain white collar, buttoned cuffs. Red and brown striped silk tie, windsor knot; bar-pin. 21 Collar-attached brushed-cotton shirt, linked cuffs, green striped silk tie, bar-pin. 22 Handstitched yellow textured-leather gloves, press-stud fastening at back of wrist. 23 Olive-green felt hat, shallow crown creased all round, narrow band, straight brim. 24 Grey and blue leather lace-up shoes, stacked heels. 25 Brown leather lace-up shoes, apron fronts, handstitching. 26 Tan leather gloves, felt linings, button fastening at back of wrist.

The Complete Look 1929–1942

1 1929. Double-breasted beige wool coat, light-brown slub, single loop-and-button fastening at side-hip, wide lapels, fur collar, matching trim on inset sleeves. Long blue silk scarf, striped in brown on points. Blue felt hat, turned-up brim, inverted pleat at one side. Short brown leather gloves, embroidered trim. Tan leather bag, orange plastic clasp. Brown leather T-strap shoes, openwork detail above pointed toes. 2 1935. Two-piece brown wool suit: hip-length jacket, full-length inset sleeves, padded shoulders; mid-calf-length skirt. Natural-sable cravat made from eight matching skins. Brown felt hat worn at an angle, shallow crown, turned-down brim, brown plastic band-and-bow trim. Brown leather gauntlets, deep cuffs bound in green. Green leather envelope-shaped bag. Brown suede shoes, bow trim, high heels. 3 1937. Two-piece brown checked wool-tweed suit: single-breasted jacket, flap pockets; plus-fours. Light-brown ribbed-wool stockings. Collar-attached brushed-cotton shirt, buttoned collar points; checked green wool tie. Knitted sweater. Wool-tweed peaked cap. Fur-lined yellow leather gloves. Yellow and tan leather lace-up shoes, pointed toecaps, stacked heels. 4 1940. Blue striped wool blouse, short cuffed sleeves, hip-level patch pockets under blue leather belt, hexagonal bone buckle, knee-length plain wool skirt. Checked silk scarf tied into large bow. Small dark-blue felt hat, shallow crown, striped trim at back, brim turned down at front and back. Short grey leather gloves, embroidered trim. Large blue cloth bag gathered onto metal frame, monogrammed trim in one corner. Blue leather shoes, high tongues, platform soles, wedge heels. 5 1942. Single-breasted wool jacket, wide lapels, flap pockets. Collarless tan wool waistcoat. Brown and white striped cotton shirt, plain white collar; blue silk tie; gold clip. Grey wool trousers. Light-brown felt hat, creased crown, narrow band, turned-down brim. Handstitched brown leather gloves. Blue and grey leather lace-up shoes, rubber soles and heels.

1943

1943

1943

1944

1944

1944

1945

1945

1945

1946

1946

1946

1946

1947

1947

1947

1947

1948

1948

1948

1948

1949

1949

1949

1949

1950

1950

1951

1951

1952

1952

1952

1952

1953

1953

1953

1953

1954

1954

1954

1954

1955

1955

1955

1956

1956

1956

1957

1957

1957

1957

1943

1943

1943

1945

1943

1944

1944

1945

1947

1948

1948

1948

1948

1947

1949

1949

1950

1950

1950

1951

1952

1952

1952

1955

1954

1953

1955

1956

1956

1956

1957

1957

1957

Women's Bags 1943–1957

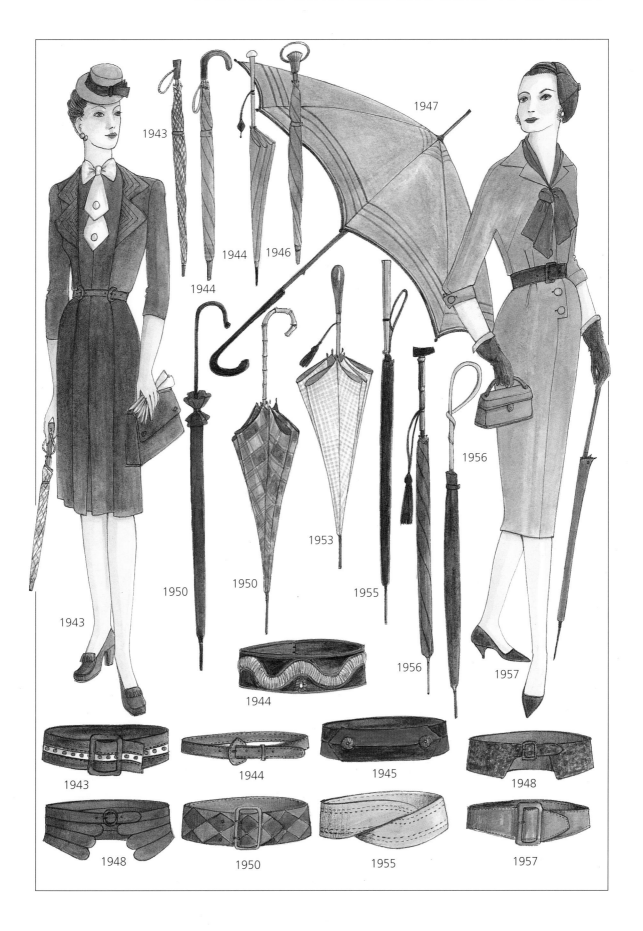

1943
1944
1944
1946
1947
1950
1950
1953
1955
1956
1956
1957
1943
1944

1943
1944
1945
1948
1948
1950
1955
1957

1943

1944

1945

1944

1946

1946

1946

1947

1947

1946

1948

1950

1947

1950

1949

1953

1954

1952

1956

1955

1956

1956

1957

1957

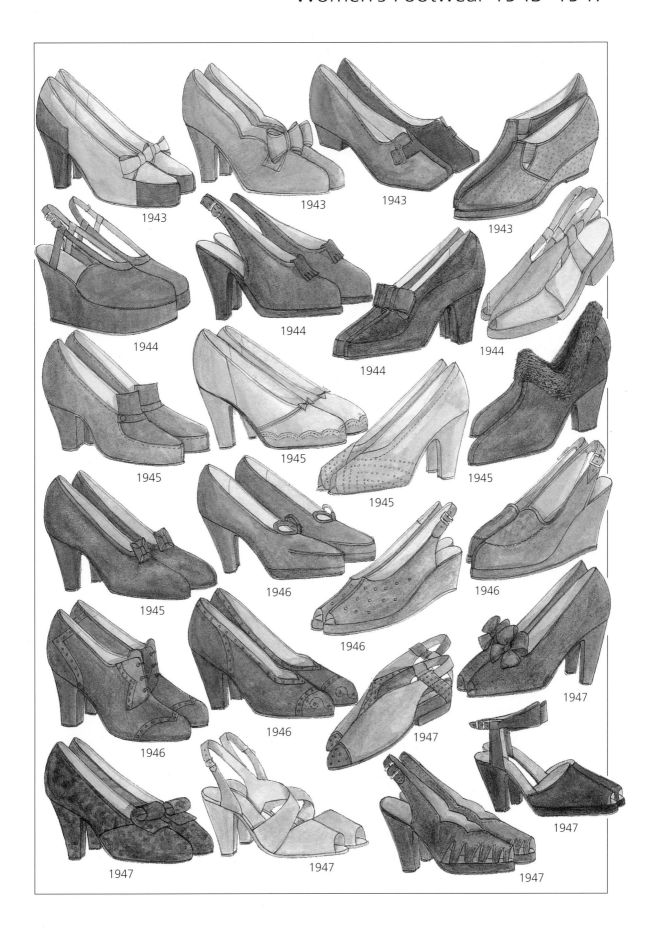

1943

1943

1943

1943

1944

1944

1944

1944

1945

1945

1945

1945

1945

1946

1946

1946

1946

1946

1947

1947

1947

1947

1947

1947

1948

1948

1948

1948

1948

1949

1948

1949

1949

1950

1949

1949

1950

1950

1950

1950

1950

1950

1951

1951

1951

1951

1951

1952

1952

1952

1952

1952

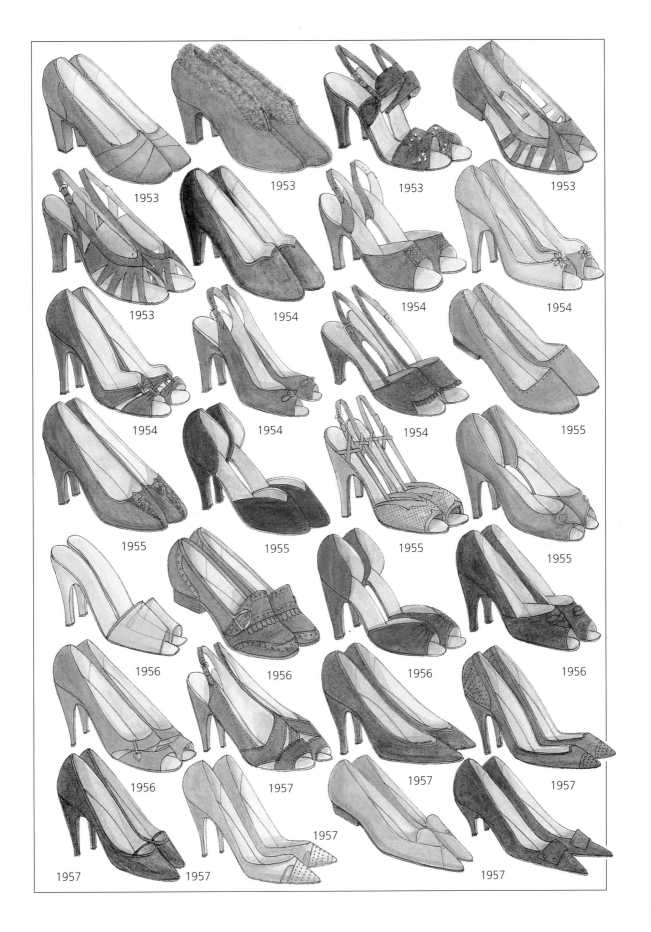

1953

1953

1953

1953

1953

1954

1954

1954

1953

1954

1954

1955

1954

1954

1955

1955

1955

1955

1955

1955

1956

1956

1956

1956

1956

1957

1957

1957

1956

1957

1957

1957

1957

1957

Men's Footwear 1943–1957

1943

1943

1945

1945

1947

1947

1947

1950

1952

1953

1954

1954

1955

1956

1956

1956

1957

1956

1957

1957

1957

1957

1943

1946

1947

1945

1946

1956

1948

1950

1950

1956

1957

1949

1943

1943

1957

1957

The Complete Look 1943

[1] Yellow wool dress, wrapover bodice, three-quarter-length inset sleeves, padded shoulders, knee-length skirt, wide box pleat, brown leather belt, metal buckle. Imitation-pearl necklace, gold leaf-shaped brooch set with blue stones. Small natural-straw hat worn at an angle, looped blue ribbon trim, narrow brim, short veil. Black suede gloves, flared cuffs. Brown leather reticule-style bag. Black suede shoes, peep toes, high heels. [2] Pink cotton dress, spotted in white, button-through top, short inset sleeves, padded shoulders, lower bodice fitted under bust to hip-level, narrow self-fabric belt, matching buckles, knee-length skirt, gathers at front. Blue taffeta turban. White cloth gloves, hand-stitched cuffs. Dark-pink plastic bangle. Blue snakeskin bag, metal frame, double handles. Two-tone blue and white leather shoes, high heels. [3] Two-piece striped wool suit: fitted double-breasted jacket, wide lapels; straight-cut trousers with turn-ups. Collar-attached white cotton shirt; striped silk tie. Grey felt trilby, creased crown, black petersham-ribbon band, turned-down brim. Black leather gloves; matching lace-up shoes, pointed toecaps, stacked heels. [4] Red wool dress, small open panels either side V-shaped neckline, gathered shaping between padded shoulders and bustline, three-quarter-length inset sleeves, self-fabric belt and covered buckle, knee-length skirt. Black straw hat, tiny crown, wide petersham-ribbon band-and-bow trim, wide flat brim. Long black cloth gloves, pointed edges. Bead bracelet; matching clip earrings. Black leather bag, metal frame, clasp fastening, wide handle; matching shoes, blunt toes, high heels. [5] Two-piece blue-grey wool suit: collarless fitted jacket, darted seams under bust, diamond-shaped plastic buttons, full-length inset sleeves, padded shoulders; knee-length skirt, unpressed pleats. Pink coral necklace and earrings. Navy-blue straw hat, tiny crown, white ribbon trim, wide brim turned up at back and down at front. Pink cloth bag, zip fastening. Navy-blue leather gloves, linked bracelet, set with black stones. Navy-blue leather shoes, buckle trim, blunt toes, high heels.

Women's Hats 1943–1947

[1] 1943. Small blue felt boater-shaped hat, worn tilted forwards, flat-topped shallow crown, wide white taffeta-ribbon band spotted in blue, flat brim, topstitched detail. [2] 1943. Brown felt hat worn at an angle and tilted forwards, tiny crown, flat top, creased edge, dark-brown petersham-ribbon band and bow, wide turned-down brim. [3] 1943. Red felt beret with two pointed corners, topstitched edges, matching bow-knot trim on centre-front. [4] 1944. Brimless fawn felt hat, sectioned flared crown, flat top, self-felt pointed flaps, button trim. [5] 1944. Small hat worn tilted forwards, tiny black felt crown, flat top, padded fur brim, matching pompon trim at back. [6] 1944. Felt hat, flared crown, topstitched self-felt band and bow, wide peak. [7] 1945. Small blue felt hat, worn tilted forwards, wide securing band at back, tiny flat-topped crown, self-felt band and bow, appliqué white felt spots, turned-up brim, pale-blue chiffon veil spotted in blue. [8] 1945. Grey felt hat, turned-back brim, crown covered in grey and pink feathers, grey tulle and open-net veils. [9] 1945. Olive-green felt hat, turned-up bonnet brim, shaped two-tier crown, flat top, pleated contrast-colour leather band, feather trim. [10] 1946. Light-green fur-felt hat, tall crown, centre crease, black ribbon band, wide turned-down brim. [11] 1946. Brimless yellow felt hat, wide crown, flat top, curled feather trim. [12] 1946. Small grey straw hat, worn tilted forwards, multicoloured velvet flower trim between narrow rolled brim and shallow flat-topped crown. [13] 1947. Outsized grey straw beret, long hatpin through crown. [14] 1947. Grey felt hat, wide turned-back brim, broad black velvet-ribbon trim on centre-front. [15] 1947. Orange felt hat, worn at an angle, split brim, threaded black quill trim. [16] 1947. Brown felt beret, large self-colour feather pompon trim at one side.

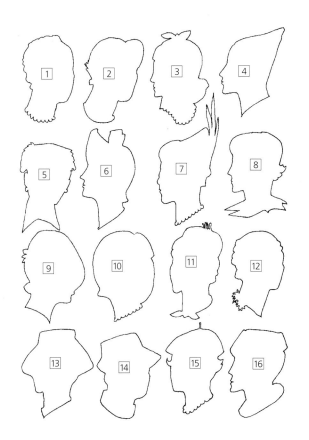

Women's Hats 1948–1952

1 1948. Small net hat worn on side of head, covered in multi-coloured silk roses and leaves, hat and face covered with open-net veil. 2 1948. Brown felt cloche hat, turned-up bonnet brim, side feather trim, self-felt bow. 3 1948. Green cloth snood, knotted bow on centre-front, open crown, gathered bag at back for hair. 4 1948. Brimless felt hat, twisted and pointed crown. 5 1949. Green velvet pillbox hat, self-colour ostrich plume trim at each side. 6 1949. Beige felt hat, wide upswept bonnet brim, machine-stitched and wired edge, shallow crown, self-colour satin bow. 7 1949. Light-brown straw hat, narrow turned-up brim, pointed crown, pleated cloth band, black feather trim. 8 1949. Grey felt cloche hat, shallow bonnet brim, pleated crown. 9 1950. Natural-straw hat, shallow crown, red velvet-ribbon band, yellow and red silk roses and leaves set under wide upswept brim. 10 1950. Off-white plastic straw hat, tiny crown, pleat around top edge, wide brim, off-white silk band and flat bow trim. 11 1951. Natural-straw hat, small crown, wide black ribbon band, narrow rolled brim, velvet flower trim. 12 1951. Half-hat of net covered in lilac silk, flat crown, wired leaf-shaped pieces above ears. 13 1952. Light-brown felt hat, shallow flat-topped crown, wide black silk band and end, matching lining of wide turned-down brim. 14 1952. Brown wool hat, tall crown, pleat around top edge, inset and topstitched band, button trim, hat worn at an angle, turned-down brim at one side, topstitched edges and detail. 15 1952. Net beret-shaped hat, covered in black fur, hat worn straight, felt stalk trim on top. 16 1952. Green felt hat, close brim, peak-shaped at front, flat crown under pleat.

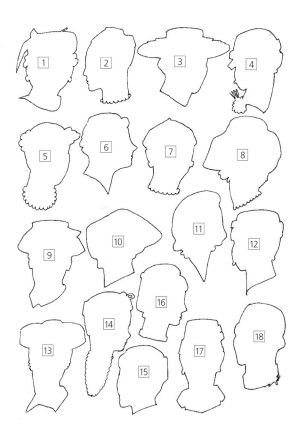

Women's Hats 1953–1957

1 1953. Brimless red felt hat, flattened domed crown, black feather and quill trim, open-mesh veil. 2 1953. Net half-hat covered in graded green and yellow feathers, hat worn to back of head. 3 1953. Black net picture hat, shallow crown draped and pleated in black silk-organdie, matching wide brim, centre-front crease. 4 1953. Brimless beige fur-felt hat, crown pleated around top edge, padded self-felt band and knot trim. 5 1954. Small net skullcap covered in white satin, trimmed with large self-fabric wired bow above centre-front point. 6 1954. Pink grosgrain half-hat, wired points. 7 1954. Green silk hat, panelled crown ending in point under button trim, brim cut in matching panels, seams and edges piped and bound in black. 8 1954. Pink plastic-straw hat, wide scalloped brim finished with grey velvet binding. 9 1955. Natural-straw hat, shallow crown, pleat around top edge, red silk trim threaded through white plastic rings, wide turned-down shaped brim. 10 1955. Dark-blue straw hat, wide turned-down brim and combined crown. 11 1955. White glazed-cotton beret, topstitched sectioned crown, wide blue cotton-satin band. 12 1956. Grey felt hat, domed crown and close brim moulded in one piece, eye-level net veil from under black velvet-ribbon band and bow, paste buckle trim. 13 1956. Pink felt hat, wide brim and shallow crown moulded in one piece, grey tulle trim draped through self-felt loops around outer brim edge. 14 1956. Small orange felt hat, close-fitting crown and seamed brim, wired satin leaves on centre-front, rouleau bow trim. 15 1957. Moulded blue-green half-hat, brooch trim at one side of pleats and folds. 16 1957. Red velvet beret, worn on back of head, sectioned crown, button trim, narrow band. 17 1957. Green felt hat, moulded crown and brim, self-felt bow trim on one side. 18 1957. Corded-velvet hat, red and black patchwork crown, narrow rolled brim in black.

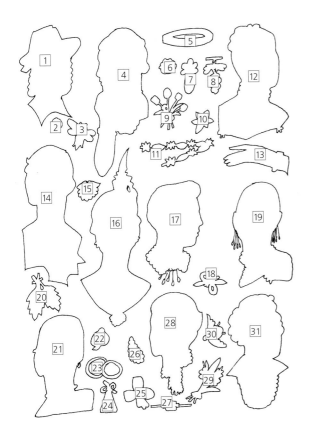

Jewelry 1943–1957

1 1943. Yellow glass-bead clip earrings. 2 1943. Gold brooch, bead and spike detail. 3 1944. Gold and black wasp brooch. 4 1943. Gold fan-shaped hairbrooch. Cream bead necklace from twisted cord. Imitation-ruby-and-pearl linked bracelet. 5 1945. Linked silver bracelet set with imitation amethysts. 6 1943. Enamel brooch, bird motif. 7 1944. Imitation-pearl and diamanté brooch. 8 1945. Small glass pendant brooch of grapes and leaves, silver pin. 9 1947. Gold brooch set with rubies, sapphires, amethysts and pearls. 10 1948. Flower-shaped brooch set with coloured stones and pearls. 11 1947. Linked gold bracelet, set with imitation emeralds. 12 1948. Clip earrings, imitation pearls and diamonds, double pendant. Imitation-pearl choker. Small diamanté dress clips. 13 1948. Silver bracelet, set with pearls, flower motifs. 14 1949. Gold clip leaf-shaped earrings, set with rubies; matching necklace. 15 1949. Diamond and ruby brooch, textured-gold leaf motifs. 16 1950. Diamond and pale-sapphire spiked brooch; matching earrings. 17 1950. Wide pearl collar, teardrop pearls suspended from rows of tiny pearls on centre-front; matching earrings. 18 1952. Gold bow, knot of tiny pearls. 19 1951. Clip earrings, teardrop pearls suspended from wired hoops of seed pearls. Pearls and crystal beads twisted to form short necklace, tassel detail on centre-front. 20 1952. Brooch of black enamel entwined leaves, trimmed in gold, set with small diamonds. 21 1953. Bow-shaped white-gold earrings, set with diamonds. Short choker of large pearls. 22 1952. Small round gold brooch, leaf motifs, set with sapphires. 23 1954. Red and blue leather cuff-link bracelet, gilt chain link. 24 1955. Blue glass pendant, gold bow trim. 25 1956. Silver and diamond looped bow brooch. 26 1955. Large imitation-pearl-and-turquoise brooch. 27 1956. Silver pin brooch, pearl each side of blue stone. 28 1956. Cut-glass-bead choker necklace, off-centre tassel detail. 29 1957. Gold brooch, glass-bead flowers. 30 1957. Glass beetle brooch, gold wings and legs. 31 1957. Long gilt chain and bead necklaces.

Women's Bags 1943–1957

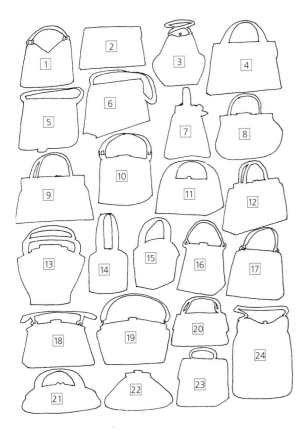

1 1943. Blue leather bag, shaped frame, flap-and-stud fastening, double handles. 2 1944. Beige calf-leather clutch bag, deep flap slotted through wide strap, topstitched detail. 3 1944. Embroidered cream silk evening bag, shaped gold-coloured frame, ribbon handle. 4 1945. Light-brown leather bag, deep flap, strap fastening, wide handles. 5 1945. Tan leather bag, full-length flap, cream canvas panel, strap-and-stud fastening, long handle. 6 1946. Tan leather shoulder bag, stud fastening under shaped flap, long handle. 7 1947. Brown felt bag, elasticated opening under short handle, self-fabric bow trim. 8 1948. Brown suede bag, metal frame, brass clasp, double rouleau handles. 9 1949. Crocodile bag, brass trim, rouleau handles. 10 1950. Round brown leather bag, topstitched detail, brass trim, long handle. 11 1950. Black leather bag, wide handle from base of deep side panels, brass trim. 12 1953. Blue leather bag, brass trim, two flat handles. 13 1953. Plum-coloured leather shell-shaped bag, pleated detail, brass trim, flat handles. 14 1954. Small drum-shaped red and white striped leather bag, black leather lid, long handle and trim. 15 1954. Small oblong grey leather bag, scalloped flap, deep sides, wide handle, topstitched detail. 16 1955. Brown leather bag, clasp fastening, brass trim, rouleau handle. 17 1955. Tall tan leather bag, clasp fastening and brass trim, flat handle. 18 1955. Large black leather bag, brass trim, short flat handle. 19 1956. Shiny olive-green leather bag, brass trim, long handle. 20 1956. Small light-blue plastic bag, scalloped flap, brass trim, long rouleau handles. 21 1956. Small light-brown textured-leather bag, dark-orange plastic trim, short handles. 22 1957. Black silk evening bag, gold wire trim. 23 1957. Brown leather bag, deep side panels, flap, lockable brass fastening, topstitched trim, short handle. 24 1957. Outsized green pitted-leather bag, shaped frame, clasp, brass trim, long handle.

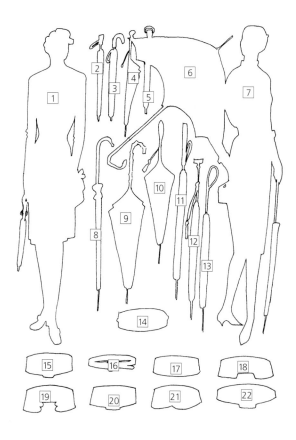

Women's Umbrellas and Belts 1943–1957

1 1943. Brown wool dress, mock lapels, cream satin bow and jabot, elbow-length sleeves, narrow suede belt, two covered half-buckles. Small natural-straw hat, ribbon trim. Cloth gloves. Checked cotton umbrella, wooden handle and ferrule, cord carrier. 2 1943. Checked cotton umbrella, painted wooden handle, cord carrier. 3 1944. Cotton umbrella, contrast-colour stripe, leather handle and carrier. 4 1944. Cotton umbrella, wooden handle, bone cap, cord carrier. 5 1946. Cotton umbrella, carved bone handle, cord carrier. 6 1947. Nylon umbrella, contrast-colour stripe, black edging, long wood and plastic handle, metal ferrule. 7 1957. Beige wool dress, bodice buttoned through to hip from under collar, red silk scarf, three-quarter-length sleeves, wide blue leather belt, covered buckle. Blue felt beret. Blue leather gloves; matching shoes, pointed toes, low spike heels. Red umbrella, long wooden handle, metal ferrule, nylon cover. 8 1950. Long umbrella, plastic handle, nylon cover, frilled collar. 9 1950. Multicoloured checked nylon umbrella, contrast-colour lining, bent bamboo handle. 10 1953. Checked nylon umbrella, contrast-colour lining, plastic handle, cord and tassel carrier. 11 1955. Umbrella, plastic handle, nylon cover, cord carrier. 12 1956. Nylon umbrella, long metal handle, cord and tassel carrier. 13 1956. Long umbrella, twisted-plastic handle, nylon cover. 14 1944. Black velvet belt, white ruched-silk detail, braid trim, back fastening. 15 1943. Blue fabric belt, covered buckle, two-colour braid trim. 16 1944. Brown leather belt, half-buckle, topstitched detail. 17 1945. Blue and red leather belt, brass button fastenings. 18 1948. Wide brown textured-leather belt, narrow strap-and-buckle fastening. 19 1948. Red suede belt, tiered scalloped detail under narrow strap-and-buckle fastening. 20 1950. Tan and green patchwork leather belt, brass buckle. 21 1955. Twisted grey suede belt, topstitched detail, concealed fastening. 22 1957. Shaped gold kid belt, covered buckle, topstitched detail.

Women's Gloves 1943–1957

1 1943. Short checked cloth gloves, open gusset at back below wrist. 2 1944. Brown fake-fur gloves, leather palms. 3 1944. Beige textured-leather gloves, decorative topstitched edges and detail in wool. 4 1945. Grey textured-leather gloves, scalloped detail at one side below wrist, topstitched decoration. 5 1946. Fine blue kid gloves, multicoloured embroidered flower design. 6 1946. Cream kid gloves, three-tier scalloped cuffs, scalloped edges, two outer rows in blue, perforated detail. 7 1946. Beige suede gloves, edges drawn down to one side and held by self-suede knot. 8 1947. Blue kid gloves, pointed scalloped cuffs, self-colour silk cord embroidery and trim. 9 1947. Beige kid gloves, flared cuffs, scalloped edges, openwork, matching flower in one corner. 10 1948. Black nylon evening gloves, diagonal thread embroidered motifs. 11 1949. Multicoloured checked fabric gloves, leather palms and trim. 12 1950. Black silk evening gloves, flared stiffened cuffs, braid embroidery, paste stones. 13 1950. Brown kid gloves, scalloped edges and wrapover detail. 14 1953. Red suede gloves, padded cuffs, embroidery. 15 1954. Short green cloth gloves, inset ruched detail and button trim at one side. 16 1955. Long blue nylon evening gloves, scattered bead and sequin trim, scalloped edges. 17 1956. Pink-brown leather gloves, gathers from under buckle trim. 18 1952. Grey suede gloves, two-tier gathered cuffs, pointed scalloped edges, embroidered trim. 19 1956. Short tan leather gloves, turned-down cuffs, open at one side. 20 1956. Long brown cloth gloves, ruched detail, self-fabric covered-button trim. 21 1957. Long transparent yellow nylon evening gloves, ruched detail above wrist. 22 1957. Short brown suede gloves, red leather binding, topstitching, loop-and-button fastening at back below wrist.

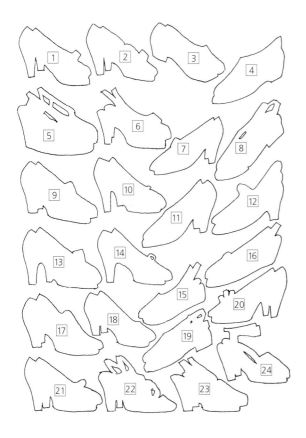

Women's Footwear 1943–1947

1 1943. Two-tone leather shoes, bow trim, blunt toes, high heels. 2 1943. Suede shoes, scalloped sides, bow trim, blunt toes, high heels. 3 1943. Blue and red two-tone leather shoes, square toes, flat heels. 4 1943. Tan textured-leather shoes, high vamps, elasticated gussets, platform soles, low wedge heels. 5 1944. Brown suede sling-back shoes, cut-away sides, blunt toes, platform soles, wedge heels. 6 1944. Blue suede sling-back shoes, fringed tongues, blunt toes, platform soles, high heels. 7 1944. Black leather shoes, high vamps, bow trim, apron fronts, high heels. 8 1944. Beige leather sling-back sandals, wrapover fronts, peep toes, hinged wooden soles, flat heels. 9 1945. Brown leather shoes, high tongues, buttoned straps, medium heels. 10 1945. Beige leather shoes, scalloped suede trim, matching tiny bow trim and high heels. 11 1945. Cream suede shoes, wrapover fronts, perforated decoration, peep toes, high heels. 12 1945. Olive-green suede ankle-boots, black fur trim, medium heels. 13 1945. Red suede shoes, covered buckle trim, blunt toes, high heels. 14 1946. Blue leather shoes, high vamps, rouleau trim, platform soles, high heels. 15 1946. Blue suede sling-back shoes, peep toes, perforated decoration, platform soles, wedge heels. 16 1946. Yellow leather sling-back shoes, orange textured-leather inserts, platform soles, wedge heels. 17 1946. Brown leather lace-up shoes, high vamps, brogued detail, high heels. 18 1946. Tan leather shoes, blunt toes, brogued detail, high heels. 19 1947. Beige and blue leather sling-back shoes, perforated decoration, flat heels. 20 1947. Black leather shoes, rosette trim, peep toes, high heels. 21 1947. Lizardskin shoes, scroll trim, blunt toes, high heels. 22 1947. Beige strap sandals, peep toes, high heels. 23 1947. Brown leather sling-back shoes, scalloped sides, cut-out pattern on sides, peep toes, platform soles, high heels. 24 1947. Navy-blue sling-back shoes, ankle-straps, open sides, peep toes, platform soles, high heels.

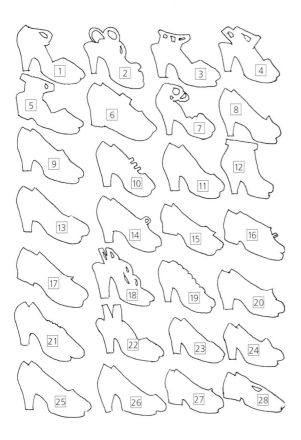

Women's Footwear 1948–1952

1 1948. Suede shoes, ankle-straps, high heels. 2 1948. Suede strap sandals, platform soles, high heels. 3 1948. Leather sling-back shoes, ankle-straps, open sides, peep toes, high heels. 4 1948. Leather sling-back shoes, bar-straps, open sides, cut-away side detail, peep toes, high heels. 5 1948. Suede sling-back shoes, open sides, peep toes, perforated detail, platform soles, wedge heels. 6 1949. Leather bar-strap shoes, perforated detail, platform soles, wedge heels. 7 1949. Leather shoes, ankle-straps, open sides, scalloped decoration, high heels. 8 1949. Leather shoes, pleated detail, peep toes, platform soles, high heels. 9 1949. Lizardskin shoes, folded tongues, high heels. 10 1949. Leather triple-bar-strap shoes, bar trim, high heels. 11 1950. Leather shoes, topstitched detail, high heels. 12 1950. Two-tone leather ankle-boots, side-zip fastening under narrow cuff, platform sole, medium heels. 13 1950. Suede shoes, perforated crossed-strap detail, high heels. 14 1950. Leather shoes, rouleau bow trim, high heels. 15 1950. Leather shoes, double tongue trim, button detail, square toes, low heels. 16 1950. Leather lace-up shoes, snakeskin trim, flat heels. 17 1950. Suede shoes, knot trim, flat heels. 18 1951. Leather strap sandals, high heels. 19 1951. Leather shoes, twisted openwork edge, high heels. 20 1951. Suede shoes, leather trim, topstitched trim, medium heels. 21 1951. Leather shoes, asymmetric vamps, scalloped edges, perforated detail, contrast leather strap-and-buckle trim, high heels. 22 1951. Leather sling-back shoes, open sides, high heels. 23 1951. Leather shoes, grey suede inset trim, high heels. 24 1952. Leather shoes, buckled tongues, stacked heels. 25 1952. Multicoloured and silver Lurex evening shoes, peep toes, high heels. 26 1952. Leather shoes, topstitched and perforated detail, high heels. 27 1952. Two-tone leather and suede shoes, bow trim, low heels. 28 1952. Suede shoes, open at one side, buckled strap, perforated detail, flat heels.

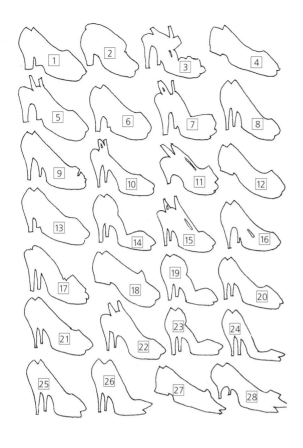

Women's Footwear 1953–1957

1 1953. Suede shoes, seamed detail, square toes, high heels. 2 1953. Suede ankle-boots, fur trim, high heels. 3 1953. Suede strap sandals, high heels. 4 1953. Leather shoes, open strap detail on one side, open toes, flat heels. 5 1953. Leather sling-back shoes, openwork detail on sides, open toes, high heels. 6 1954. Leather shoes, shaped fronts, slender heels. 7 1954. Leather sling-back shoes, open sides, ruched detail above open toes, slender heels. 8 1954. Leather shoes, low vamps, flower trim, open toes, slender heels. 9 1954. Suede shoes, ruched fronts, leather connecting bars, open toes, slender heels. 10 1954. Suede sling-back shoes, buttoned-strap detail, open toes, slender heels. 11 1954. Leather sling-back shoes, self-leather fringe above open toes, slender heels. 12 1955. Leather shoes, cut-away sides, topstitched detail, flat heels. 13 1955. Leather shoes, embroidered-leather inset, slender heels. 14 1955. Suede shoes, open sides, slender heels. 15 1955. Leather sling-back shoes, leather-trimmed canvas fronts, open toes, slender heels. 16 1955. Leather shoes, cut-away on one side, low vamps, wrapover detail, button trim, open toes, slender heels. 17 1956. Transparent plastic mules, open toes, slender heels. 18 1956. Leather shoes, shaped strap and buckle, leather fringe, brogued detail, flat heels. 19 1956. Leather shoes, open sides, low vamps, ruched detail, open toes, slender heels. 20 1956. Leather shoes, low vamps, wrapover detail, rouleau trim, open toes, slender heels. 21 1956. Suede shoes, cut-out detail, open toes, spike heels. 22 1957. Leather sling-back shoes, asymmetric strap fronts, open toes, spike heels. 23 1957. Leather shoes, pointed toes, slender heels. 24 1957. Leather shoes, pointed toecaps, perforated detail, slender heels. 25 1957. Patent-leather shoes, bar-straps, low vamps, pointed toes, spike heels. 26 1957. Suede shoes, low vamps, pointed toecaps, perforated detail, stiletto heels. 27 1957. Leather shoes, wrapover fronts, pointed toes, flat heels. 28 1957. Leather shoes, low vamps, buttoned straps, pointed toes, low stiletto heels.

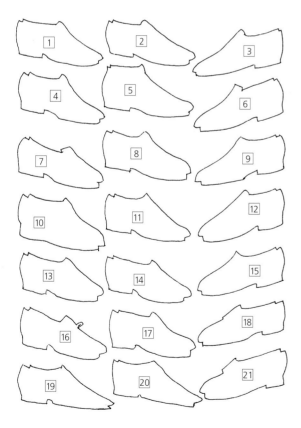

Men's Footwear 1943–1957

1 1943. Suede lace-up shoes, topstitched detail, no toecaps, stacked heels. 2 1943. Textured-leather lace-up shoes, plain leather strap, perforated detail, no toecaps, stacked heels. 3 1945. Leather shoes, topstitched detail, apron fronts, stacked heels. 4 1945. Textured-leather lace-up shoes, topstitched detail, brogued toecaps, stacked heels. 5 1947. Suede lace-up ankle-boots, no toecaps, stacked heels. 6 1947. Leather step-in shoes, high tongues, brogued detail, stacked heels. 7 1947. Leather step-in shoes, short tongues, half bar-strap, apron fronts, stacked heels. 8 1950. Patent-leather lace-up shoes, no toecaps, stacked heels. 9 1952. Leather lace-up shoes, no toecaps, stacked heels. 10 1953. Leather lace-up shoes, apron fronts, combined platform soles and wedge heels. 11 1954. Leather lace-up shoes, apron fronts, topstitched detail, stacked heels. 12 1954. Leather shoes, double strap-and-buckle fastening, grey leather apron fronts and trim, combined crepe soles and heels. 13 1955. Leather shoes, strap-and-buckle fastening, apron fronts, stacked heels. 14 1956. Leather step-in shoes, high tongues, wide straps, cut-out detail, apron fronts, topstitched detail, stacked heels. 15 1956. Leather shoes, combined strap and tongue, apron fronts, stacked heels. 16 1956. Leather lace-up shoes, leather laces with tassels, apron fronts, stacked heels. 17 1956. Leather lace-up shoes, topstitched detail, stacked heels. 18 1957. Leather shoes, high tongues, fringing under strap and buckle, apron fronts, stacked heels. 19 1957. Leather lace-up shoes, no toecaps, brogued detail, stacked heels. 20 1957. Leather lace-up shoes, no toecaps, pointed toes, stacked heels. 21 1957. Suede shoes, laced under fringed tongues, apron fronts, brogued detail, stacked heels.

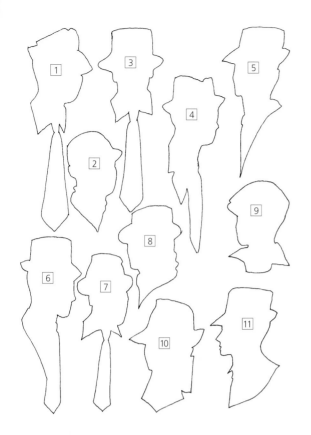

Men's Hats and Neckwear 1943–1957

1 1943. Green felt trilby, creased crown, narrow black petersham-ribbon band, wide brim turned up at back and side. Green and white striped cotton collar-attached shirt. Brown checked wool tie. 2 1945. Close-fitting natural-straw cap, wide curved peak. Striped cotton neckscarf. 3 1946. Natural-straw hat, tall crown, flat top, wide pink and blue spotted silk band, wide brim. Grey cotton collar-attached shirt, buttoned-down collar. Cream silk tie, bird print below plain knot. 4 1947. Blue-grey fur-felt homburg, tall crown, central crease, wide black petersham-ribbon band, matching bound edge of stiff upturned brim. Blue and white striped shirt, separate white collar. Red patterned silk tie. 5 1946. Rough natural-straw hat, tall crown, flat top, wide green patterned silk band, twisted on one side, wide brim. Checked brushed-cotton collar-attached shirt. Three-colour striped silk tie. 6 1948. Tan felt trilby, tall crown, flat top, brown petersham-ribbon band, wide brim, turned up at back. Brown and white striped cotton collar-attached shirt. Brown patterned silk tie. 7 1950. Beige felt hat, creased crown, narrow olive-green petersham-ribbon band, straight brim. Cream cotton collar-attached shirt, cut-away collar points. Patterned silk tie. 8 1950. Fawn felt hat, shallow crown, creased edge, wide ribbon band, bow trim, straight brim. 9 1956. Brown wool cap, shallow curved peak covered by front crown. Brown cotton collar-attached shirt, cut-away collar points, worn open. Patterned silk cravat. 10 1956. Felt trilby, tall creased crown, wide grey petersham-ribbon band and bow trim, turned-down brim. Red and blue patterned silk scarf. 11 1957. Brown tweed hat, seamed band and bow, narrow brim turned up at back. Pale-grey cotton shirt, plain white attached collar. Green knitted-silk tie, central pattern of red diamond shapes.

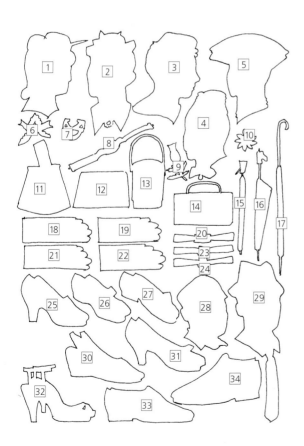

Accessories at a Glance 1943–1949

1 Small felt hat, shallow crown, flat top, side flap, feather trim. Double-loop clip earrings. 2 Small felt hat, shallow crown, flat top, satin-ribbon trim, narrow brim, turned-up edge. Star clip earrings; flower-wreath enamelled brooch. 3 Small felt hat, securing band at back, felt flower trim on centre-front, net veil. Gold clip earrings. 4 Brimless ruched-velvet hat. 5 Crownless felt hat, wide folded brim, rouleau flower trim. Double row of imitation pearls; matching clip earrings. 6 Bird brooch. 7 Clip brooch. 8 Gold wire bracelet, centre dome set with turquoise stones. 9 Gold thistle brooch, set with ruby. 10 Onyx, pearl and gold brooch. 11 Leather bag, single-loop handle. 12 Embroidered silk evening bag. 13 Leather bucket-shaped bag, strap-and-stud fastening. 14 Oblong leather bag, topstitched detail, rouleau handles. 15 Checked cotton umbrella, wooden handle, cord carrier. 16 Cotton umbrella, dog's-head handle, cord and tassel. 17 Long nylon umbrella, leather handle. 18 Leather gloves, ruched detail on outer side below wrist. 19 Fabric gloves, scalloped edge, button trim. 20 Narrow belt, covered oblong buckle. 21 Leather gloves, open gusset at front below wrist. 22 Leather gloves, inset pattern in contrast colour below wrist. 23 Narrow leather belt, covered half-buckle. 24 Narrow leather belt, covered buckle, topstitching. 25 Leather shoes, high vamps, side splits, blunt toes, high heels. 26 Leather bar-strap shoes, openwork detail, wedge heels. 27 Two-tone leather shoes, perforated detail, flat heels. 28 Wool-tweed peaked cap. Patterned silk scarf. 29 Felt trilby, creased crown. Collar-attached striped cotton shirt, buttoned collar points. Striped silk tie. 30 Suede sling-back shoes, peep toes, wedge heels. 31 Two-tone shoes, bow trim, high heels. 32 Suede strap sandals, platform soles, high heels. 33 Leather step-in shoes, brogued detail. 34 Lace-up leather ankle-boots, no toecaps, stacked heels.

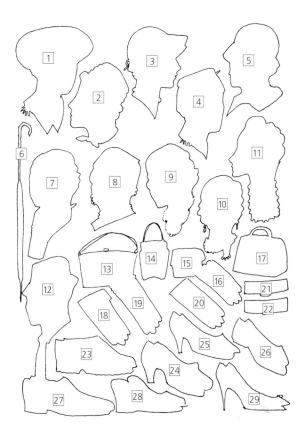

Accessories at a Glance 1950–1957

1 Crownless straw hat, edge bound in contrast colour. Stylized flower brooch; matching clip earrings. 2 Natural-straw hat, narrow turned-up brim, tall crown draped in multicoloured patterned silk. Bead clip earrings. 3 Straw skullcap, short transparent veil, satin rouleau bow trim on back. Imitation-pearl necklace and clip earrings. 4 Felt cloche, topstitched shaped edge to turned-down brim, leather bow trim on centre-front. Snailshell clip earrings; large flower-and-leaf paste brooch. 5 Felt hat, domed crown, narrow turned-down brim. Pearl stud clip earrings. 6 Long umbrella, bamboo handle, nylon cover. 7 Paste hair decoration; matching earrings and bracelet. Long silk gloves. 8 Plastic bead choker; matching earrings. 9 Wired glass bead necklace; clip earrings. 10 Plastic bead necklace, side bow decoration and tassel trim; matching drop earrings. 11 Long plastic bead necklace; matching clip earrings. 12 Felt trilby, creased crown, leather band, narrow brim. Checked cotton collar-attached shirt, cut-away collar. Narrow knitted tie. 13 Leather bag, curved frame, clasp fastening, strap handle. 14 Small velvet evening bag, covered frame, ribbon handle. 15 Multicoloured silk clutch purse, flap, decorative stud fastening. 16 Leather bag, brass lock and trim, short rouleau handle. 17 Leather gloves, pointed turned-down cuffs, button trim. 18 Suede gloves, ruched detail below wrist. 19 Short fabric gloves, scalloped edge. 20 Suede gloves, scalloped edge. 21 Wide leather belt, covered buckle, double spikes and eyelets. 22 Wide suede belt, covered half-buckle. 23 Lace-up leather shoes, brogued detail, crepe soles. 24 Leather shoes, folded flaps, blunt toes, high heels. 25 Suede shoes, low vamps, spike heels. 26 Leather shoes, contrast trim, flat heels. 27 Step-in leather shoes, bar-strap, apron fronts, stacked heels. 28 Leather mules, open toes, perforated detail, wedge heels. 29 Leather shoes, low-cut vamps, pointed toes, rosette trim, stiletto heels.

The Complete Look 1943–1957

1 1943. Striped wool three-piece suit: single-breasted jacket, wide lapels, flap pockets; collarless single-breasted waistcoat; straight-cut trousers, turn-ups. Collar-attached shirt; silk tie, contrast-colour pattern. Felt trilby, crown with central crease, wide band, turned-down brim. Leather gloves. Leather lace-up shoes, blunt toecaps. 2 1943. Fitted hip-length striped wool jacket, single-breasted fastening, inset sleeves, padded shoulders, plain wool collar and lapels. Round enamelled brooch. Knee-length skirt, centre-front inverted box pleat, matching fabric. Silk scarf. Straw hat, tiny crown, deep striped band, wide brim, turned-up edge. Kid gloves, scalloped cuffs. Leather handbag, shaped flap, double-stud fastening, padded rouleau handle. Leather shoes, blunt toes, large bow trim, high heels. 3 1949. Patterned silk two-piece suit: hip-length fitted jacket, single-breasted fastening, notched shawl collar, inset sleeves; mid-calf-length skirt. Crownless felt hat, double brim on centre-front. Three rows of imitation pearls; matching clip earrings. Short kid gloves. Leather bag, flap-and-stud fastening, long strap handle. Leather shoes, ruched detail, peep toes, platform soles, high heels. 4 1957. Wool-tweed dress, collarless unfitted bodice, double-breasted fastening above bustline, three-quarter-length sleeves, wide wool belt, covered buckle, below-knee-length narrow skirt. Felt hat, small crown draped in patterned silk, turned-down brim. Plastic bead choker; matching clip earrings. Suede gloves, cuffs, button detail; matching bag, covered frame, two strap handles, brass trim. Suede shoes, bar-straps above low-cut vamps, pointed toes, high stiletto heels. 5 1957. Three-piece wool suit: double-breasted jacket, wide lapels; collarless single-breasted waistcoat; narrow trousers, no turn-ups. Collar-attached shirt; silk tie, diamond pattern under plain knot. Felt trilby, creased crown, wide band, narrow brim. Step-in leather shoes, low tongues under wide straps, stacked heels.

Women's Hats 1958–1962

1958
1958
1958
1958
1959
1959
1959
1960
1960
1960
1960
1961
1961
1961
1962
1962
1962

1963

1963

1963

1963

1964

1964

1965

1965

1965

1965

1966

1966

1966

1967

1967

1967

1968

1968

1968

1968

1968

1969

1969

1969

1969

1971

1970

1971

1971

1971

1958

1958

1958

1959

1958

1959

1960

1959

1959

1960

1961

1960

1965

1966

1961

1964

1967

1964

1965

1968

1968

1971

1969

1969

1970

1970

1971

1971

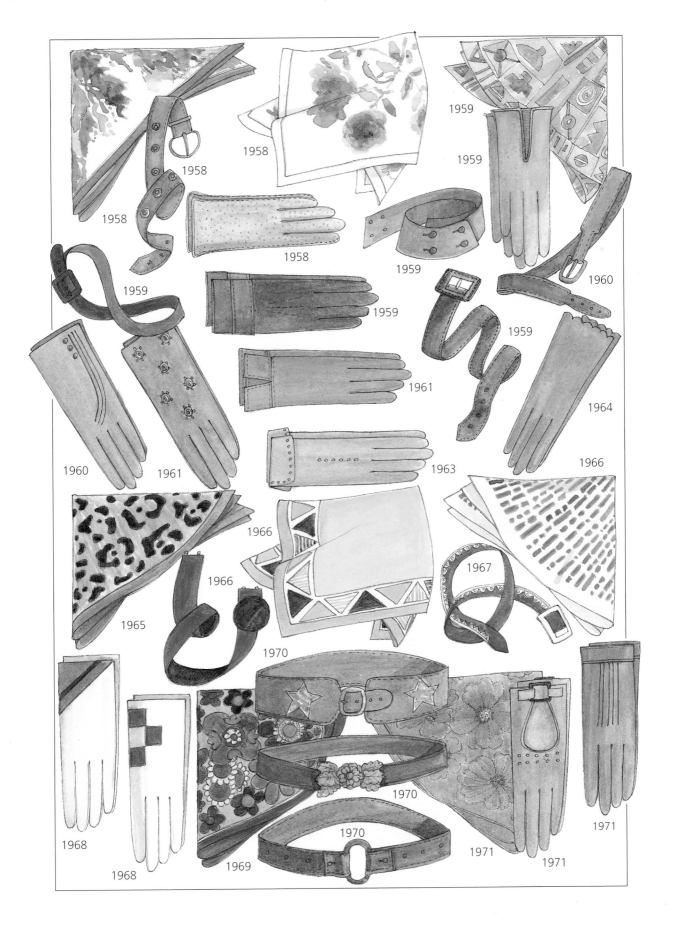

1958
1958
1958
1958
1958
1959
1959
1959
1960
1960
1961
1961
1960
1962
1961
1962
1962
1962
1963
1963
1963
1962
1964
1964
1964

1965
1965
1965
1966
1966
1966
1966
1966
1967
1967
1967
1968
1968
1968
1969
1969
1969
1970
1970
1970
1971
1971
1971
1971

Women's Boots 1958–1971

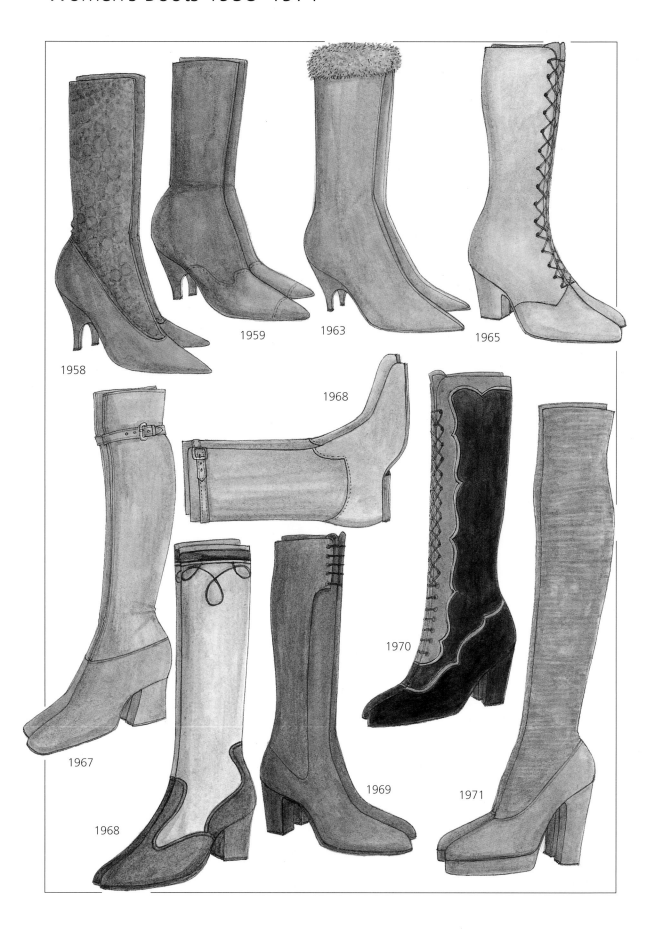

1958

1959

1963

1965

1968

1967

1968

1969

1970

1971

1958

1958

1959

1960

1960

1960

1960

1963

1963

1963

1964

1964

1964

1964

1965

1967

1968

1968

1971

1971

1971

1958

1958

1958

1959

1963

1959

1961

1963

1965

1966

1968

1969

1969

1970

1971

1971

1958 1958 1958 1958 1959 1959 1960

1961 1962 1969 1969 1965 1966

1969 1969 1970 1970 1970 1971 1971

1958

1965

1964

1971

1971

The Complete Look 1958

1 Brown linen-look cotton dress, fitted bodice, short cap sleeves, low neckline, wide stand-away plain white cotton collar, slotted with orange spotted cotton scarf, tied into bow at front, below-knee-length straight skirt. Orange straw pillbox hat. Large pearlized plastic beads; matching clip earrings and bracelet. Tan suede gloves. Brown leather bag, flap, short rouleau handle, brass fittings. Brown leather shoes, low vamps, T-strap infill, pointed toes, high stiletto heels. 2 Green wool dress, unfitted bodice, slashed neckline, short inset sleeves, wide green leather belt, covered buckle, two spikes and sets of eyelets, below-knee-length straight skirt. Multicoloured stretch-fabric turban. Green glass beads; matching clip earrings. Blue suede gloves, ruched and buttoned detail on one side; matching bag, deep flap, long strap handle, brass fittings. Blue leather shoes, low vamps, fine bar-straps, pointed toes, high stiletto heels. 3 Light-brown wool suit: single-breasted jacket, narrow lapels, flap pockets; narrow trousers, no turn-ups. Grey and white collar-attached shirt; green silk tie, single bar of blue and yellow. Felt hat, creased crown, dark ribbon band, narrow brim. Black leather step-in shoes, high tongues, bar-straps, blunt toes, apron fronts. 4 Yellow and blue spotted cotton dress, fitted bodice, high round neckline, short cap sleeves, wide self-fabric belt, covered buckle, below-knee-length flared skirt, off-centre pleat, double-breasted button trim at hip-level. Yellow straw hat, brim turned back. Large blue wooden beads; matching clip earrings. Short yellow cotton gloves, topstitched cuffs. Yellow leather clutch bag, clasp fastenings at each end of frame. Yellow leather shoes, low vamps, rouleau bow trim, square toes. 5 Brown and beige wool-tweed two-piece suit: single-breasted collarless jacket, inset sleeves, hip-level flap pockets; below-knee-length straight skirt. Blue felt hat, creased crown, inset band, wide brim. Large earrings; matching brooch. Blue and brown patterned silk scarf. Blue leather gloves. Brown leather bag, buckled strap handles, plastic clasp. Brown leather shoes, low vamps, flat bow, pointed toes, high stiletto heels.

Women's Hats 1958–1962

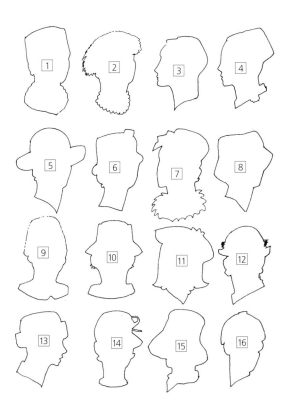

1 1958. Brimless deep-pink felt hat, deep crown, black silk braid motif trim on centre-front. 2 1958. Large black fur beret, set onto wide black satin band, large bow on centre-front. 3 1958. Blue suede cap, sectioned crown, small topstitched peak under self-suede buckled strap. 4 1958. Small pillbox hat, draped in spotted beige silk, worn on back of head. 5 1959. Large hat, tall brown velvet crown, wide tan band, wide upswept brim covered in civet-cat fur. 6 1959. Green felt hat, tall crown, wide black petersham-ribbon band and slotted detail, narrow rolled brim. 7 1960. Evening hat, orange satin pillbox, brown velvet-ribbon bow trim on centre-front, worn on back of head. 8 1960. Blue felt hat, shallow creased crown, bright-green ribbon band, knotted off-centre, long ends, wide turned-down brim. 9 1960. Brimless striped mink-fur hat, high crown. 10 1960. Blue and turquoise checked wool hat, tall crown, crease around top edge, self-fabric bow trim on centre-front, stiffened turned-down brim. 11 1961. Natural-straw hat, deep turned-back brim, single blue silk flower trim on one side edge. 12 1961. Brown and beige wool-tweed bowler hat, stiffened crown, self-fabric knotted bow trim on centre-front, fringed ends, narrow curled brim. 13 1961. Light-blue and dark-blue woven-plastic-straw hat, large crown, deep turned-up brim. 14 1962. Red velvet jockey cap, stiffened crown, cut in sections, topstitched detail, wired self-fabric rouleau bow on centre-front, large stiffened peak. 15 1962. Large leopardskin hat, tall crown, flat top, wide turned-down brim, black silk lining, scarf in matching fur. 16 1962. Multicoloured checked wool-tweed cap, large crown cut in one piece, covered button trim, large stiffened peak.

Women's Hats 1963–1967

1 1963. Beige felt hat, high crown, wide upswept brim, covered in self-coloured hessian. 2 1963. Brimless orange-yellow felt hat, domed crown. 3 1963. Turquoise felt hat, high crown, draped in patterned silk-chiffon. 4 1963. Small pink felt pillbox-style hat, domed crown, worn on back of head. 5 1964. White cotton-piqué jockey cap, stiffened crown, cut in sections, button trim on top, self-fabric band from either side of stiffened peak, matching bow trim on centre-front. 6 1964. Grey plastic-straw hat, high narrow crown, black silk band, matching wired bow and ends on centre-front and lining of deep turned-down brim. 7 1965. Small white silk beret, crown cut in sections, bright-green feathers from under self-fabric flap on centre-back, brooch trim. 8 1965. Bright-pink plastic-straw hat, high crown, flat top, pink silk-ribbon bow on centre-front, wide turned-up brim. 9 1965. Brown felt hat, domed crown, wide self-colour petersham-ribbon band knotted on centre-front, wide brim turned down on front, narrowing to back and turned up. 10 1965. Brimless olive-green plastic-straw hat, large domed crown, black ruffled plastic-straw pompon on top. 11 1966. Blue and white striped cap, shallow crown, stiffened flat top, covered button trim, wide peak. 12 1966. Grey plastic-straw hat, unstructured creased crown, trimmed on centre-front with yellow cloth flowers and leaves, wired brim turned down at front and up at back. 13 1966. Stiffened silk-organdie bonnet covered in multicoloured silk flowers, organdie ribbons tie under chin in large bow. 14 1967. Lilac-blue felt cap, large crown, domed top, narrow topstitched inset band, matching small peak. 15 1967. Domed mesh pillbox-style hat, covered with pink silk flowers, worn on back of head. 16 1967. Small orange-yellow felt beret, stalk in centre of crown, hat worn towards front of head.

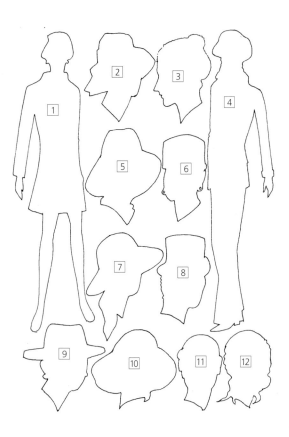

Women's Hats 1968–1971

1 1968. Yellow wool mini-length coat, double-breasted fastening to hip-level seam, wide-set collar, long inset sleeves, topstitched detail. Large navy-blue suede beret, cut in sections, set onto padded band, hat worn at an angle. Navy-blue leather gloves; matching bar-strap shoes, blunt toes. 2 1968. Brown silk-grosgrain hat, draped crown incorporating wide band, crossed over on one side, wide brim, wired edge. 3 1968. Coney-fur beret, self-fur pompon on top. 4 1971. Blue wool trouser suit: long top, large patch-and-buttoned-flap pockets set at hip-level, low round neckline, long cuffed inset sleeves; trousers flared from knee-level. Pale-blue cotton shirt, long collar. Wide patterned silk tie. Blue velvet cap, outsized sectioned crown, topstitched detail, large peak. Blue leather boots, blunt toes, high heels. 5 1968. Black straw hat, creased crown, wide brim, multicoloured patterned silk lining; matching silk scarf. 6 1969. Two-tone felt cap, large navy-blue crown, pale-grey top and peak, topstitched detail. 7 1969. Brown felt hat, multicoloured patterned silk scarf pleated around tall crown, long ends fall at back, wide brim, wired topstitched edge. 8 1969. Simulated ocelot-fur top hat, tall flat-topped crown, curled brim, brooch trim on centre-front. 9 1970. Brown trilby-style hat, creased crown, wide brown leather band, split on centre-front, linked by silver chains, topstitched edges, wide brim, turned up topstitched edge. 10 1971. Olive-green fur-felt hat, low close-fitting crown, twisted-cord band, undulating brim, topstitched edge. 11 1971. Patterned knitted-cotton pull-on cloche hat, wide turned-back cuff, large multicoloured brooch worn on one side. 12 1971. Silver-blue stretch-Lurex pull-on turban-style hat, draped to centre-front, brooch trim.

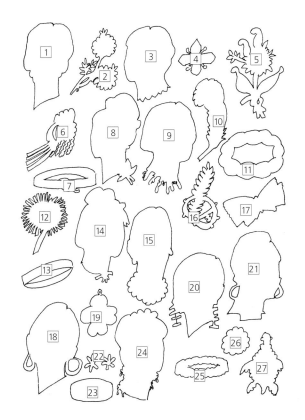

Jewelry 1958–1971

1 1958. Silver wire hair ornament threaded with pink glass beads. Pink and clear glass clip earrings. 2 1958. Flower-design orange glass brooch, gold stems and leaves. 3 1958. Gold necklace and earrings, set with multicoloured stones. 4 1958. Gold brooch set with uncut stones and pearls. 5 1959. Flower-design gilt brooch, set with imitation rubies and sapphires. 6 1959. Paste and silver dress clip. 7 1960. Gilt expanding bracelet, leaf design set with green stones on centre-front. 8 1959. Leaf-design clip earrings, set with orange stones and imitation pearls; matching brooch. 9 1960. Twisted gold wire and blue stone necklace; matching drop earrings. 10 1960. Feather-design marcasite brooch. 11 1961. Twisted gold mesh bracelet, set with turquoise stones. 12 1961. Flower-design brooch, fine gold straw petals, centre of diamonds, gold stem set with diamonds. 13 1964. Red and black plastic expanding bracelet. 14 1964. Twisted gold wire necklace, flower and bow decoration on front; matching brooch worn on black velvet ribbon in hair. 15 1965. Green plastic three-strand necklace; matching earrings. 16 1965. Twisted gold wire brooch, set with imitation emeralds and diamonds. 17 1966. Gilt butterfly brooch, set with imitation sapphires. 18 1969. Beaten-copper drop earrings. 19 1968. Multicoloured plastic pendant. 20 1967. Black and white pop-art drop earrings. 21 1968. Black and white plastic pop-art drop earrings; matching brooch. 22 1969. Flower-design blue plastic clip earrings. 23 1970. Brown plastic bangle, large orange plastic stone set on front, surrounded by gilt rope. 24 1970. Pink and blue glass-bead chandelier earrings. 25 1971. Enamelled leaf-design bracelet, set with small diamonds. 26 1971. Black and gold plastic flower-design brooch. 27 1971. Turtle-design brooch, uncut green stone back and head, dark-green stones surround, gilt body.

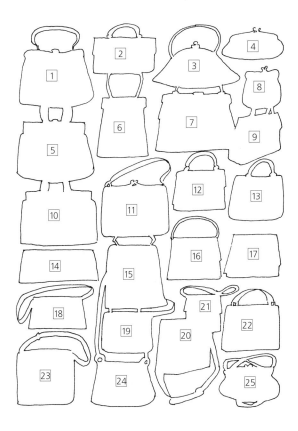

Women's Bags and Purses 1958–1971

1 1958. Leather bag, plastic clasp, strap handle, gilt fittings. 2 1958. Plastic leather-look bag, flap, stud fastening, stitched rouleau handle, gilt fittings. 3 1959. Leather bag, rouleau handle, brass fittings. 4 1960. Cloth evening purse, engraved silver frame and clasp. 5 1961. Crocodile bag, round handles. 6 1961. Leather bag, shaped flap, strap-and-stud fastening, rouleau handle, brass fittings, topstitched detail. 7 1962. Leather bag, front flap, stud fastening, stitched rouleau handle, brass clasp and fittings. 8 1962. Beaded silk evening bag, gilt frame and clasp. 9 1963. Leather bag, strap handles threaded through flap, strap-and-stud fastening. 10 1964. Textured-leather bag, strap handles from diagonal side strips. 11 1965. Plastic-raffia bag, gilt frame, clasp and fittings, strap handle. 12 1965. Leather bag, flap-and-stud fastening, stitched rouleau handle, brass fittings. 13 1966. Plastic leather-look bag, contrast-colour patches front and back, zip fastening, stitched rouleau handle, brass fittings. 14 1966. Leather clutch bag, contrast-colour flap tucked into scalloped opening. 15 1967. Leather bag, flap, stud fastening under brass bar and ring, matching fittings, rouleau handle, topstitched detail. 16 1968. Plastic-patent bag, strap handle, deep flap, gilt trim. 17 1968. Patent-leather bag, deep flap, shaped edge, contrast-colour suede trim. 18 1968. Plastic shoulder bag, flap, stud fastening under large buckle, long handle. 19 1969. Two-tone leather bag, deep flap, strap-and-stud fastening, adjustable handle. 20 1971. Leather bag, flap, buckled-strap fastening, adjustable handle. 21 1970. Beaded evening bag, contrast-colour binding, trim and handle. 22 1970. Plastic-patent bag, deep flap, strap handle, brass fittings. 23 1970. Suede bag, flap, stud fastening, adjustable strap handle. 24 1971. Suede bag, zip fastening, patch and flap on side, stud fastening, adjustable handle. 25 1971. Joined suede purses, brass frames and clasps, long strap handle.

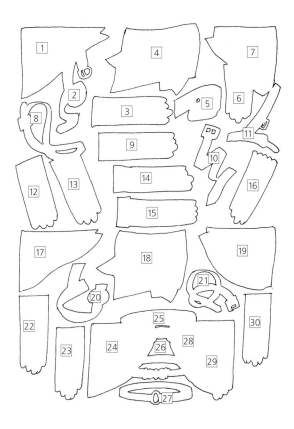

Women's Scarves, Belts and Gloves 1958–1971

1 1958. Silk headscarf, screenprint of flowers. 2 1958. Brown leather belt, decorative brass studs, matching buckle, topstitched detail. 3 1958. Textured-leather gloves, topstitched detail. 4 1958. Silk headscarf, screenprint of flowers. 5 1959. Wide green leather belt, fake double-breasted fastening, stud fastening at back. 6 1959. Cloth gloves, long elasticated gusset on centre-front. 7 1959. Silk headscarf, abstract print. 8 1959. Red and blue reversible leather belt. 9 1959. Leather gloves, contrast-colour inset band under wrist, topstitched detail. 10 1959. Green cloth belt, covered buckle, handstitched edges. 11 1960. Khaki leather belt, brass buckle, handstitched detail. 12 1960. Leather gloves, curved machine-stitched detail, covered button trim. 13 1961. Cloth gloves, embroidered and beaded motifs. 14 1961. Leather gloves, flared cuffs, split on centre-front, topstitched detail. 15 1963. Leather gloves, turned-down cuffs, perforated decoration. 16 1964. Leather gloves, scalloped edges. 17 1965. Silk headscarf, leopard print. 18 1966. Silk headscarf, wide geometric patterned border. 19 1966. Silk headscarf, screenprint design. 20 1966. Red and black reversible leather-look plastic belt, fastening under large disc on centre-front. 21 1967. Red suede belt, white machine-embroidered edge, white plastic buckle. 22 1968. White leather gloves, red and grey inset trim. 23 1968. White leather gloves, inset squares in blue. 24 1969. Silk headscarf, multicoloured flower pattern. 25 1970. Wide brown leather belt, narrow strap-and-buckle fastening, snakeskin star trim. 26 1970. Green velvet-ribbon belt, flower-and-leaf-design metal clasp. 27 1970. Brown leather belt, adjustable fastening through plastic ring. 28 1971. Silk headscarf, screenprint of flowers. 29 1971. Leather gloves, open fronts, perforated detail, strap fastening through square buckle. 30 1971. Leather gloves, machine-stitched detail.

Women's Footwear 1958–1964

1 1958. Sling-back shoes, leather straps, trim, pointed toecaps and stiletto heels, canvas fronts. 2 1958. Shoes with leather apron fronts and stiletto heels, mock snakeskin uppers. 3 1958. Printed-silk evening shoes, open gusset on sides above pointed toes, stiletto heels. 4 1958. Leather shoes, contrast-colour pleated-leather trim through buckle above pointed toes, stiletto heels. 5 1959. Suede shoes, leather bands above pointed toes, matching buttoned bar-straps, stiletto heels. 6 1959. Satin evening shoes, open sides, crossed straps, pointed toes, high heels, diamanté decoration. 7 1959. Suede shoes, contrast-colour leather buckled bar-straps, pointed toes, medium heels. 8 1960. Suede shoes, contrast-colour leather buckled bar-straps, pointed toecaps, stiletto heels and trim. 9 1960. Leather shoes, mock lacing above pointed toes, brogued detail, stiletto heels. 10 1960. Snakeskin shoes, leather trim pleated through buckle above pointed toes, low heels. 11 1961. Leather shoes, wide buckled bar-straps, elongated pointed toes, low heels. 12 1961. Leather shoes, strap-and-plastic-buckle trim above pointed toes, stiletto heels. 13 1961. Suede shoes, high tongues above pointed toes, low heels. 14 1962. Leather shoes, apron fronts, brogued detail, stacked heels. 15 1962. Patent-leather shoes, petersham-ribbon band and bow trim above pointed toes, high heels. 16 1962. Leather shoes, rouleau bow trim above pointed toes, flat heels. 17 1962. Leather shoes, bow knots above pointed toes, louis heels. 18 1963. Satin evening shoes, silk flower trim above pointed toes, stiletto heels. 19 1963. Suede shoes, contrast-colour leather apron fronts, flat heels. 20 1963. Leather shoes, contrast-colour insert and tongue above square toes, rouleau bow trim, medium heels. 21 1964. Leather shoes, wide strap above square toes, button trim, medium heels. 22 1964. Velvet evening shoes, pointed toes, louis heels. 23 1964. Suede shoes, flat bow trim above square toes, low thick heels.

Women's Footwear 1965–1971

1 1965. Leather sling-back shoes, contrast-colour squat heels, matching bow trim above blunt toes. 2 1965. Leather shoes, wide bar-straps, blunt toes, squat heels. 3 1965. Suede shoes, double crossover bar-straps, centre-front fastening under ribbon bow, squat heels. 4 1966. Suede shoes, contrast-colour leather apron fronts, tongues, buckled bar-straps and squat heels. 5 1966. Suede sling-back shoes, T-straps, open sides, blunt toes, squat heels. 6 1966. Leather sandals, buttoned T-straps, open sides and toes, stacked heels. 7 1966. Suede shoes, short buttoned T-straps, blunt toes, wedge heels. 8 1966. Leather pumps, contrast-colour buttoned bar-straps and trim, flat heels. 9 1967. Plastic-patent pumps, contrast-colour motifs above square toes, flat heels. 10 1967. Plastic-patent pumps, disc tongues above blunt toes, flat heels. 11 1967. Suede shoes, open sides, low T-straps, square toes, squat heels. 12 1968. Two-tone suede shoes, buttoned T-straps, open sides, shaped squat heels. 13 1968. Leather sling-back shoes, buckled strap detail above blunt toes, shaped heels. 14 1968. Leather shoes, high tongues, buckled straps, brogued detail, square toes, stacked heels. 15 1969. Leather shoes, high tongues, rouleau bar-and-ring trim, blunt toes, thick heels. 16 1969. Patent-leather pumps, satin trim threaded through petersham-covered buckle above square toes, flat heels. 17 1969. Suede T-strap shoes, open sides, blunt toes, thick heels. 18 1970. Satin evening shoes, buttoned ankle-straps, open sides, blunt toes, thick heels. 19 1970. Lace-up leather shoes, contrast-colour insert above blunt toes, topstitching, thick heels. 20 1970. Leather strap sandals, cork platform soles and squat heels. 21 1971. Denim shoes, open sides and toes, contrast trim, rouleau straps, platform soles, wedge heels. 22 1971. Leather strap sandals, high wedge heels. 23 1971. Leather bar-strap shoes, contrast-colour patches above blunt toes, platform soles, thick heels. 24 1971. Leather ankle-strap shoes, open sides, platform soles, thick heels.

Women's Boots 1958–1971

1 1958. Knee-high fitted boots, plain leather shoes, pointed toes, no toecaps, high slender heels, topstitched detail, mock snakeskin uppers, no fastenings. 2 1959. Mid-calf-length dark-red leather fitted boots, topstitched apron fronts, matching pointed toecaps, medium-high heels, no fastenings. 3 1963. Knee-high fitted beige suede boots, grey fake-fur cuffs, pointed toes, low stiletto heels, zip fastening on inside leg. 4 1965. Knee-high fitted grey leather boots, hook-laced from instep to cuff, blunt toes, squat heels. 5 1967. Above-knee-high light-blue plastic leather-look boots, fitted legs, buckled strap under knee, blunt toes, thick flared heels, topstitched detail, no fastenings. 6 1968. Mid-calf-length light-brown leather boots, straight legs, strap-and-buckle trim under cuff, topstitched edge to shoes, blunt toes, flat stacked heels. 7 1968. Knee-high light-grey leather boots, straight legs, black leather trim under cuffs, matching shoes, no fastenings, topstitched decoration, blunt toes, medium-high thick heels. 8 1969. Knee-high dark-green suede fitted boots, lacing at knee-level, no other fastenings, decorative panel seams, blunt toes, medium-high thick heels. 9 1970. Knee-high dark-red leather fitted boots, scalloped gold leather panels either side fastening, laced to ankle, hooked to under cuffs, edge piped in light grey, scalloped seam above shoe piped in gold, blunt toes, high thick heels. 10 1971. Above-knee-length pink boots, stretch crinkled leather-look plastic legs, leather-look plastic shoes, blunt toes, thick platform soles, thick high heels.

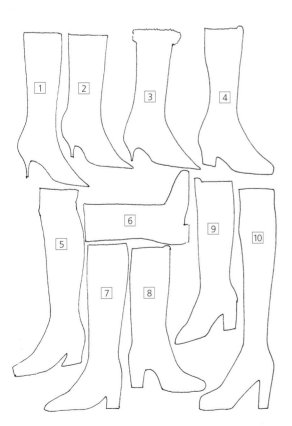

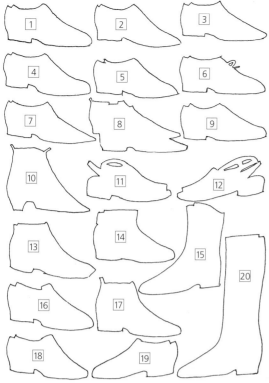

Men's Footwear 1958–1971

1 1958. Step-in leather shoes, high tongues, strap and buckle, apron fronts, square toes, stacked heels. 2 1958. Lace-up leather shoes, apron fronts, pointed toes, brogued detail, stacked heels. 3 1959. Lace-up leather shoes, pointed toes, stacked heels. 4 1960. Lace-up suede shoes, blunt toes, rubber soles and heels. 5 1960. Step-in leather shoes, strap over instep, apron fronts, blunt toes, stacked heels. 6 1960. Step-in leather shoes, high tongues, rouleau bow trim, apron fronts, topstitched detail, blunt toes, stacked heels. 7 1960. Imitation-crocodile-leather shoes, plain leather tongues, matching strap-and-buckle fastening, pointed toes, stacked heels. 8 1963. Leather ankle-boots, elasticated side gussets, elongated square toes, stacked heels. 9 1963. Step-in leather shoes, elasticated side panels, high tongues and apron fronts cut in one, stacked heels. 10 1964. Leather chelsea boots, elasticated side gussets, front and back tape pulls, topstitched detail, pointed toes, high stacked heels. 11 1964. Leather sandals, open toes, sling-back strap and buckle, topstitched detail, rubber soles and heels. 12 1964. Leather strap sandals, sling-back strap and buckle, leather soles, stacked heels. 13 1964. Corduroy lace-up ankle-boots, leather linings, square toes, crepe soles and heels. 14 1965. Canvas lace-up sneaker boots, deep cuffs, large eyelets, coloured laces, rubber soles and combined heels. 15 1967. Mid-calf-length leather cowboy boots, plastic star decoration on front, topstitched detail, blunt toes, stacked heels. 16 1968. Step-in leather shoes, high tongues, chain trim, topstitched detail, blunt toes, stacked heels. 17 1968. Leather lace-up ankle-boots, blunt toes, rubber soles and combined heels. 18 1971. Step-in suede shoes, high tongues, topstitched detail, blunt toes, rubber soles and combined heels. 19 1971. Lace-up leather shoes, blunt toecaps, rubber platform soles, thick heels. 20 1971. Knee-high leather boots, topstitched detail, blunt toes, stacked heels.

Men's Hats 1958–1971

1 1958. Brown felt trilby, creased crown, dark-brown petersham-ribbon band, brim turned up at sides. 2 1958. Olive-green felt trilby, creased crown, self-fabric plaited band, feather trim, straight brim turned up at back. 3 1958. Fawn felt trilby, creased crown, self-fabric band and knot, brim turned down at front and up at back. 4 1959. Blue felt trilby, creased crown, black petersham-ribbon band and bow, turned-down brim. 5 1959. Straw hat, flat-topped crown, wide pleated silk band in contrast colour, narrow brim turned down at front and up at back. 6 1961. Brown wool-tweed hat, creased crown, wide self-colour ribbon band and bow, narrow brim turned up at back. 7 1963. Crocheted cotton cap, large stiffened peak. 8 1963. Denim sailing cap, two-piece crown set onto narrow band, self-colour cord trim, large stiffened peak. 9 1965. Brown ski cap, fur crown, large leather peak, band and trim. 10 1966. Brown checked wool-tweed pork-pie hat, flat-topped crown, creased edge, leather band, matching edge of narrow brim turned up at sides. 11 1968. Brown wool cap, peak hidden under crown. 12 1969. Light-brown brushed-felt hat, creased crown, self-fabric plaited band, narrow brim turned down at front and up at back. 13 1969. Fawn felt trilby, creased crown, self-colour leather band, buckle trim, narrow brim turned up at back. 14 1970. Large olive-green fur-felt hat, tall flat-topped crown, black petersham-ribbon band, wide sweeping brim. 15 1971. Large black felt hat, tall creased crown, deep self-colour petersham-ribbon band, sweeping brim, hat worn at an angle. 16 1971. Large maroon fur-felt hat, tall creased crown, self-colour satin-ribbon band and bow, wide flat brim.

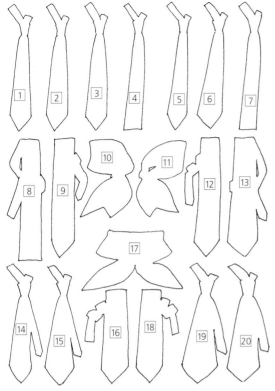

Men's Neckwear 1958–1971

1 1958. Textured-silk tie, broad blue and gold stripes, narrow body, pointed hem. 2 1958. Red silk tie, wide blue bar edged in yellow under small knot, narrow body, pointed hem. 3 1958. Cream silk tie, patterned with brown and yellow squares, narrow body, pointed hem. 4 1958. Gold-coloured silk tie, woven-cord band down centre-front, matching three horizontal stripes half-way down front, red motifs on crossover points, matching bar above square hem, narrow body. 5 1959. Pink silk tie, wide silver-grey diagonal stripe under knot, narrow body, pointed hem. 6 1959. Blue silk tie, woven striped design under knot, plain grey pointed panel above dark-grey bar, narrow body, pointed hem. 7 1960. Purple wool tie, stripes of various blues and greys, narrow body, square hem. 8 1961. Yellow and brown acrylic tie, narrow body, square hem. 9 1962. Multicoloured striped silk tie, narrow body, pointed hem. 10 1969. Multicoloured patterned cream silk neckscarf, wide borders of blue and green, handrolled hems, points drawn through scarf-ring. 11 1969. Fine cream silk-crepe neckscarf, scatter pattern of blue flowers, rolled hems. 12 1965. Acrylic tie, brown and cream stripes, matching diagonal striped pattern half-way down front, medium-wide body, pointed hem. 13 1966. Green silk tie, pattern of graded stripes, medium-wide body, pointed hem. 14 1969. Two-tone silk tie, plain red knot, matching asymmetric raised pattern on light-grey body, pointed hem. 15 1969. Light-red silk tie, multicoloured all-over pattern, wide body, pointed hem. 16 1970. Two-tone brown silk scarf square, pattern of stylized flowers and leaves, points drawn through scarf-ring. 17 1970. Blue acrylic tie, all-over pattern in brown, wide body, pointed hem. 18 1970. Multicoloured printed-flower-pattern silk tie, wide body, pointed hem. 19 1971. Brown textured-silk tie, yellow and red uneven diagonal stripes, wide body, pointed hem. 20 1971. Multicoloured all-over-pattern cream silk tie, wide body, deep border above pointed hem.

Accessories at a Glance 1958–1964

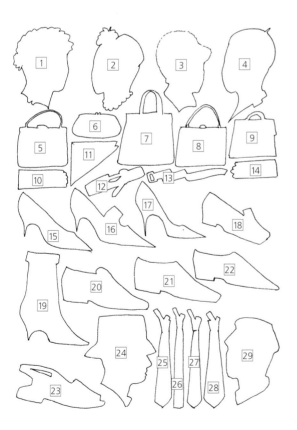

1 Brimless hat, crown of pink silk-organdie petals set onto wide band. Gold clip earrings; matching brooch. 2 Silk-covered pillbox hat, silk rose trim on centre-front. Clip earrings; matching necklace. 3 Peaked fur cap. Large clip earrings; matching necklace. 4 Brimless red felt hat, domed crown, stalk trim. Square clip earrings; matching brooch. 5 Grey leather bag, covered frame, clasp fastening, strap handle. 6 Blue satin evening purse, gilt frame and clasp fastening. 7 Beige leather bag, flap on side, strap-and-stud fastening, strap handles. 8 Blue leather bag, gilt frame, clasp fastening, strap handle. 9 Black leather bag, stitched rouleau handle, brass lock, fastening and trim. 10 Beige kid gloves, split cuffs. 11 Silk scarf square, poppy print. 12 Olive-green suede belt, gilt buckle, top-stitched detail. 13 Red leather belt, self-leather covered buckle, large eyelets. 14 Grey cloth gloves, turned-down scalloped cuffs. 15 Leather shoes, contrast-colour draped trim under matching covered buckles, pointed toes, stiletto heels. 16 Mock-snakeskin shoes, wide buttoned bar-straps, elongated pointed toes, low stiletto heels. 17 Leather shoes, low vamps, cut-out detail above square toes, stiletto heels. 18 Two-tone leather shoes, high tongues and square toes cut in one, flat stacked heels. 19 Mid-calf-length leather boots, turned-down cuffs, low stiletto heels, square toes. 20 Step-in leather shoes, stitched bar under high tongues, apron fronts, blunt toes, stacked heels. 21 Leather shoes, elasticated side gussets, square toes, stacked heels. 22 Lace-up leather shoes, pointed toes, stacked heels. 23 Leather sandals, open toes, strap-and-buckle fastenings, rubber soles incorporating low heels. 24 Brown felt hat, creased crown, wide ribbon band, turned-down brim. 25 Green silk tie, all-over pattern, narrow body, pointed hem. 26 Blue knitted-wool tie, narrow body, square hem. 27 Pink silk tie, pattern under knot, narrow body, pointed hem. 28 Cream silk tie, diagonal stripes, medium-wide body, pointed hem. 29 Denim cap, large peak.

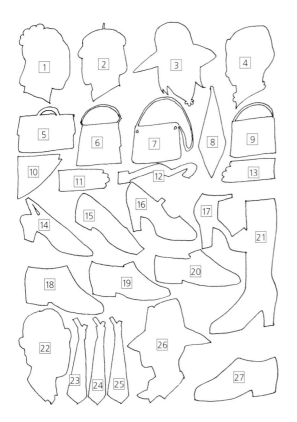

Accessories at a Glance 1965–1971

1 Brimless green felt hat, decorated with silk roses on top of domed crown. Gilt knot brooch, set with paste stones. 2 Yellow felt peaked cap, small crown, spike trim. 3 Tan felt hat, tall crown, wide band, buckle trim, sweeping brim. Flower-design enamelled pendant. 4 Pull-on knitted-wool hat. Two-tone clip earrings; matching necklace. 5 Black leather bag, flap, metal clip fastening and trim, stitched rouleau handle. 6 Blue leather bag, concealed fastening under flap, brass trim, rouleau handle. 7 Brown suede shoulder bag, purse with flap on side, large stud fastening, top zip, long adjustable handle. 8 Acrylic scarf, stylized flower pattern. 9 Cream leather bag, deep flap, brass trim, strap handle. 10 Acrylic scarf, graded spot pattern. 11 Leather gloves, contrast-colour trim. 12 Two-tone leather belt, reversible square buckle. 13 Red suede gloves, keyhole, stud fastening. 14 Red leather sling-back shoes, small blue bow on back strap, matching trim and low thick heels. 15 Blue leather pumps, black motif above square toes, flat heels. 16 Patterned fabric shoes, buttoned bar-straps, blunt toes, platform soles, thick heels. 17 Grey leather shoes, cut-out detail under ankle-straps, open side, peep toes, platform soles, thick heels. 18 Blue lace-up suede ankle-boots, rubber soles and heels. 19 Brown step-in leather shoes, tasselled ties, high tongues, apron fronts, topstitched detail, stacked heels. 20 Brown step-in suede shoes, blunt toes, rubber soles and heels. 21 Long denim boots, topstitched detail, blunt toes, platform soles, thick heels. 22 Beige felt hat, brown ribbon band, narrow curled brim. 23 Patterned cream silk tie, wide body, pointed hem. 24 Pink patterned silk tie, wide body, pointed hem. 25 Acrylic tie, multicoloured pattern, wide body, pointed hem. 26 Green felt hat, tall crown, brown ribbon band, wide sweeping brim. Spotted silk neckscarf. 27 Olive-green lace-up suede shoes, blunt toecaps, perforated detail, rubber soles and heels.

The Complete Look 1958–1971

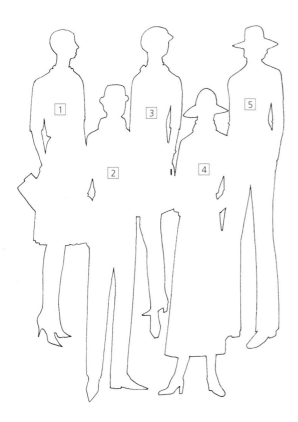

1 1958. Knee-length red wool dress, black leather belt slotted through bloused bodice, bow trim, gold crescent-shaped brooch on one side low neckline, elbow-length sleeves, pleated skirt. Brimless red felt hat. Gold and imitation-pearl clip earrings. Two-strand imitation-pearl necklace. Short white cloth gloves, button detail on split cuffs. Black leather bag, stud fastening under flap, brass trim, rouleau handle. Red and white patterned silk shoes, pointed toes, high stiletto heels. 2 1965. Short beige wool-tweed jacket, zip fastening, fur collar, cuffed sleeves, welt pockets. Cream collar-attached shirt; striped knitted-wool tie, narrow body. Straight-cut brown wool trousers, no turn-ups. Brown leather step-in shoes, elasticated side gussets, pointed toes, stacked heels. Light-brown felt hat, shallow crown, self-felt band, narrow curled brim. 3 1964. Turquoise wool coat-dress, checked in yellow, button-through semi-fitted bodice, stand-away collar, elbow-length sleeves, buttoned flap pockets above and below hip-level blue leather belt, round buckle, mini-length flared skirt. Fitted knee-length yellow leather boots, squat heels, square toes. Yellow leather bag, two strap handles, strap-and-stud fastening. Short white leather gloves. Large fur hat, brown leather peak. Yellow plastic clip earrings; matching bead necklace. 4 1971. Mid-calf-length beige wool coat, fly fastening, self-fabric belt, large orange plastic buckle, long sleeves, knitted cuffs. Multicoloured patterned silk scarf. Tan felt hat, tall crown, brown band, wide sweeping brim. Short brown leather gloves, keyhole. Tan leather shoulder bag, strap-and-flap fastening, long adjustable strap. Brown leather shoes, white trim, blunt toes, platform soles, thick heels. 5 1971. Single-breasted blue wool jacket, wide lapels, large flap-and-patch pockets, topstitched detail. Cream and brown striped collar-attached shirt; beige patterned silk tie, wide body. Grey wool flared trousers, no turn-ups. Beige suede lace-up shoes, rubber soles and heels. Olive-green felt hat, tall crown, ribbon band, sweeping brim.

Women's Hats 1972–1978

1972

1972

1973

1973

1973

1973

1974

1974

1975

1976

1976

1977

1977

1978

1978

1978

1979

1979

1979

1980

1980

1980

1981

1981

1982

1982

1983

1983

1984

1984

1985

1985

Jewelry 1972–1985

1972

1972

1972

1972

1972

1974

1974

1979

1979

1979

1975

1979

1980

1980

1981

1982

1983

1982

1982

1982

1982

1984

1982

1985

1985

1985

1985

1984

1985

1972

1973

1974

1981

1972

1973

1975

1978

1983

1979

1984

1985

1977

1975

1980

1985

1985

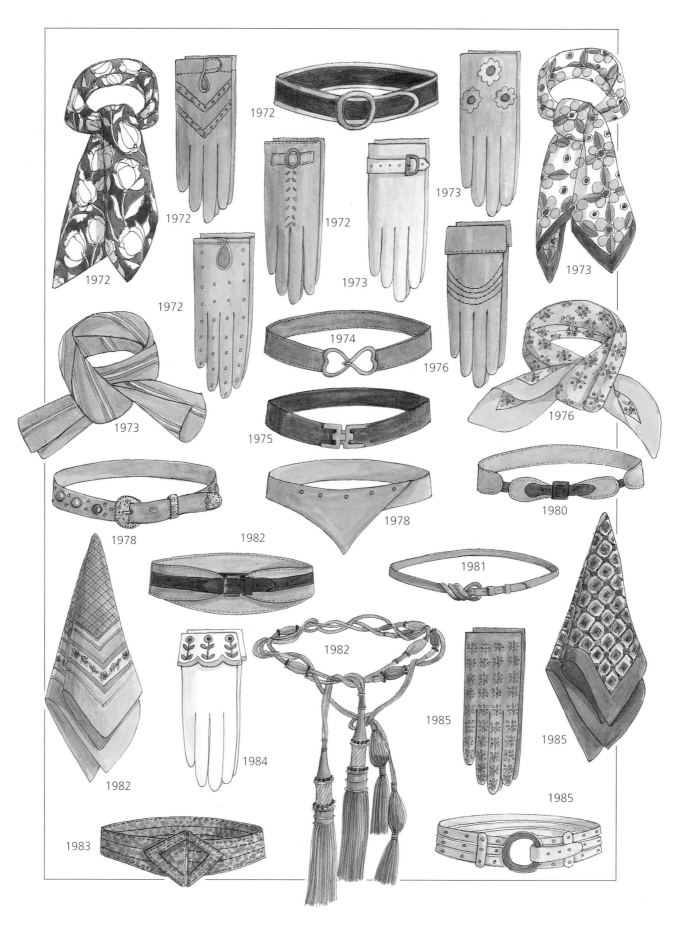

1972

1972

1972

1972

1972

1972

1973

1973

1973

1973

1973

1974

1975

1976

1976

1976

1978

1978

1980

1978

1981

1982

1982

1982

1982

1984

1985

1985

1985

1983

1972

1972

1973

1973

1974

1974

1974

1975

1975

1975

1976

1976

1976

1976

1977

1977

1977

1977

1979

1978

1978

1979

1979

1979

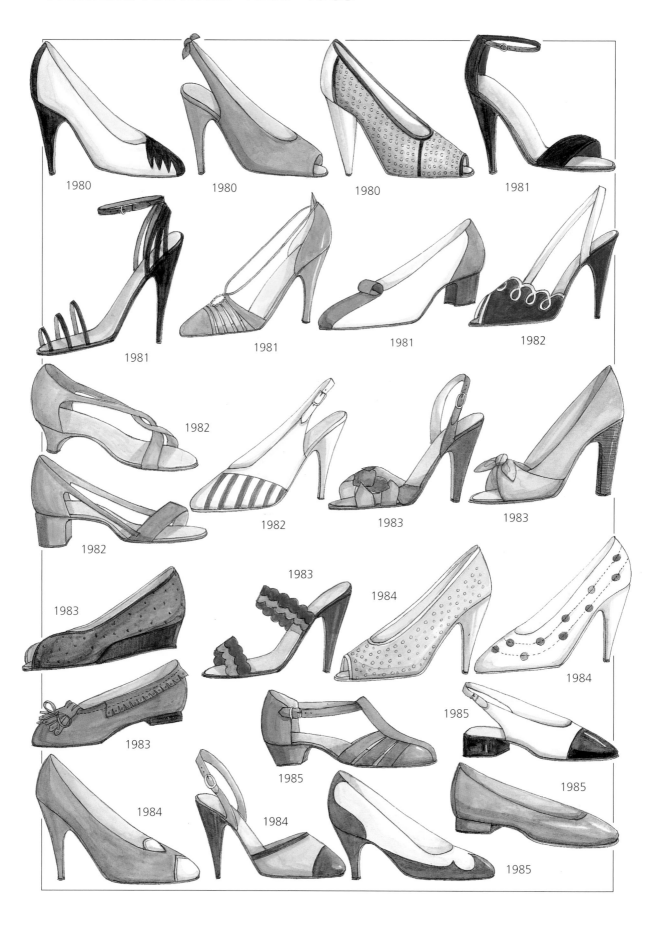

1980

1980

1980

1981

1981

1981

1981

1982

1982

1982

1982

1983

1983

1983

1984

1984

1983

1983

1985

1984

1985

1985

1984

1984

1985

1985

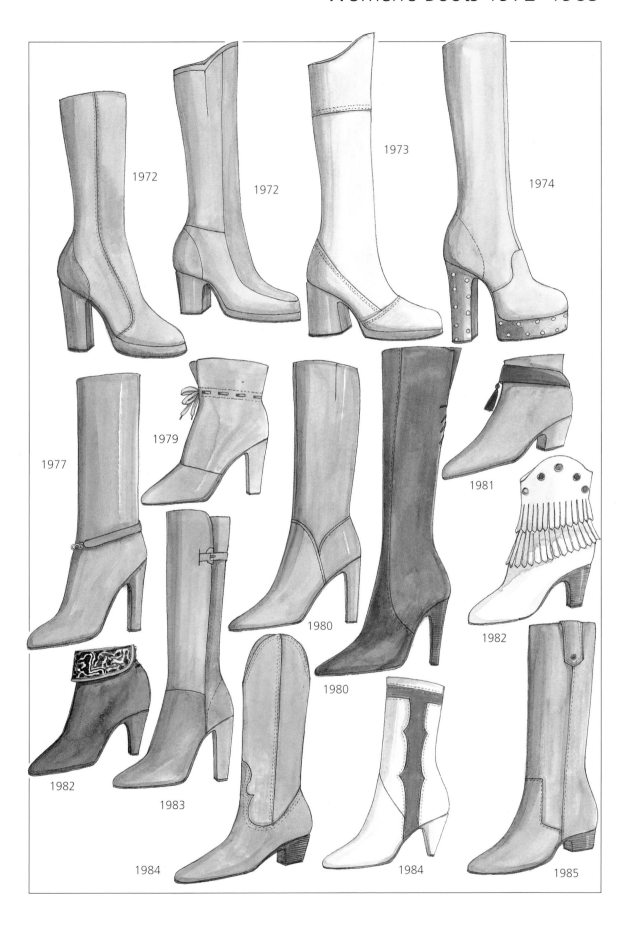

1972

1972

1973

1974

1977

1979

1980

1980

1981

1982

1982

1983

1984

1984

1985

1972

1972

1972

1973

1973

1973

1974

1974

1975

1976

1976

1976

1976

1978

1979

1979

1981

1981

1983

1985

1985

1972

1973

1973

1973

1973

1974

1976

1979

1976

1978

1979

1981

1983

1985

1972

1974

1974

1973

1974

1972

1972

1972

1974

1974

1976

1976

1979

1980

1980

1980

1982

1983

1984

1979

1985

1985

1984

1985

1985

1972

1974

1979

1982

1985

The Complete Look 1972

[1] Short-sleeved checked wool dress, round neckline, knee-length flared skirt, wide patent-leather belt, large round buckle; wool-crepe blouse, bow-tied neckline, long sleeves gathered into cuffs. Brimless mock-leather beret, narrow band. Graded painted-wooden-bead necklace. Short leather gloves. Suede shoulder bag, zip fastening, long adjustable handle. Leather sling-back shoes, square patent-leather toecaps, matching platform soles and thick heels. [2] Edge-to-edge wool jacket, long inset sleeves, button detail above wrist; wool sweater, low neckline, long sleeves; checked wool mini-length pleated skirt. Felt hat, tall crown, wide turned-up brim edged with petersham. Outsized plastic-bead necklace. Leather shoulder bag, deep flap, double strap-and-buckle fastening, long adjustable strap. Leather sling-back shoes, peep toes, thick platform soles and heels, stud trim. [3] Single-breasted checked wool jacket, wide lapels, large patch pockets. V-neck leather jerkin, topstitched detail. Cotton collar-attached shirt; multicoloured checked wool tie, large knot, wide body. Flared wool trousers, hip-level pockets. Felt hat, self-colour petersham-ribbon band, narrow sweeping brim. Leather shoulder bag, deep flap, brass plate and lock, matching trim, long adjustable handle. Leather step-in shoes, high tongues, knotted rouleau trim, apron fronts, stacked heels. [4] Hip-length single-breasted wool jacket, welt pockets, narrow leather belt, sectioned clasp fastening, multicoloured patterned silk scarf, bow brooch, plastic bangles; mid-calf-length wool-tweed skirt. Felt cloche-style hat, no band. Ribbed-wool stockings. Lace-up leather shoes, apron fronts, brogued detail, platform soles. [5] Ribbed-acrylic sweater, low neckline, long sleeves; acrylic blouse, pointed collar; flared sailcloth trousers, hip yoke, fly opening, deep waistband, wide leather belt, large oval buckle. Multicoloured patterned acrylic turban. Plastic leather-look shoulder bag, three purses, long handle, brass trim. Striped stockings. Plastic clogs, stud trim, cork platform soles and heels.

Women's Hats 1972–1978

[1] 1972. Brown felt cloche-style hat, narrow brown leather band, turned-down brim, topstitched edge. [2] 1972. Gold silk-crepe turban, draped to cross-over under large deep-pink silk flower, open crown. [3] 1973. Brimless black and cream pull-on wool-jersey hat, self-fabric flower on side. [4] 1973. Cream straw hat, high domed crown, two-tone orange velvet ribbon, button trim, narrow self-straw band, wide turned-down brim, wired edge. [5] 1973. Red wool beret, stalk trim, narrow band. [6] 1973. Purple velvet cap, outsized crown, gathers under self-fabric button trim, pink leather band, matching large peak. [7] 1974. Cream felt hat, tall creased crown, perforations above deep brown-velvet band, wide curled brim. [8] 1974. Brimless evening hat, embroidered with pink, blue and purple sequins, matching large padded-leaf motif on side. [9] 1975. Green lacquered-plastic-straw hat, shallow crown, white organza daisies and yellow spotted tulle, wide turned-down brim. [10] 1976. Blue felt hat, sectioned crown, topstitched seams, self-fabric rouleau flower on centre-front, top-stitched brim turned up at front. [11] 1976. White felt hat, domed crown threaded with white petersham ribbon, wide brim, scalloped edge. [12] 1977. Rust-red suede-fabric hat, sectioned crown, topstitched seams, inset self-suede band, turned-down brim, topstitched edge. [13] 1977. Animal-print cotton hat, tall creased crown, twisted black plastic-patent band, wide turned-down brim, wired edge. [14] 1978. Yellow felt cap, preformed crown, small peak. [15] 1978. Brown knitted-wool pull-on hat, fitted crown, wide plaited and padded rouleau band, self-colour and contrast. [16] 1978. Pale-grey felt hat, shallow crown, self-felt band and bow on centre-front, narrow turned-down brim.

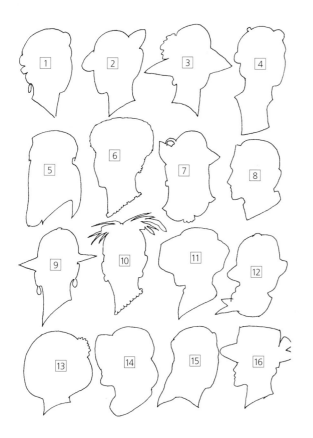

Women's Hats 1979–1985

1 1979. Small pink plastic-straw hat, shallow crown, self-colour velvet-ribbon band and bow trim, narrow rouleau brim. 2 1979. Natural-straw hat, shallow crown, yellow petersham-ribbon band and bow, matching binding on edge of wide brim, turned up at back, wired edge. 3 1979. Blue lacquered-plastic-straw hat, domed crown, self-colour petersham-ribbon band, large pink silk flower at one side, wide turned-down brim, wired edge. 4 1980. Small pale-blue felt hat, shallow crown, self-fabric stalk on top, narrow brim. 5 1980. Beige knitted-wool pull-on hat, jacquard pattern in contrast colours, ribbed edge. 6 1980. Large brimless black fox-fur hat. 7 1981. Blue felt hat, shallow crown, yellow silk rouleau band and bow trim, narrow turned-down brim, wired edge. 8 1981. Pale-blue wool-jersey pull-on hat, deep turned-back hand-knitted rib in pink and blue, hat worn over self-fabric balaclava helmet. 9 1982. Olive-green straw hat, moulded crease from front to back of petersham-ribbon band over tall crown, wide brim, wired edge. 10 1982. Small blue-grey straw pillbox hat, trimmed on back with self-straw bow and long blue-grey feathers. 11 1983. Beige felt hat, large crown, deep turned-back brim, wired and topstitched edge. 12 1983. Moulded green flecked tweed hat, tall crown, self-fabric covered button on top, matching inset band, piped either side, turned-down stiffened brim. 13 1984. Black lacquered-straw hat, wide turned-back brim, red silk flower trim. 14 1984. Outsized tan felt bowler-style hat, large high crown, wide brim, curled edge. 15 1985. Pull-on green plastic-straw brimless hat, tall crown incorporating deep cuff. 16 1985. Black lacquered-plastic-straw hat, flat-topped crown, wide black petersham-ribbon band and large bow on back, matching binding on edge of wide flat brim, wired edge.

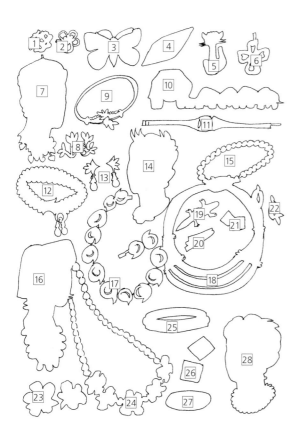

Jewelry 1972–1985

1 1972. Small gold brooch, abstract design, set with red stones. 2 1972. Small gold wire brooch, set with pearl beads. 3 1972. Gold wire butterfly brooch, set with pink stones. 4 1972. Leaf-shaped metal brooch, enamelled in three colours. 5 1974. Small gold brooch, stylized cat design. 6 1974. Gold pendant, stylized flower design. 7 1975. Necklace, multicoloured enamelled hearts set onto gold chains. Gold snailshell clip earrings. 8 & 9 1979. Narrow gold bracelet, set with imitation diamonds, rubies and pearls. Matching gold clip earrings, set with imitation diamonds and rubies. 10 1979. Linked gold bracelet, elephant design, set with various imitation stones. 11 1979. Gold bracelet, lotus-flower design, coloured enamel, imitation diamonds. 12 & 13 1980. Three-strand imitation-pearl choker, clasp fastening under gilt leaves, set with imitation diamonds and sapphires, two pearl drops under. Matching gilt clip earrings, set with imitation diamonds and sapphires, pearl drops under. 14 1981. Twisted black velvet ribbon and silver wire choker, plastic jade and imitation diamond, three-clasp fastening; matching clip earrings. 15 1982. Imitation-pearl choker, linked flat gilt beads, fastening to side of large imitation pearl on centre-front, set with coloured-glass stones. 16 1982. Necklace, large flat leather discs threaded onto cord; matching drop earrings. 17 1982. Linked gilt bracelet, set with two-colour plastic-amber stones. 18 1984. Gold wire necklace, large plastic plates joining three-strand lower necklace. 19 1982. Enamelled metal brooch, lizard design, set with coloured stones. 20 1982. Gilt brooch. 21 1982. Square ceramic clip earrings, two-colour glaze. 22 1983. Gilt and plastic-jade clip earrings. 23 1984. Coloured-glass clip earrings, flower design. 24 1985. Frosted coloured-glass bead necklace, contrast-colour flowers on base. 25 1985. Plastic bangle, set with various coloured stones. 26 1985. Ceramic clip earrings, set with coloured glass. 27 1985. Oval metal brooch, set with large stone. 28 1985. Two-colour twisted bead choker; matching drop earrings.

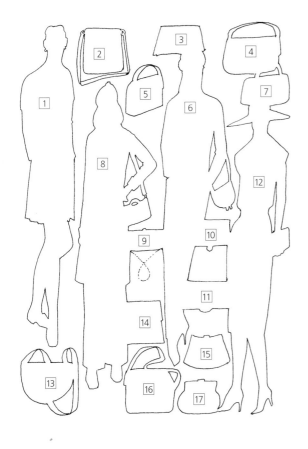

Women's Bags 1972–1985

1 1972. Suit: hip-length top, scooped neckline, short sleeves, checked panel; matching pleated skirt. Blouse, pointed collar, sleeves gathered into cuffs. Suede bag, low zip fastening, keyhole, brass trimmings, long rouleau handle. Long socks. Leather step-in shoes. 2 1972. Suede bag, deep flap, tongue threaded through covered buckle, topstitched detail, long strap handle, brass fittings. 3 1973. Textured-leather bag, flap threaded through self-leather bar, contrast-colour trim. 4 1974. Leather bag, short flap, strap threaded through coloured plastic trim, short adjustable strap handle. 5 1973. Leather bag, deep side panels, scalloped flap, decorative catch, strap handle. 6 1981. Double-breasted jacket, shawl collar, long sleeves. Tapered trousers, hip-level pockets. Blouse, low neckline. Leather bag, deep flap, contrast-colour binding ending in tassels, matching other trim, long strap handle. Sandals, high heels. 7 1975. Leather bag, deep sides, full-length flap, short strap handle, brass trim. 8 1975. Mid-calf-length coat, wide lapels, topstitched edges and detail, wide belt. Patterned blouse, pointed collar. Flared trousers. Leather shoes, platform soles. Turban hat. Two-tone leather bag, deep flap incorporating carrier handle, long detachable shoulder strap, brass fittings. 9 1978. Evening bag, sequin embroidery, chain handle. 10 1983. Two-tone leather clutch bag, top and bottom flaps connected by strap and buckle, handstitched detail. 11 1984. Evening clutch bag, three scalloped flaps edged in contrast colour, matching colour of embroidery on top flap. 12 1985. Patterned dress, capped sleeves and scooped neckline bound in plain colour, matching wide belt and straw hat. Leather shoes, pointed toes. Leather bag, contrast strap and trim. 13 1977. Half-moon-shaped bag, strap fastening, brass trim, long handle. 14 1979. Suede clutch bag, deep flap, threaded-strap fastening, topstitched edges and detail. 15 1985. Three-colour snakeskin striped bag, metal frame and clasp fastening. 16 1980. Leather bag, contrast bindings and trim, long handle, brass fittings. 17 1985. Beaded evening bag, silver frame, jeweled clasp.

Women's Scarves, Gloves and Belts 1972–1985

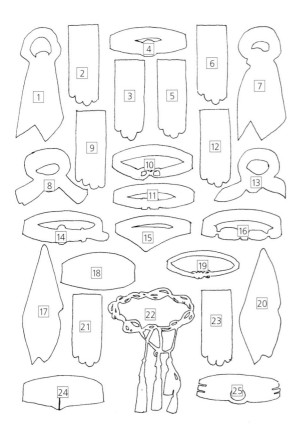

1 1972. Red and white silk scarf, rose pattern. 2 1972. Blue-grey leather gloves, Velcro fastening above keyhole, V-shaped perforated design. 3 1972. Tan leather gloves, strap-and-buckle trim above perforated pattern. 4 1972. Stiffened-cloth belt, contrast-colour leather-look plastic binding, matching round buckle. 5 1973. White cloth gloves, self-fabric strap, perforated detail, plastic buckle. 6 1973. Green cloth gloves, appliqué flower pattern. 7 1973. Multicoloured cotton scarf, stylized flower pattern, plain border. 8 1973. Plnk and grey striped silk scarf. 9 1972. Pink leather gloves, keyhole, button fastening, perforated pattern. 10 1974. Olive-green leather belt, linked heart-shaped metal clasp fastening. 11 1975. Brown leather belt, brass clasp fastening. 12 1976. Beige cloth gloves, deep cuffs, curved topstitched detail. 13 1976. Blue patterned silk scarf, wide cream border. 14 1978. Leather belt set with coloured stones and silver studs, matching engraved buckle, carrier and end. 15 1978. Blue-grey suede belt, deep point on centre-front, stud trim and fastening. 16 1980. Beige leather belt, sides and front linked with red, matching strap and covered buckle fastening. 17 1982. Green acrylic scarf square, contrast-colour borders and patterns, checked centre panel. 18 1982. Wide tan and blue leather belt, red strap and brass buckle fastening. 19 1981. Narrow pink leather belt, asymmetric brass buckle. 20 1985. Multicoloured patterned silk scarf square, wide brown border. 21 1984. White cloth gloves, deep cuffs, scalloped edge, embroidered finish, matching stylized flowers. 22 1982. Three interwoven silk cord and bead belts, large tassel ends. 23 1985. Blue leather gloves, perforated flower design. 24 1983. Purple textured-leather belt, hook-and-bar fastening under mock self-leather buckle, topstitched detail. 25 1985. White three-strand leather belt, self-leather connecting bars either side large green plastic buckle, silver stud trim.

Women's Footwear 1972–1979

[1] 1972. Leather sling-back shoes, peep toes, contrast-colour edges, thick heels, platform soles. [2] 1972. Moulded-plastic mules, two Lurex bar-straps, thick heels, platform soles. [3] 1973. Velvet mules, fronts scattered with sequins, high wedge heels and platform soles covered with sequins, matching bow knot on centre-front. [4] 1973. Clogs, leather uppers attached to carved wooden soles and heels with metal studs. [5] 1974. Sling-back leather sandals, high wedge heels, platform soles, plaited-string trim. [6] 1974. Suede sling-back shoes, open sides, peep toes, platform soles, thick heels. [7] 1974. Leather shoes, high tongues under wide straps, apron fronts, high wedge heels, platform soles. [8] 1975. Distressed-leather shoes, buckled bar-straps over high vamps, apron fronts, platform soles, plastic stacked heels. [9] 1975. Two-tone leather shoes, buckled T-straps, blunt toecaps, thick heels. [10] 1975. Multicoloured patterned canvas shoes, suede straps and trim, peep toes, high wedge heels, platform soles. [11] 1976. Leather bar-strap shoes, open sides, pointed toes, high heels. [12] 1976. Leather clogs, high vamps, pointed toes, contrast-colour high heels. [13] 1976. Leather bar-strap shoes, open sides, peep toes, perforated edges, plastic stacked heels. [14] 1976. Leather sling-back shoes, crossover straps form peep toes, squat heels. [15] 1977. Two-tone leather sling-back shoes, high vamps, toecaps, topstitching, squat heels. [16] 1977. Suede shoes, ankle-straps, open sides, low scalloped vamps, perforated detail, tapered heels. [17] 1977. Green mock-snakeskin leather shoes, high tongues, bow trim, apron fronts, square toes, squat heels. [18] 1979. Red leather shoes, low vamps, strap fronts, tapered heels. [19] 1978. Pink perforated-suede lace-up shoes, beige trim, crepe combined soles and heels. [20] 1978. Leather mules, high vamps, pointed tongues, open toes, plastic stacked heels. [21] 1979. Leather T-strap sandals, open sides, openwork detail, blunt toes, flat heels. [22] 1979. Leather sandals, open sides, strap fronts, rouleau leg ties, stacked heels. [23] 1979. Leather strap sandals, tapered heels.

Women's Footwear 1980–1985

[1] 1980. Two-tone leather shoes, asymmetric design above pointed toes, tapered heels. [2] 1980. Canvas sling-back shoes, knot on back strap, peep toes, tapered heels. [3] 1980. Two-tone leather shoes, perforated detail on main body, contrast-colour bindings, peep toes, round heels. [4] 1981. Suede shoes, ankle-straps, open sides, asymmetric strap fronts, tapered heels. [5] 1981. Leather strap sandals, ankle-straps, tapered heels. [6] 1981. Satin evening shoes, open sides, fine rouleau straps, openwork detail and bead motif above pointed toes, tapered heels. [7] 1981. Two-tone leather shoes, central panel with scroll detail above pointed toes, squat heels. [8] 1982. Suede sling-back shoes, asymmetric heel straps, low scalloped vamps, contrast-colour bindings and trim, peep toes, tapered heels. [9] 1982. Leather shoes, open sides, twisted straps form open toes, low heels. [10] 1982. Leather shoes, open sides, asymmetric front bar and side straps, squat heels. [11] 1982. Leather sling-back shoes, contrast-colour-stripe side panels, pointed toes, tapered heels. [12] 1983. Leather sling-back shoes, asymmetric patchwork fronts, open sides and toes, tapered heels. [13] 1983. Leather shoes, low vamps, bow-knot trim above open toes, plastic stacked heels. [14] 1983. Ostrich-leather shoes, open toes, wedge heels. [15] 1983. Leather mules, two two-tone straps, scalloped edges, tapered heels. [16] 1984. Perforated-leather shoes, peep toes, contrast-colour bindings, matching tapered heels. [17] 1984. Leather shoes, decorated multicoloured discs, topstitched detail, pointed toes, tapered heels. [18] 1983. Leather shoes, fringed cuffs, matching tongues above pointed toes, bow trim, flat heels. [19] 1985. Leather T-strap sandals, open sides, openwork detail on sides, pointed toes, squat heels. [20] 1985. Two-tone leather sling-back shoes, pointed toecaps, squat heels. [21] 1984. Leather shoes, contrast-colour pointed toecaps and small tongues, tapered heels. [22] 1984. Two-tone leather sling-back shoes, pointed toecaps, tapered heels. [23] 1985. Two-tone leather shoes, pointed toes, tapered heels. [24] 1985. Leather pumps, pointed toes, flat heels.

Women's Boots 1972–1985

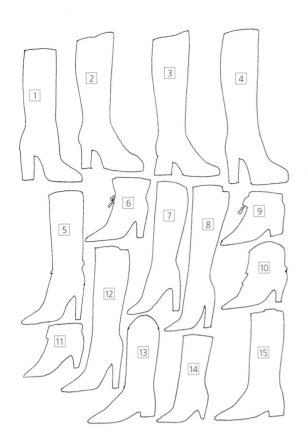

1 1972. Long fitted leather boots, curved panel seams either side centre-front, topstitched detail, inside-leg zip fastening, high thick heels, platform soles. 2 1972. Knee-length fitted leather boots, front panel incorporating apron fronts, inside-leg zip fastening, high thick heels, platform soles. 3 1973. Above-knee-length fitted suede boots, double topstitched seams and detail, flared medium-high thick heels, platform soles. 4 1974. Above-knee-length fitted leather boots, inside-leg zip fastening, high thick heels, perforated pattern of spots over contrast-colour leather, matching platform soles. 5 1977. Knee-length leather boots, ankle-strap and chain trim, high heels, pointed toes. 6 1979. Kid ankle-boots, threaded laces at ankle-level, high heels, pointed toes. 7 1980. Knee-length fitted leather boots, inside-leg zip fastening, topstitched seams and detail, pointed toes, high heels. 8 1980. Above-knee-length fitted suede boots, laced at back mid-calf-level, topstitched panel seams, pointed toes, high stacked heels. 9 1981. Leather ankle-boots, contrast-colour leather sash and centre-front tassel trim, pointed toes, squat heels. 10 1982. Short leather boots, multicoloured stones set above two rows of self-leather fringing, pointed toes, medium-high stacked heels. 11 1982. Suede ankle-boots, patterned-leather cuffs, back lacing, pointed toes, high heels. 12 1983. Above-knee-length leather boots, wrapover panels, adjustable strap and clasp under knee, pointed toes, high heels. 13 1984. Leather cowboy-style boots, decorative seaming, double rows of topstitching, matching detail, pointed toes, squat stacked heels. 14 1984. Short leather boots, contrast-colour leather inserts, topstitched detail, pointed toes, tapered heels. 15 1985. Leather boots, straight legs, decorative strap and stud, topstitched seams and detail, pointed toes, low stacked heels.

Men's Footwear 1972–1985

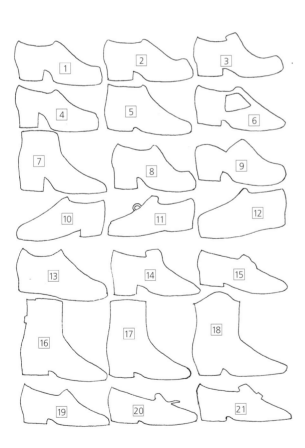

1 1972. Leather lace-up shoes, brogued detail, blunt toecaps, stacked heels, platform soles. 2 1972. Leather lace-up shoes, brogued detail, apron fronts, platform soles. 3 1972. Leather step-in shoes, topstitched detail, high tongues, blunt toecaps, stacked heels, platform soles. 4 1973. Two-tone leather lace-up shoes, covered heels, platform soles. 5 1973. Suede lace-up ankle-boots, blunt toes, rubber soles and heels. 6 1973. Leather sandals, buckled T-straps, open sides, perforated detail, crepe soles and heels. 7 1974. Leather-look ankle-boots, inset bands of contrasting colours over instep, stacked heels. 8 1974. Leather lace-up shoes, topstitched detail, covered heels, platform soles. 9 1975. Clogs, leather uppers attached to wooden soles and heels with metal studs. 10 1976. Two-tone leather lace-up shoes, double apron fronts, side flash, covered heels. 11 1976. Leather step-in shoes, rouleau bow and trim, rubber soles and wedge heels. 12 1976. Leather lace-up shoes, topstitched detail, square toecaps, thick rubber combined soles and wedge heels. 13 1976. Canvas, leather and suede lace-up sports shoes, contrast-colour flash on sides, coloured rubber soles. 14 1978. Leather step-in shoes, two buckled bar-straps under high tongues, stacked heels. 15 1979. Leather step-in shoes, strap-and-covered-ring trim under low tongues, apron fronts, stacked heels. 16 1979. Leather boots, strap-and-buckle detail at back, topstitched detail, stacked heels. 17 1981. Leather boots, contrast-colour stitched cuffs, matching diamond-shaped inset panels, topstitched detail, stacked heels. 18 1981. Leather cowboy-style boots, topstitched detail, square toes, stacked heels. 19 1983. Three-colour leather step-in shoes, low tongues, apron fronts, stacked heels. 20 1985. Leather step-in shoes, knotted rouleau under low tongues, apron fronts, stacked heels. 21 1985. Leather step-in shoes, buckled strap under high tongues, stacked heels.

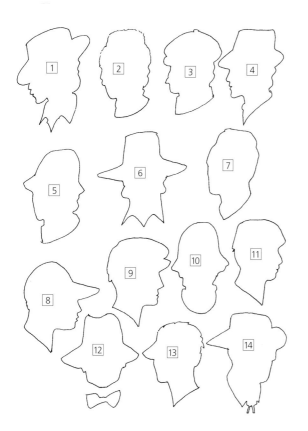

Men's Hats 1972–1985

1 1972. Beige felt hat, high creased crown, wide bright-red band and bow, matching binding on edge of wide brim. 2 1973. Fur hat, mock brim turned back close to crown, hat worn at an angle. 3 1973. Multicoloured checked wool cap, large crown cut in sections, wide peak. 4 1973. Felt hat, high creased crown, wide contrast-colour satin band and knot, feather trim, wide brim turned up at back. 5 1973. Brown cotton-needlecord hat, high panelled crown, self-fabric band and knot, narrow topstitched brim, hat worn at an angle. 6 1974. Black leather hat, high crown, flat top, deep petersham-ribbon band, wide sweeping brim. 7 1976. Green knitted-wool pull-on hat, wide ribbed turned-back cuff. 8 1976. White cotton-canvas sports hat, fitted crown, cut in sections, topstitched seams, aeration eyelets, small back opening, adjustable strap, wide topstitched visor. 9 1978. Brown herringbone wool-tweed cap, large unstructured crown, wide peak. 10 1979. Cotton-canvas hat, multicoloured camouflage pattern, aeration eyelets, inset self-fabric band, topstitched detail, matching unstiffened trim. 11 1979. Multicoloured checked wool-tweed cap, crown covering small peak. 12 1981. Natural-straw hat, high creased crown, narrow contrast-colour petersham-ribbon band, wide sweeping brim. 13 1983. Crownless sports hat, wide white topstitched canvas headband, large transparent blue plastic visor. 14 1985. Off-white felt cowboy-style hat, high creased crown, narrow self-fabric band, wide brim swept up at each side.

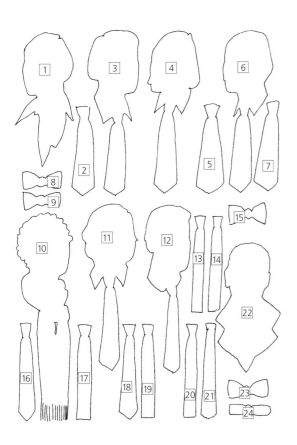

Men's Neckwear 1972–1985

1 1972. Red, white and blue silk neckscarf square, abstract pattern, wide border, rolled edge. 2 1974. Multicoloured patterned silk tie, large knot, wide body, pointed hem. 3 1972. Multicoloured silk tie, abstract pattern, large knot, wide body, pointed hem. 4 1972. Multicoloured rayon tie, abstract pattern, large knot, wide body, pointed hem. 5 1974. Red, white and blue silk tie, check and spot pattern, large knot, wide body, pointed hem. 6 1973. Brown and white silk tie, random design, large knot, wide body, pointed hem. 7 1974. Patterned rayon tie, large knot, wide body, pointed hem. 8 1974. Spotted silk bow-tie. 9 1974. Blue silk bow-tie, random pattern. 10 1976. Long green knitted-chenille scarf, fringed hem. 11 1976. Patterned rayon tie, large knot, medium-wide body, pointed hem. 12 1979. Matt-silk tie, diagonal stripes of contrast colours, small knot, narrow body, pointed hem. 13 1979. Silk tie, horizontal stripes, small knot, narrow body, square hem. 14 1980. Turquoise knitted wool tie, small knot, narrow body, fringed square hem. 15 1980. Blue and white silk-satin evening bow-tie. 16 1980. Blue silk tie, diagonal pattern in pink, small knot, narrow body, pointed hem. 17 1982. Matt-rayon tie, diagonal stripes in contrast colour, small knot, narrow body, square hem, gold cat pin. 18 1983. Rayon tie, multicoloured random pattern, small knot, narrow body, pointed hem. 19 1984. Pink silk tie, fine horizontal red stripes, small knot, narrow body, square hem. 20 1984. Orange knitted-cotton tie, three blue stripes part way down narrow body, small knot, square hem. 21 1985. Dark-blue leather tie, small knot, narrow body, pointed hem. 22 1985. Long red cashmere-and-silk-mixture scarf. 23 1985. Pink silk evening bow-tie, contrast-colour and metallic stripes. 24 1985. Narrow red silk bow-tie, pattern in contrast colours.

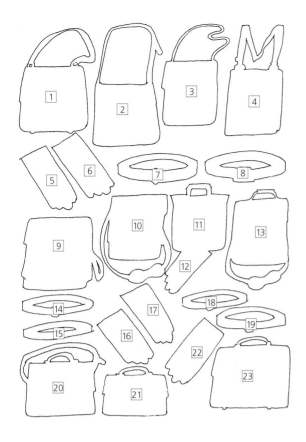

Men's Bags, Gloves and Belts 1972–1985

[1] 1972. Leather shoulder bag, deep flap, strap-and-buckle fastenings, long adjustable strap handle. [2] 1973. Leather shoulder bag, shaped flap, strap-and-stud fastening, outside pocket, long adjustable strap handle. [3] 1974. Leather shoulder bag, deep flap, lockable brass fastening, matching trim, long narrow adjustable strap handle. [4] 1974. Leather shoulder bag, concealed fastening under topstitched panel, matching edges and detail, long adjustable strap handle. [5] 1972. Leather gloves, perforated detail, button fastening above keyhole. [6] 1974. Leather gloves, elasticated band inside large keyhole. [7] 1972. Canvas belt, leather-look plastic bindings, brass buckle and trim. [8] 1973. Leather belt, metal stud trim, leather-covered buckle. [9] 1976. Shoulder bag, patterned canvas front and back, two flaps, brass catches, leather sides, matching long adjustable strap handle. [10] 1976. Leather shoulder bag, shallow flap, brass catch, matching trim, outside pocket with flap, long strap handle, shoulder pad. [11] 1978. Leather bag, short flat handles, zip fastening, lockable brass catch on side. [12] 1979. Leather gloves, handstitched detail. [13] 1979. Leather shoulder bag, flap, brass catch, matching handle and trim, two outside pockets, single flap, long adjustable strap handle, shoulder pad. [14] 1977. Leather belt, contrast-colour leather edging, brass buckle and trim. [15] 1978. Plaited-leather belt, metal buckle. [16] 1980. Leather gloves, handstitched detail. [17] 1979. Leather gloves, handstitched detail. [18] 1980. Cut-leather belt, gilt buckle. [19] 1985. Two-colour striped canvas belt, leather strap and metal buckle fastening. [20] 1982. Leather shoulder bag, deep flap, brass catches, matching trim, embossed detail on centre-front, stitched rouleau handle, long adjustable strap handle. [21] 1984. Woven-leather bag, deep flap, leather binding, brass catch, stitched rouleau handle. [22] 1985. Leather gloves, perforated detail, large keyhole, strap and stud. [23] 1985. Leather bag, deep flap, brass catch, matching trim, securing straps, stitched rouleau handle.

Accessories at a Glance 1972–1979

[1] Natural-straw hat, tall crown, wide band and bow, wide turned-down brim. [2] Knitted-chenille pull-on hat, deep cuff. Gold bow-shaped clip earrings. [3] Wool peaked cap, stalk trim. Sapphire and pearl clip earrings. [4] Plastic-straw hat, shallow crown, ribbon band, cloth flower trim, wide turned-down brim. Enamel, gilt and bead choker necklace. [5] Small gilt brooch, set with coloured stones. [6] Gold wire bracelet, butterfly motif, set with coloured stones. [7] Leather bag, deep flap, brass catch and trim, stitched rouleau handle and long strap handle. [8] Leather bag, handle integrated in main body, long strap handle, zip fastening. [9] Leather bag, two flaps, strap fastening, matching adjustable strap handle. [10] Corded-silk evening bag, mock strap-and-buckle fastening. [11] Multicoloured silk scarf. [12] Leather gloves, two keyholes. [13] Striped canvas belt, brass buckle and trim. [14] Leather belt, gilt flower-shaped clasp, belt and clasp set with coloured stones. [15] Cloth gloves, gathers each side keyhole. [16] Multicoloured acrylic scarf. [17] Leather sling-back shoes, strap fronts, open toes, platform soles, thick heels. [18] Leather shoes, high tongues above inset panel, blunt toes, thick heels. [19] Suede shoes, ankle-straps, open sides, contrast-colour suede leaf trim, almond-shaped toes, tapered heels. [20] Spotted silk bow-tie. [21] Leather strap sandals, ankle-straps, stiletto heels. [22] Long leather boots, topstitched seams, platform soles, thick heels. [23] Suede peaked cap, button trim. Patterned silk scarf. [24] Silk tie, self-colour raised stripe, large knot, wide body. [25] Silk tie, self-colour spot-and-stripe pattern, medium-wide body. [26] Narrow slubbed-silk tie, square hem. [27] Leather gloves, keyhole, perforated decoration. [28] Striped silk bow-tie. [29] Leather step-in shoes, contrast-colour inset panels, platform soles, thick heels. [30] Leather belt, round buckle, topstitched detail. [31] Leather bag, deep flap, brass catch and trim, long strap handle. [32] Leather step-in shoes, inset panel and fringed detail under high tongues, apron fronts, low stacked heels.

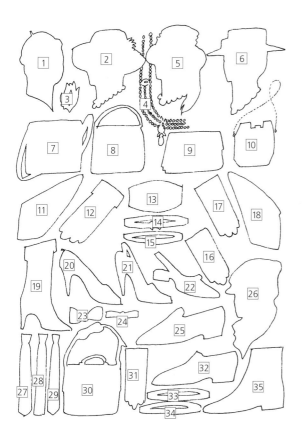

Accessories at a Glance 1980–1985

1 Natural-straw beret, stalk trim, small veil. Gold earrings, set with coloured stones, pearl drops. 2 Small leaf-shaped gilt brooch set with coloured stones. 3 Felt hat, swept back brim, silk flower trim. Glass drop earrings; matching necklace. 4 Two- and three-strand pearl necklace, gilt trim set with coloured stones; matching pendant with large pearl drop. 5 Straw hat, crown draped with panne-velvet, wide brim. Stainless steel earrings, set with large coloured stone, matching centrepiece of bead necklace. 6 Straw hat, flat-topped crown, wide ribbon and bow, flat brim. 7 Leather bag, zip fastening, panelled front, adjustable strap handle. 8 Leather bag, flap, brass catch and trim, topstitched detail, short strap handle. 9 Textured-leather bag, topstitched contrast-colour panel on one side, matching bound edges. 10 Plastic evening bag, clasp fastening, long chain handle. 11 Silk scarf, pineapple design. 12 Leather gloves, scalloped edge, perforated pattern. 13 Wide two-colour mock-snakeskin belt, back fastening. 14 Narrow leather belt, double buckle. 15 Three coloured leather rouleau belts attached to single strap, buckle fastening. 16 Leather gloves, perforated flower design. 17 Leather gloves, perforated detail. 18 Screen-printed silk scarf. 19 Boots, turned-down cuffs, tapered heels, pointed toes. 20 Suede shoes, open toes, contrast-colour binding and trim. 21 Leather sling-back shoes, clear plastic fronts, open toes, leather bindings, stiletto heels. 22 Two-tone leather sling-back shoes, bow trim above pointed toecaps. 23 Checked silk bow-tie. 24 Spotted silk bow-tie. 25 Step-in shoes, inset bands of self-leather above rounded tongues, low stacked heels. 26 Wool-tweed peaked cap. Patterned silk scarf. 27 Striped acrylic tie, small knot. 28 Knitted-silk tie. 29 Narrow suede tie. 30 Leather bag, flap, brass clasp, rouleau handle and adjustable strap handle, shoulder pad. 31 Perforated-leather gloves, keyhole. 32 Step-in shoes, strap and buckle over high tongues. 33 Leather belt, contrast strap. 34 Canvas belt, leather strap. 35 Leather boots, topstitched detail, stacked heels.

The Complete Look 1972–1985

1 1972. Single-breasted flecked wool-tweed jacket, two-button fastening, wide lapels, patch pockets, side openings, topstitched edges and detail. Flared wool trousers, turn-ups. Silk shirt, long collar points. Silk scarf, flower pattern, wide border. Wool hat, creased crown, turned-down topstitched brim. Leather bag, deep flap, brass catches and trim, long adjustable strap handle. Lace-up leather shoes, contrast-colour inset strap, platform soles, thick heels. 2 1974. Striped silk blouse, pointed collar, cuffed sleeves, flap pockets, button trim, strap opening, shirt ends tied above waist. Stretch-wool hipster trousers, worn tucked into knee-high leather boots, shaped over knees, topstitched detail, platform soles, thick heels. Wide leather belt, metal eyelet trim, large buckle. Felt hat, swept-back brim, stitched edge. Large pearl clip earrings. Leather bag, deep flap, stud fastening, self-leather fringed hem, long strap handle. 3 1979. Wool-tweed shirt, narrow collar. Knitted-wool tie, small knot, narrow body, embroidered cat motif. Collarless leather waistcoat. Straight-cut wool trousers, turn-ups, narrow leather belt, gilt buckle. Leather step-in shoes, low tongues, strap-and-tassel trim, apron fronts. Cotton sports cap, sectioned crown, wide topstitched peak. Leather bag, deep flap, inset bands in contrast colour. 4 1982. Silk camisole top, narrow shoulder straps; silver pin set with coloured stones worn on low neck edge; trousers in matching fabric, gathered from under curved suede belt, narrow hems. Sling-back shoes, open sides and toes, shaped fronts, silk bow trim in contrast colour, stiletto heels. Silver clip earrings, set with coloured stones; matching necklace. Silk bag, rounded flap, long chain handle. 5 1985. Patterned acrylic-crepe dress, three-quarter-length sleeves, yoke, flared skirt; small scarf worn on high neckline; leather belt gathered into contrast-colour twisted-leather buckle. Leather bag, gathered flap, rouleau trim, long strap handle. Short leather gloves, keyhole, perforated detail. Straw hat, deep crown, wide brim. Large two-tone clip earrings. Three-colour leather shoes, pointed toes.

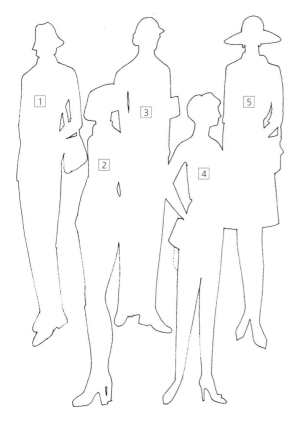

1986

1986

1986

1987

1987

1987

1987

1988

1988

1988

1990

1990

1992

1992

1992

1993

1993

1993

1995

1995

1996

1996

1996

1997

1998

1998

1999

1999

1986   1986   1986   1986   1987   1987

1987   1987   1988   1988   1988   1989

1989   1989   1990   1990   1991   1991

1992   1994   1996   1996   1999   1999

1986

1986

1988

1986

1987

1988

1987

1988

1989

1988

1989

1995

1998

1999

1992

1993

1997

1995

1998

1999

1997

1998

1999

1999

1999

1999

1986

1986

1986

1987

1986

1987

1988

1988

1988

1988

1988

1989

1990

1990

1990

1990

1990

1990

1991

1991

1991

1991

1991

1992

1992

1992

1992

Women's Footwear 1993–1999

1993

1993

1993

1994

1994

1994

1994

1995

1995

1995

1995

1995

1996

1996

1996

1996

1996

1996

1998

1998

1998

1998

1998

1998

1999

1999

1999

1999

1999

1999

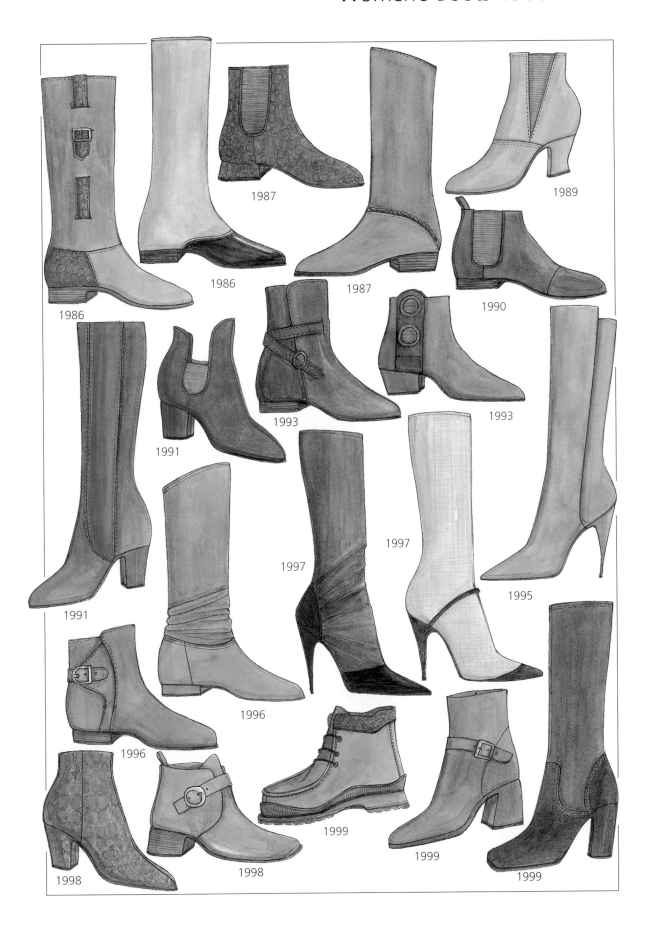

1986

1986

1987

1987

1989

1990

1991

1991

1993

1993

1996

1997

1997

1995

1996

1998

1998

1999

1999

1999

1986

1986

1986

1987

1987

1988

1989

1989

1990

1990

1990

1990

1991

1991

1992

1992

1992

1993

1993

1993

1994

1994

1994

1994

1995

1995

1996

1996

1997

1997

1998

1998

1999

1999

1999

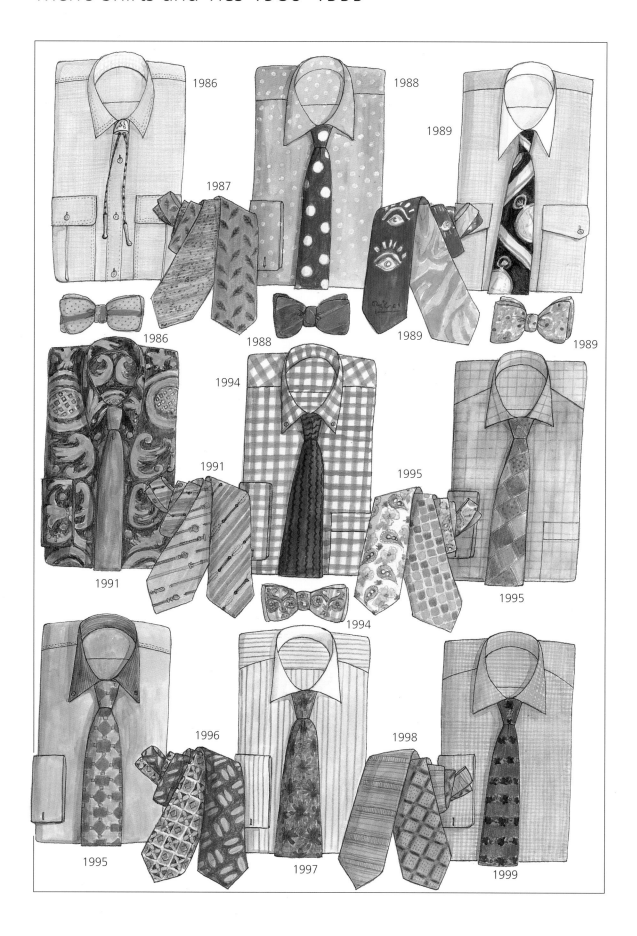

1986

1987

1988

1989

1986

1988

1989

1989

1994

1991

1995

1991

1994

1995

1996

1998

1995

1997

1999

1986

1987

1988

1986

1988

1989

1986

1998

1992

1991

1991

1996

1996

1999

1998

1995

1997

1999

1999

The Complete Look 1986–1999

1986

1988

1992

1999

1996

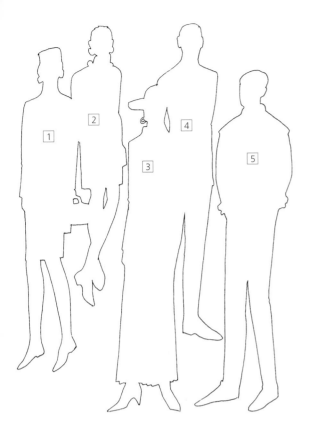

The Complete Look 1986

[1] Single-breasted checked wool jacket, single-button fastening, wide lapels, collar worn turned up, padded shoulders; knee-length skirt in plain colour; silk blouse with round neckline. Felt pillbox hat, worn tilted forward. Large silver clip earrings, set with square stones. Two-tone checked wool scarf, fringed hems. Short leather gloves; matching bag, shaped flap, two-stud fastening, short stitched rouleau handle, brass trim. Two-tone leather shoes, apron fronts, pointed toes, flat heels. [2] Sleeveless knitted-wool dress, ribbed polo collar, short straight skirt, wide leather belt, metal stud and topstitched decoration, central tassel trim, matching decoration on flap of leather clutch bag. Outsized plastic clip earrings, handpainted tiger-stripe decoration; matching short necklace. Leather step-in shoes, high tongues above decorative straps, apron fronts, pointed toes, crepe soles and combined heels. [3] Hip-length checked wool jacket, side-button fastening in sets of two, padded shoulders, long sleeves; silk scarf worn tucked into round neckline; ankle-length pleated wool skirt. Large natural-straw hat, high crown, wide petersham-ribbon band, wide turned-up brim. Large gold hoop earrings. Short leather gloves, V-shaped open gusset, button trim; matching large bag, brass catch, lock and trim, long strap handle. Leather shoes, narrow vamps, pointed toes, medium-high tapered heels. [4] Two-piece striped cotton suit: single-breasted jacket, two-button fastening, welt pockets, wide shoulders; narrow trousers, no turn-ups. Collar-attached shirt; silk tie, handpainted mermaid design on medium-wide body. Leather step-in shoes, high tongues, elasticated side gussets, padded edges, contrast-colour rubber soles and combined heels. [5] Cotton jacket, zip fastening under strap front, wide shoulders, long sleeves worn rolled up, topstitched edges and detail. Collar-attached shirt, small collar; plain cotton tie, narrow body. Narrow cotton trousers, turn-ups, pleats from wide waistband; leather belt, large oval brass buckle. Lace-up canvas sports shoes, rubber toecaps, matching soles and combined heels.

Women's Hats 1986–1992

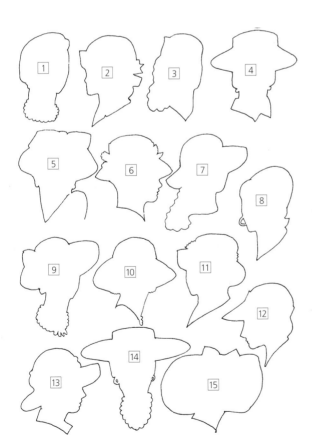

[1] 1986. Red wool beret. [2] 1986. Beige felt hat, large crown, wide contrast-colour petersham-ribbon band, bow and ends, turned-back brim, hat worn low on head. [3] 1986. Brimless grey felt hat, small crown, creased inner edge, hat worn tipped forward. [4] 1987. Plastic-straw hat, navy-blue flat-topped crown, wide beige brim, wired edge, contrast-colour ribbon band, bow and ends. [5] 1987. Red lacquered-straw hat, tiny domed crown, narrow contrast-colour satin band, matching edges of wired organdie looped bows on back and bound edge of wide wired brim. [6] 1987. Green felt hat, large crown, creased inner edge, band of various felt leaves with scalloped edges, turned-down brim, hat worn low on head. [7] 1987. Natural-straw hat, large crown, patterned silk draped band, wide swept-up brim, wired edge, hat worn low on head. [8] 1988. Pale-grey felt cloche-style hat, close-fitting crown, self-felt band, narrow turned-back brim. [9] 1988. Black lacquered-straw hat, small crown, draped in spotted silk, large bow tied on one side, wide brim, wired edge. [10] 1988. Natural-straw hat, large crown, wide swept-back contrast-colour brim, wired edge, hat worn low on head. [11] 1990. Brown felt hat, large crown, wide fake-fur band, brim turned back all around, hat worn low on head. [12] 1990. Green lacquered-straw crownless hat, large peak set onto wide band. [13] 1992. Dark-blue felt hat, large crown, fake-astrakhan draped band, kilt-pin trim, wide brim turned up at front, hat worn low on head. [14] 1992. Red lacquered-straw hat, shallow flat-topped crown, draped stiffened silk band, matching outsized bow and ends on centre-front, wide flat brim, wired edge. [15] 1992. White plastic-straw hat, shallow crown, outsized brim folded back on itself on centre-front, black and white slotted ribbon trim.

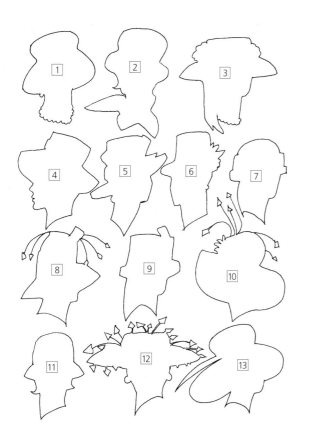

Women's Hats 1993–1999

1 1993. Blue natural-straw hat, wide waisted crown, inset cream bands matching edge of wide turned-down brim. 2 1993. Brown natural-straw hat, high waisted crown, wide petersham-ribbon band, turned-up brim. 3 1993. Dark-cream natural-straw hat, wide-based shallow crown, band of silk roses and velvet leaves, wide turned-down brim, wired edge. 4 1995. Black natural-straw hat, very high crown, looped silk-organdie bow trim, wide brim, turned-up wired brim. 5 1995. Pink natural-straw hat, high crown, silk ribbon band, large bow trim on centre-front, wide brim, turned-up wired edge. 6 1996. Grey stylized top hat shape covered in silk, wide self-fabric pleated band, flat brim, narrow turned-up edge, silk roses trim at one side. 7 1996. Blue felt hat, wide crown, deep band of checked wool, bow trim on centre-front, narrow turned-up brim, hat worn low on head. 8 1996. Blue-black natural-straw hat, high banded crown, looped detail on top, shaved-feather trim, wide turned-down brim, wired edge. 9 1997. Green woven-straw hat, wide flat-topped crown, narrow self-straw band, knot and ends, turned-up brim, wired edge. 10 1998. Grey woven-straw hat, high domed crown, wide inset self-straw band, feather decoration on centre-front, shaved-feather trim, wide trim, wired edge, binding. 11 1998. Blue woven straw hat, wide domed crown draped with silk-chiffon, narrow turned-down brim, wired edge. 12 1999. Dark-green natural-straw hat, shallow crown, wide turned-down brim, wired edge, hat covered with black shaved feathers. 13 1999. Brown natural-straw hat, long feather threaded through base of high waisted crown at one side, wide brim, wired edge.

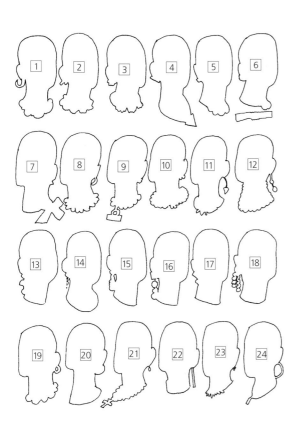

Jewelry 1986–1999

1 1986. Split hoop gilt earrings, triangular-shaped detail, set with cut stones. Outsized gilt chain necklace. 2 1986. Knotted plastic rouleau clip earrings; matching necklace. 3 1986. Two-colour gold clip earrings, flower design set with coloured stones; matching necklace. 4 1986. Silver arrow-shaped clip earrings, set with clear stones; matching pendant necklace. 5 1987. Gold and enamel clip earrings, set with clear stones; matching necklace. 6 1987. Gilt clip earrings, set with coloured stones; matching necklace and bracelet. 7 1987. Gold and pearl clip earrings, insect design, set with coloured stones. Bow-shaped brooch, set with coloured and clear stones. 8 1987. Transparent coloured plastic clip earrings, set with coloured stones. Necklace of linked flowers and leaves separated by large pearl beads. 9 1988. Gilt and pearl clip earrings. Gilt, pearl and enamel necklace, barrel pendant on centre-front. 10 1988. Choker necklace, twisted ropes of glass beads, side fastening under gilt flowers; matching clip earrings. 11 1988. Gilt earrings, two pendants, heart-shaped ends set with coloured stones. Gilt necklace, centre-front fastening under winged beetle clasp. 12 1989. Mixed plastic-bead choker and necklace; matching drop earrings. 13 1989. Drop earrings, set with pearls and clear stones. 14 1989. Gilt clip earrings, linked bead drops. Engraved gilt collar. 15 1990. Plastic-gilt pendant earrings. 16 1990. Square silver earrings, set with pearls and clear stones, matching pendant. 17 1991. Coloured clear plastic clip earrings, pendant from pewter trim. 18 1991. Plastic-jet clip earrings, set in pewter, bead pendants. 19 1992. Gold chain necklace, enamelled stripe on links; matching earrings. 20 1994. Gilt snailshell clip earrings. Gilt collar set with coloured stones. 21 1996. Gold drop earrings set with coloured stones. Plastic cross set with coloured stones, bead chain. 22 1996. Silver pendant earrings; matching dog collar. 23 1999. Bronze and coloured crystal necklace, flower design; matching earrings. 24 1999. Twisted gold wire hoop earrings. Gold watchchain necklace with fob.

Women's Bags 1986–1999

1 1986. Leather tote bag, side strap around middle, knotted centre-front, side panels extended to form thick handle, topstitched details. 2 1986. Two-tone leather bag, decorative straps with buckle trim extended to form handles, zip fastening. 3 1987. Quilted leather bag, flap, decorative gilt stud, matching long bead-chain handle. 4 1987. Leather bag, flap topstitched panel, gilt fastening and trim, short strap handle. 5 1988. Patterned-leather tote bag, plain leather strap around middle, matching long strap handle. 6 1989. Leather bag, flap, diagonal topstitched panel, gilt clasp and trim, short rouleau handle. 7 1990. Two-tone half-moon-shaped leather bag, zip fastening, silk cord handle. 8 1991. Leather bag, round textured metal handle, zip fastening. 9 1989. Leather belt incorporating two small purses, one under zip fastening, the other an outside patch and flap. 10 1994. Plastic bag, flat sides, base and top, flap, stud fastening, short bead handle. 11 1994. Leather bag, flap striped in two colours, stud fastening, thick strap handle. 12 1992. Leather tote bag, strap around middle, decorated with gilt discs, matching eyelets and trim, long strap handle. 13 1994. Small round leather bag, zip fastening, heart-shaped gilt tag, matching shapes to ends of rouleau handles. 14 1996. Heart-shaped leather bag, gilt clasp fastening, matching trim, stitched rouleau handle. 15 1998. Canvas duffle bag, leather bindings, matching rouleau handles, brass eyelets. 16 1996. Leather bag, zip fastening, encased in fake-fur tote bag, long knotted handle. 17 1997. Canvas tote bag, contrast-colour leather handles and trim. 18 1999. Canvas bag, flap embroidered with raffia flowers, bead trim, long strap handle, topstitched details. 19 1999. Tiny leather bag, flat sides, flap, long strap handle. 20 1999. Leather backpack, large bag, zip fastening, small external bag, all-round zip fastening, adjustable shoulder straps. 21 1999. Leather tote bag, scalloped edge, perforated pattern, strap handles. 22 1999. Hatbox-style bag, lid decorated with silk flowers and leaves, looped rouleau handle.

Women's Scarves, Gloves and Belts 1986–1999

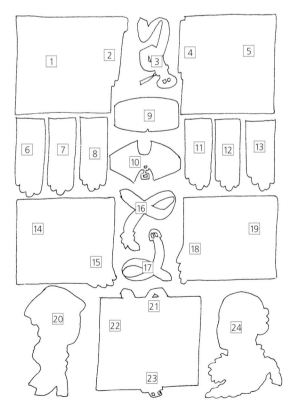

1 1986. Silk scarf, 1920s-style figure against black and white spotted background. 2 1986. Leather gloves, fox-fur cuffs. 3 1986. Tooled-leather belt, engraved silver buckle, matching eyelets and carrier with tasselled trim. 4 1987. Leather gloves, three-button trim on one side. 5 1988. Multicoloured patterned scarf, fringed edges. 6 1987. Suede gloves, laced detail on upper hand. 7 1988. Cloth gloves, applied contrast-colour ribbon stripes. 8 1989. Leather gloves, central V-shaped cut, topstitched detail, button trim. 9 1988. Wide leather belt, narrow mock-snakeskin strap and trim in contrast colour, brass buckle. 10 1989. Leather belt, widening to cut-away centre-front, machine topstitched detail, gilt fastening, matching chain drops. 11 1995. Cloth gloves, self-fabric bow trim. 12 1998. Suede gloves, curved panels from centre-front, gilt button trim. 13 1999. Leather gloves, large centre-front eyelets, matching small eyelets on each side. 14 1992. Multicoloured silk scarf, playing-card pattern, decorative border. 15 1995. Cloth gloves, appliqué-leather trim in contrast colour. 16 1993. Leather belt, adjustable open gilt buckle, leaf motif. 17 1997. Leather belt, textured-metal studs, matching eyelets and buckle. 18 1999. Leather gloves, raised square metal studs. 19 1997. Rayon scarf, pattern of roses and butterflies, contrast-colour border, rosebud pattern. 20 1998. Long devoré scarf, shaded in two colours. 21 1998. Leather belt, round and diamond-shaped studs in silver and gold, large buckle. 22 1999. Devoré scarf, cut-pile flowers on textured background, wide border. 23 1999. Wide leather belt, metal-stud decoration, narrow strap fastening, metal buckle. 24 1999. Three-colour looped chenille boa.

Women's Footwear 1986–1992

1 1986. Leather shoes, piped in gold, matching lining, scalloped edges and round heels. 2 1986. Leather shoes, square metal toecaps, matching plate above tapered heels. 3 1986. Patent-leather shoes, applied leaf shapes on one side, pointed toes, tapered heels. 4 1987. Leather shoes, extension above tapered heels, pointed toes. 5 1986. Leather step-in shoes, contrast-colour apron fronts, strap-and-buckle fastening. 6 1987. Two-tone step-in leather shoes, apron fronts, rubber soles and heels. 7 1988. Two-tone patent-leather step-in shoes, apron fronts under bar, stacked heels. 8 1988. Moulded plastic sandals, open sides, woven fronts, strap-and-buckle fastening. 9 1988. Lace-up leather shoes, topstitched detail, low heels. 10 1988. Suede lace-up shoes, apron fronts, perforated detail, pointed toes, stacked heels. 11 1988. Leather sling-back shoes, wedge heels above small metal heels, matching pointed toecaps. 12 1989. Suede shoes, high vamps with point, matching back above tapered heels, pointed toes. 13 1990. Two-tone leather pumps, pointed toecaps. 14 1990. Leather shoes, self-leather and metal bow trim, tapered heels. 15 1990. Leather sling-back shoes, narrow vamps, pointed toes, tapered stacked heels. 16 1990. Leather sling-back shoes, snakeskin T-straps, matching bars, pointed toes, flat heels. 17 1990. Two-tone leather shoes, low vamps, laced bar-straps, apron fronts, pointed toes, straight heels. 18 1990. Leather sandals, single strap, rubber soles. 19 1991. Suede sling-back shoes, front straps form knot above pointed toes. 20 1991. Leather mules, buckled bar-straps, pointed toes, stiletto heels. 21 1991. Leather sling-back shoes, contrast-colour spot decoration, pointed toes, set-back heels. 22 1991. Two-tone leather pumps, low vamps, bow trim, flat heels. 23 1992. Satin shoes, buckled bar-straps, open sides, peep toes, stiletto heels. 24 1992. Lace-up two-tone leather shoes, apron fronts, stacked heels. 25 1992. Suede pumps, metal-stud trim, pointed toes, flat heels. 26 1992. Two-tone leather shoes, narrow vamps, pointed toecaps, square heels.

Women's Footwear 1993–1999

1 1993. Leather shoes, bow trim, pointed toes, stacked heels. 2 1993. Leather shoes, strap-and-buckle fastening under tongues, stacked heels. 3 1993. Suede shoes, crossed bar-straps, buckle fastening, pointed toes, low heels. 4 1994. Suede sling-back shoes, crossed straps, low heels. 5 1994. Two-tone leather shoes, perforated decoration, wedge heels. 6 1994. Leather sling-back shoes, perforated decoration, peep toes, stacked heels. 7 1995. Suede shoes, thin straps above open sides, flat heels. 8 1995. Leather shoes, bar-straps, buckle fastening, rubber soles and heels. 9 1995. Leather mules, re-embroidered lace band, high heels. 10 1995. Canvas lace-up sports shoes, bound edges, topstitched detail, rubber soles and heels. 11 1996. Leather shoes, ankle straps, front bar-straps in contrast colour, platform soles, wedge heels. 12 1996. Leather sling-back shoes, buckled bar-straps, waisted heels. 13 1996. Leather sling-back shoes, peep toes, rubber soles and heels. 14 1996. Satin strap sandals, platform soles, high heels. 15 1996. Canvas shoes, ankle-straps, open sides, peep toes, platform soles. 16 1996. Moulded plastic mules, contrast-colour straps, platform soles. 17 1998. Two-tone leather shoes, bar-straps, low squat heels, wavy edge to soles, turned-up toes. 18 1998. Patent-leather shoes, ankle-straps, open sides, pointed toes, metal stiletto heels, upper part covered in leather. 19 1998. Leather lace-up shoes, high vamps, topstitched toecaps, flared stacked heels. 20 1998. Step-in suede shoes, apron fronts, topstitched detail, moulded-in rubber soles and heels. 21 1998. Leather mules, wide bar-strap, thin toe-strap. 22 1999. Leather shoes, square toes, angular two-piece waisted heels. 23 1999. Two-tone leather mules, wide straps, square toes, platform soles, angled heels. 24 1999. Leather mules, contrast-colour bar-straps, apron fronts, ridged-rubber base to combined heels and platform soles continues up centre-front and back. 25 1999. Two-tone leather mules, wide fronts, tasselled trim, open toes, wedge heels, platform soles, angled on centre-front. 26 1999. Leather shoes, square patent-leather toecaps, high set-back heels.

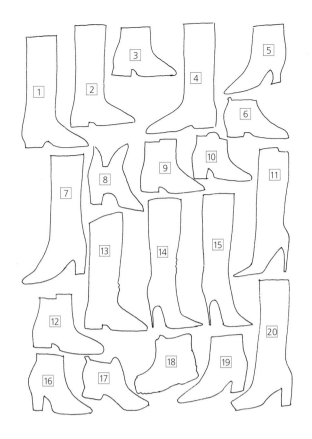

Women's Boots 1986–1999

1 1986. Leather boots, mock-snakeskin threaded buckled strap on outside straight legs, matching panel above stacked heels, pointed toes. 2 1986. Suede boots, straight legs, contrast-colour patent-leather apron fronts, stacked heels. 3 1987. Short mock-lizardskin boots, elasticated gussets, flared heels. 4 1987. Leather boots, straight legs, curved seam over instep, twisted-leather inset, pointed toes, stacked heels. 5 1989. Short leather boots, elasticated gussets, pointed toes, louis heels. 6 1990. Leather ankle-boots, elasticated gussets, pointed toecaps, stacked heels. 7 1991. Fitted leather boots, side panels in contrast colour, pointed toes, thick heels. 8 1991. Velvet ankle-boots, elasticated gussets, pointed toes, thick heels. 9 1993. Short leather boots, wrapover fronts, threaded straps, buckled on side, pointed toes, stacked heels. 10 1993. Leather ankle-boots, elasticated gussets under side panel, brass-ring decoration, pointed toes, low heels. 11 1995. Fitted leather boots, wrapover fronts, pointed toes, stiletto heels. 12 1996. Leather ankle-boots, wrapover fronts, strap-and-buckle fastening on side, stacked heels. 13 1996. Leather boots, straight legs, creased-suede inset at ankle-level, pointed toes. 14 1997. Long fitted boots, patent-leather fronts with pointed toes, matching stiletto heels, stretch-fabric uppers, pleated at ankle-level. 15 1997. Fitted stretch-fabric boots, patent-leather pointed toecaps, stiletto heels and decorative bar-strap. 16 1998. Fitted mock-snakeskin boots, pointed toes, thick heels. 17 1998. Leather ankle-boots, high tongues under strap-and-buckle fastening, square toes, shaped stacked heels. 18 1999. Lace-up leather boots, fake-fur-trim cuffs, high tongues and apron fronts cut in one piece, ridged-rubber trim above matching soles and heels. 19 1999. Short leather boots, strap-and-buckle trim, platform soles, flared stacked heels. 20 1999. Patent-leather boots, high vamps, square toes, thick heels, plain leather semi-fitted legs.

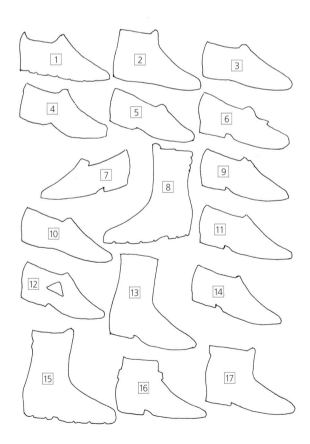

Men's Footwear 1986–1992

1 1986. Suede and leather lace-up sports shoes, padded sides and upper heels, ridged-rubber soles and combined heels. 2 1986. Canvas lace-up sports boots, rubber toecaps, matching soles and combined heels. 3 1986. Suede lace-up shoes, topstitched detail, man-made soles and heels. 4 1987. Two-tone lace-up shoes, leather laces and side trim, man-made soles and heels. 5 1987. Leather step-in shoes, low vamps under decorative strap and buckle, apron fronts, openwork detail, matching sides, man-made soles and heels. 6 1988. Leather step-in shoes, fringed tongues under strap and buckle, apron fronts, stacked heels. 7 1989. Leather step-in shoes, high tongues, threaded-leather trim, tassel trim, matching sides, apron fronts, square toes, stacked heels. 8 1990. Two-tone lace-up leather boots, padded sides, blunt toes, ridged-rubber soles and heels. 9 1989. Textured-leather shoes, strap-and-buckle fastening, stacked heels. 10 1990. Canvas lace-up sports shoes, rubber toecaps, matching combined soles and heels. 11 1990. Leather step-in shoes, elasticated side vents, brogued detail above almond-shaped toes, stacked heels. 12 1990. Suede sandals, T-strap-and-buckle fastening, open sides, wrapover strap fronts, stacked heels. 13 1991. Leather lace-up boots, topstitched detail, blunt toecaps, stacked heels. 14 1991. Two-tone leather lace-up shoes, apron fronts, brogued detail, stacked heels. 15 1992. Two-tone lace-up boots, panelled sides, blunt toes, ridged man-made soles and heels. 16 1992. Mock-crocodile-skin ankle-boots, diagonal strap-and-buckle fastening above wrapover fronts, stacked heels, almond-shaped toes. 17 1992. Leather lace-up ankle-boots, padded tops, canvas side panels, man-made soles and heels.

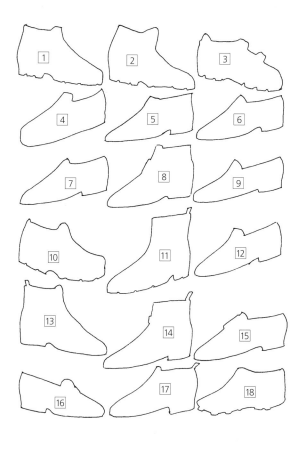

Men's Footwear 1993–1999

1 1993. Canvas lace-up ankle-boots, rubber toecaps, ridged man-made soles and heels. 2 1993. Leather lace-up boots, contrast-colour inserts, topstitched detail, apron fronts, ridged man-made soles and heels. 3 1993. Multicoloured man-made-fabric sports shoes, strap-and-Velcro fastenings, ridged soles and combined heels. 4 1994. Suede step-in shoes, high tongues under wide straps, man-made platform soles and heels. 5 1994. Leather step-in ankle-boots, high mottled leather tongues and combined apron fronts, stacked heels. 6 1994. Leather step-in shoes, high tongues under wide straps, apron fronts, pointed toes, man-made soles and heels. 7 1994. Leather lace-up shoes, apron fronts, brogued detail, blunt toes, stacked heels. 8 1995. Leather step-in ankle-boots, high tongues under wide straps, elasticated gussets, blunt toes, stacked heels. 9 1995. Leather step-in shoes, high tongues under wide straps, apron fronts, blunt toes, stacked heels. 10 1996. Leather lace-up shoes, high fronts and sides, apron fronts, stitched side panels, wedge heels, ridged man-made soles. 11 1996. Leather ankle-boots, elasticated gussets, blunt toes, ridged man-made soles and heels. 12 1997. Leather step-in shoes, high tongues under wide straps, metal trim, apron fronts, blunt toes, stacked heels. 13 1997. Leather ankle-boots, laced through side straps, apron fronts, blunt toes, stacked heels. 14 1998. Leather ankle-boots, elasticated side vents under strap-and-buckle fastening, blunt toes, man-made soles and stacked heels. 15 1998. Leather step-in shoes, double strap-and-buckle fastening over short tongues, topstitched toecaps, stacked heels. 16 1999. Leather step-in shoes, strap-and-Velcro fastening, tongues combined with apron fronts, man-made soles and heels. 17 1999. Leather lace-up ankle-boots, tongues combined with stitched front panels, square toes, rubber soles and heels. 18 1999. Leather step-in sports shoes, elasticated gussets, topstitched detail, ridged moulded-rubber soles and combined heels roll up on front, back and sides.

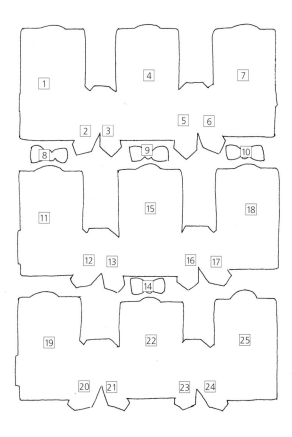

Men's Shirts and Ties 1986–1999

1 1986. Pale-blue collar-attached shirt, gingham-lined collar, pleated patch-and-buttoned-flap pockets, topstitched edges and detail. Two-colour silk cord tie, bone toggle, silver ends. 2 1987. Striped flecked silk tie. 3 1987. Blue silk tie, feather pattern. 4 1988. Grey and white spotted cotton collar-attached shirt, cut-away collar. Red silk tie, patterned with large white spots. 5 1989. Silk tie with reproduction Picasso design. 6 1989. Silk tie, abstract pattern. 7 1989. Pink cotton shirt, white collar, long points, patch-and-buttoned-flap pockets. Silk tie, patterned with large pocket watches between three-colour stripes. 8 1986. Spotted silk bow-tie, contrast-colour stripe through middle. 9 1988. Three-colour striped silk bow-tie. 10 1989. Multicoloured rayon bow-tie, abstract flower pattern. 11 1991. Patterned silk shirt, buttoned-down collar points. Multi-coloured screenprinted silk tie. 12 1991. Silk tie, patterned with period walking sticks. 13 1991. Multicoloured striped silk tie. 14 1994. Silk bow-tie, pattern on striped ground. 15 1994. Red and white checked cotton shirt, buttoned-down collar points, patch pocket. Red silk tie, wavy stripes. 16 1995. Silk tie, paisley pattern combined with flowers. 17 1995. Silk tie, patterned with multicoloured squares. 18 1995. Checked brushed-cotton shirt, cut-away collar points, patch pockets. Multicoloured patchwork silk tie. 19 1995. Brushed-cotton shirt, contrast-colour needlecord collar, buttoned-down points. Silk tie, pattern of squares and diamonds. 20 1996. Multicoloured patterned rayon tie. 21 1996. Silk tie, random pattern. 22 1997. Striped cotton shirt, plain white collar. Rayon tie, patterned with abstract flowers. 23 1998. Green striped wool tie. 24 1998. Spotted silk tie with satin check. 25 1999. Pink checked cotton collar-attached shirt. Blue silk tie, striped with flower pattern.

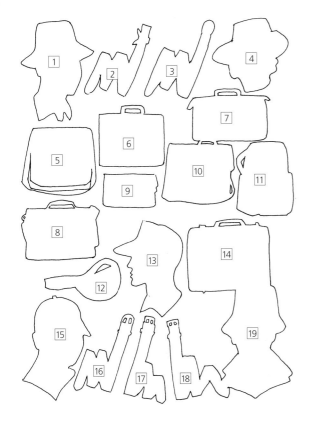

Men's Hats, Belts and Bags 1986–1999

1 1986. Woven natural-straw hat, deep draped band, wide brim.
2 1986. Reversible leather belt, embossed design on one side, metal eagle over fastening. 3 1987. Leather belt, embossed design and logo, engraved oval buckle. 4 1988. Leather hat, flat-topped crown, eyelet holes above plaited self-fabric band, wide brim, stitched edge. 5 1986. Leather bag, flap, lockable metal fastening, matching buckle on long adjustable handle, topstitched edges and detail. 6 1988. Crocodile-skin briefcase, retractable handles, topstitched detail, strap-and-clasp fastening. 7 1989. Leather briefcase, top zip fastening, stitched handles, decorative straps. 8 1996. Nylon bag, deep flap, double strap-and-clasp fastenings, long adjustable and detachable handle, short stitched rouleau carrying handle. 9 1992. Small leather bag, two flaps, stud fastenings. 10 1991. Leather bag, flap, lockable metal clasp, long adjustable and detachable handle, short carrying handle. 11 1998. Small nylon rucksack, two zipped side pockets, folded back pocket with flap, main bag fastening with straps, two shoulder straps, topstitched edges and detail. 12 1996. Nylon bumbag, two zipped compartments, logo, open back pocket, adjustable waist-strap. 13 1991. Crownless nylon sports visor, wide front band, logo, elasticated back, wide peak, topstitched edges. 14 1999. Matt silver-coloured aluminium briefcase, rigid handle, lockable fastenings. 15 1998. Cotton sports cap, sectioned crown, button trim on top, eyelet holes, logos on centre-front, large topstitched peak. 16 1995. Textured-leather belt, gilt buckle, eyelets, stud and carrier. 17 1997. Striped woven-nylon belt, topstitched leather trim, matching carrier, metal buckle. 18 1999. Leather belt, topstitched edges, metal carrier, eyelets and leather-trimmed metal buckle. 19 1999. Waterproofed checked nylon sports hat, flat-topped crown, narrow turned-down brim.

Accessories at a Glance 1986–1992

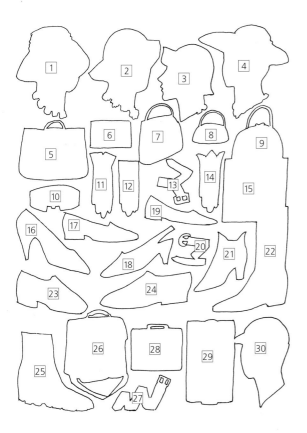

1 Straw hat, self-colour draped chiffon band, wide turned-down brim. Gilt clip earrings, coloured stones; matching necklace. 2 Two-tone topstitched silk hat, large crown, wide brim swept back. Gold clip earrings, flower design; matching necklace. 3 Felt hat, large crown, contrast-colour draped band, brim swept back at front. Gold and jet drop earrings; matching gold brooch. 4 Straw hat, small crown, contrast-colour silk drapery, wired brim. Large clip earrings set with coloured stones; matching necklace. 5 Linen tote bag, contrast-colour plastic handles and trim. 6 Leather envelope bag, gilt corners and trim. 7 Leather bag, zip fastening strap-and-stud trim, rouleau handle. 8 Leather bag, strap-and-stud fastening, rouleau handle. 9 Suede bag, gilt clasp, matching trim, rouleau handles. 10 Leather belt, narrow strap-and-buckle fastening in contrast colour. 11 Leather gloves, keyhole. 12 Leather gloves, strap-and-gilt-clasp trim. 13 Leather belt, engraved buckle and carrier. 14 Leather gloves, perforated detail, scalloped edges. 15 Multicoloured patterned silk scarf. 16 Leather shoes, contrast-colour appliqué trim, tapered heels. 17 Two-tone step-in leather shoes, apron fronts, man-made soles and heels. 18 Leather sling-back shoes, stacked tapered heels. 19 Two-tone leather pumps, flat heels. 20 Suede belt, two-pronged metal buckle. 21 Leather ankle-boots, elasticated gussets, low heels, pointed toes. 22 Leather boots, topstitched detail, blunt toes, stacked heels. 23 Leather lace-up shoes, man-made combined soles and heels. 24 Leather step-in shoes, elasticated gussets, toecaps, stacked heels. 25 Leather boots, buckled straps above lacing, ridged-rubber soles and heels. 26 Leather bag, flap, strap fastenings, front pockets, long handle, carrying handle. 27 Striped nylon belt, metal buckle and carrier. 28 Leather briefcase, retractable handles, metal trim. 29 Checked cotton shirt, patch pockets, buttoned flaps. Striped silk tie. 30 Cotton peaked cap.

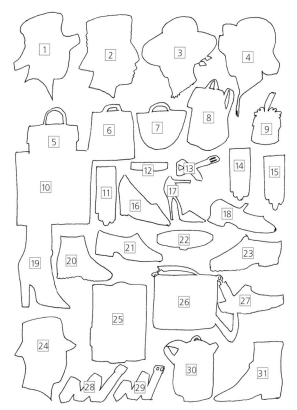

Accessories at a Glance 1993–1999

1 Straw hat, waisted crown, wide band and bow. Gilt clip earrings. 2 Straw hat, wide crown, draped band, turned-down brim. Two-tone clip earrings. 3 Straw hat, shaved-feather trim under draped band, wired brim. Clip earrings, flower design, set with coloured stones; matching necklace. 4 Straw hat, large crown, organza band and bow, swept-back brim. Tasselled drop earrings; matching necklace. 5 Leather bag, contrast-colour spots on flap, rouleau handle. 6 Mock-crocodile-skin bag, integral handle, gilt trim. 7 Mock-zebra-skin tote bag, zipped pocket on front. 8 Nylon backpack, flap, Velcro fastening, front pocket. 9 Silk hatbox-style bag, trimmed with silk roses. 10 Patterned devoré scarf. 11 Cloth gloves, multicoloured spots. 12 Leather belt, metal-stud decoration, matching buckle and carrier. 13 Leather belt, perforated decoration, metal buckle and carrier. 14 Leather gloves, perforated detail. 15 Cloth gloves, appliqué decoration. 16 Leather shoes, peep toes, brogued decoration, wedge heels. 17 Satin shoes, open sides, pointed, contrast-colour ankle-straps and stiletto heels. 18 Two-tone leather pumps, bar-straps, Velcro fastenings; soles roll up on front, back and sides; squat heels. 19 Leather boots, buckled-strap decoration, thick heels. 20 Leather ankle-boots, wedge heels, ridged soles. 21 Leather step-in shoes, apron fronts, man-made soles and heels. 22 Textured-leather belt, two-pronged metal buckle. 23 Leather lace-up shoes, ridged soles and heels. 24 Cotton sports hat, seamed band, metal eyelets, topstitched brim. 25 Checked cotton shirt. Checked silk tie. 26 Nylon bag, strap-and-clasp fastening, long handle. 27 Leather mules, elasticated gussets; soles roll up on front, back and sides. 28 Leather belt, metal clasp. 29 Striped belt, leather trim, metal buckle. 30 Nylon backpack, front pocket, zip fastenings, contrast-colour trim. 31 Leather ankle-boots, buckled-strap decoration over side vents.

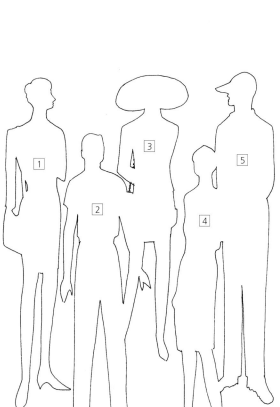

The Complete Look 1986–1999

1 1986. Two-piece wool suit: edge-to-edge fitted jacket, edges bound in contrast colour, long sleeves, padded shoulders, wide leather belt, narrow strap-and-buckle fastening; above-knee-length skirt. Small brimless felt hat. Triangular-shaped gilt clip earrings; matching brooch. Leather bag, crossed-strap detail, long handle. Leather gloves, topstitched detail below wrists. Leather shoes, wide ankle-straps, open sides, pointed toes, tapered heels. 2 1988. Linen shirt, buttoned-down collar points, short sleeves, patch pockets. Multicoloured patterned silk tie. Wool trousers, straight legs, no turn-ups, hip-level piped pockets, leather belt, wide sides, narrow strap-and-brass-buckle fastening. Leather lace-up shoes, apron fronts, man-made soles and heels. 3 1992. Two-piece checked wool suit: short edge-to-edge jacket, wide lapels, padded shoulders; mini-length skirt, wide leather belt, two-pronged metal buckle. Silk blouse, low neckline. Straw hat, wide turned-back brim, wired edge. Textured-gilt clip earrings; matching heart-shaped brooch and chain necklace. Small leather bag, quilted flap, long gilt bead-and-chain handle. Leather gloves, strap-and-button detail. Leather shoes, contrast-colour spots, almond-shaped toes. 4 1999. Short sleeveless wool top, small collar, zip fastening, topstitched detail, worn over contrast-colour T-shirt. Leather hipster skirt, side zip fastening, open to knee-level, topstitched edges, leather belt, metal-stud decoration, matching buckle, carrier and end. Nylon backpack, two patch-and-flap pockets, wide straps. Short leather gloves, bow trim. Leather shoes, topstitched detail, square toes, low set-back shaped heels. 5 1996. Nylon jacket, zip fastening, patch-and-flap pockets, Velcro fastenings, topstitched detail. Striped cotton collar-attached shirt, collar worn open. Two-colour checked silk tie. Cotton trousers, straight legs, turn-ups, leather belt, metal buckle and carrier. Cotton sports cap, large peak. Leather lace-up shoes, apron fronts, topstitched detail, ridged-rubber soles and heels.

Women's Hats 1900–1949

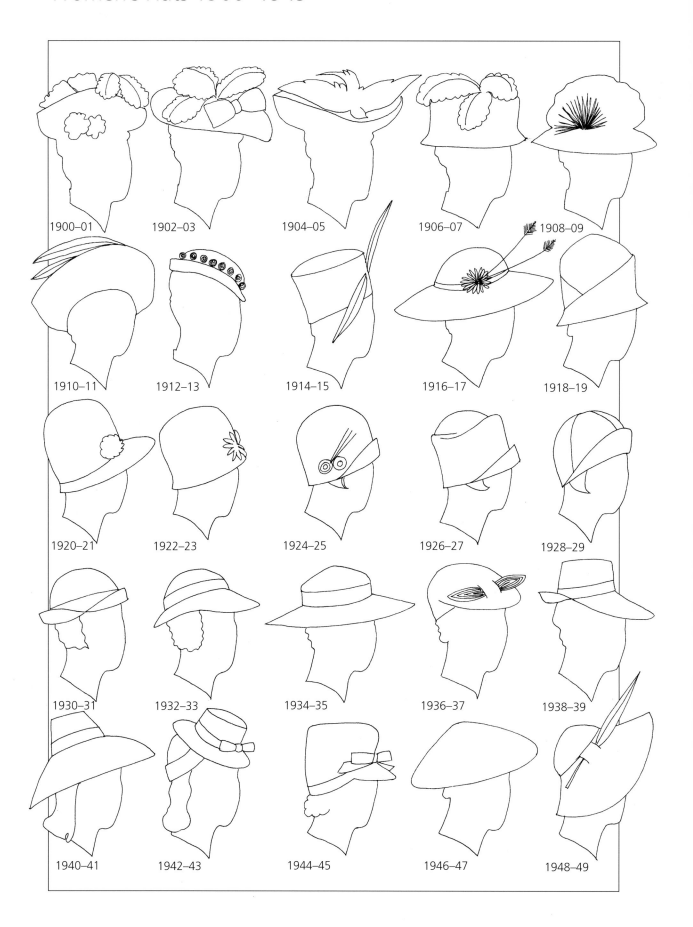

1900–01

1902–03

1904–05

1906–07

1908–09

1910–11

1912–13

1914–15

1916–17

1918–19

1920–21

1922–23

1924–25

1926–27

1928–29

1930–31

1932–33

1934–35

1936–37

1938–39

1940–41

1942–43

1944–45

1946–47

1948–49

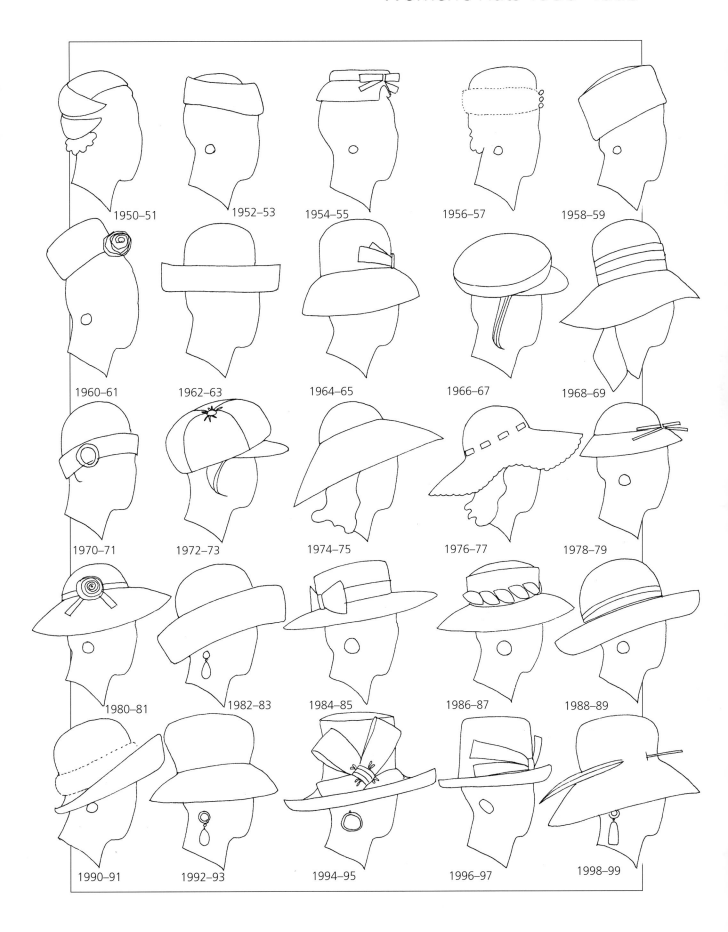

1950–51

1952–53

1954–55

1956–57

1958–59

1960–61

1962–63

1964–65

1966–67

1968–69

1970–71

1972–73

1974–75

1976–77

1978–79

1980–81

1982–83

1984–85

1986–87

1988–89

1990–91

1992–93

1994–95

1996–97

1998–99

Women's Footwear 1900–1949

1900

1907

1908

1915

1916

1924

1925

1932

1933

1940

1941

1949

1950

1957

1958

1965

1966

1974

1975

1982

1983

1990

1991

1999

Women's Boots 1900–1999

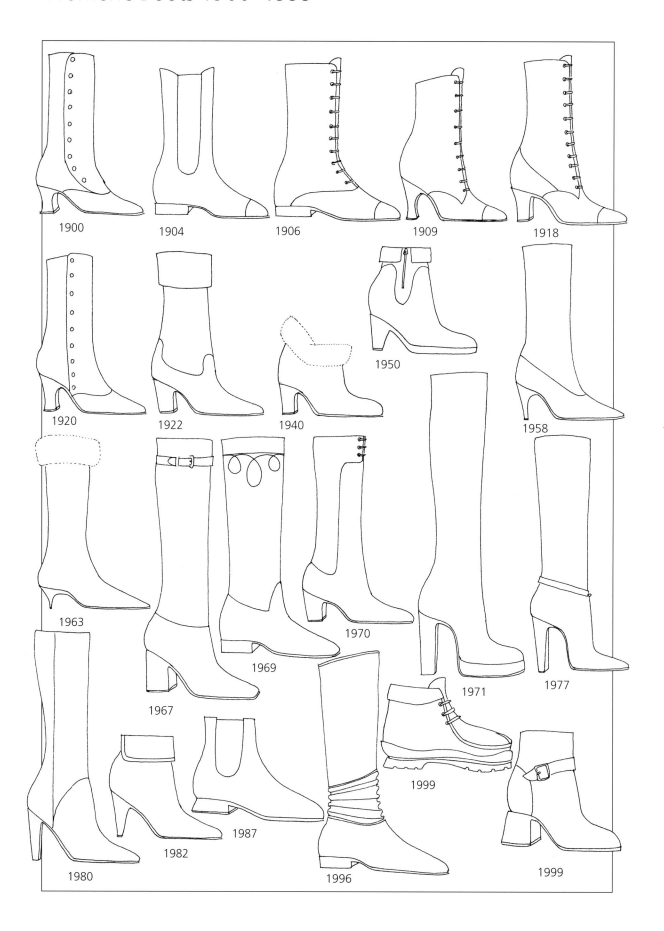

1900

1904

1906

1909

1918

1920

1922

1940

1950

1958

1963

1967

1969

1970

1971

1977

1980

1982

1987

1996

1999

1999

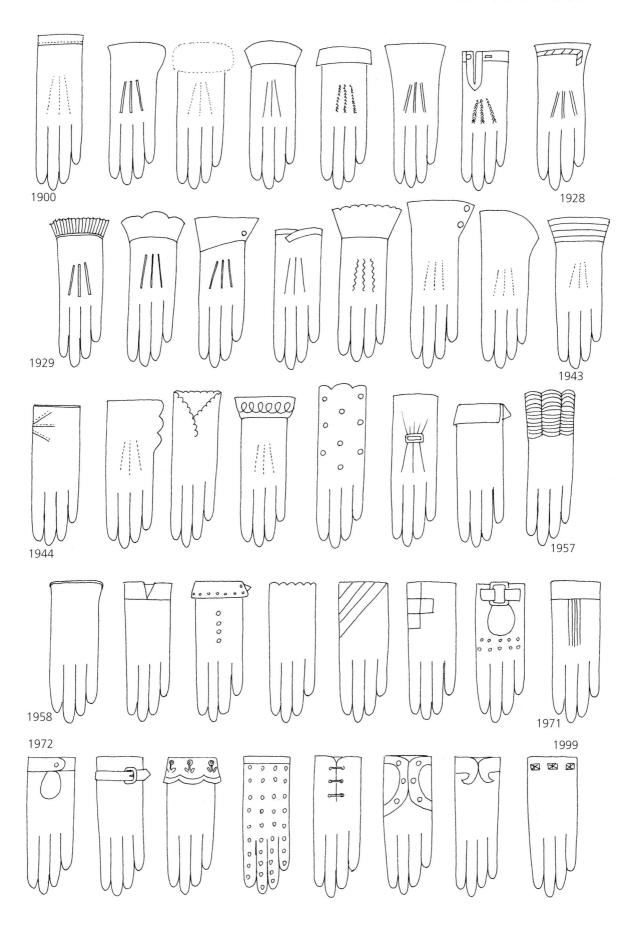

1900   1928

1929   1943

1944   1957

1958   1971

1972   1999

Women's Bags 1900–1999

1900

1919

1920

1939

1940

1959

1960

1979

1980

1999

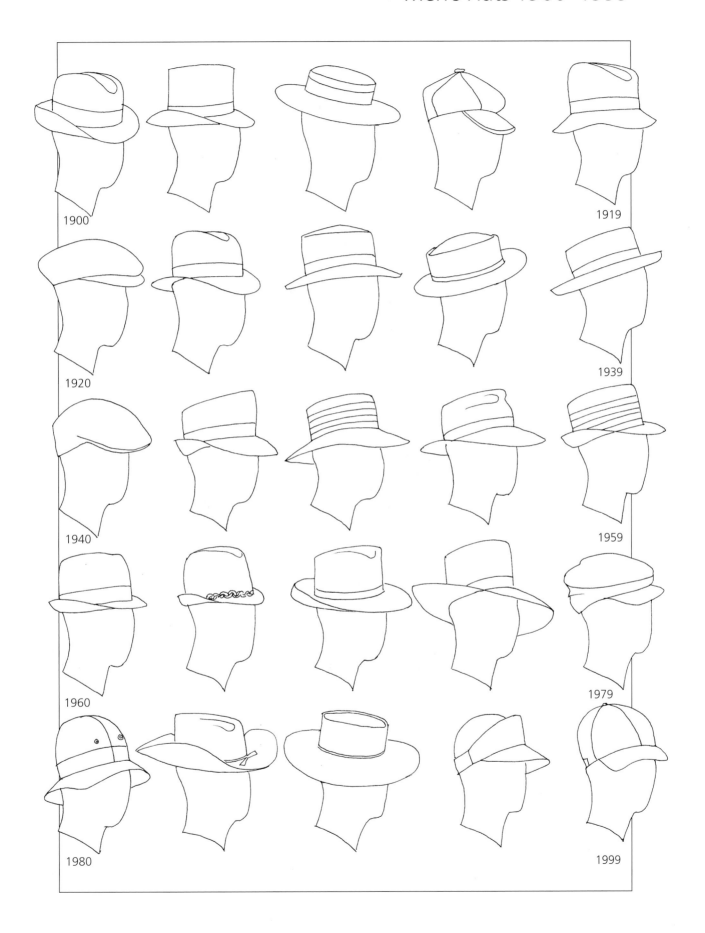

1900

1919

1920

1939

1940

1959

1960

1979

1980

1999

1900

1919

1920

1939

1940

1959

1960

1972

1973

1985

1986

1999

Concise Biographies of Designers and Companies

Adidas. Sports shoe company. Germany. Founded by Adi (Adolf) Dassler (1900–78; Herzogenaurach). In 1925 Dassler, with his brother Rudolf, began to produce high-performance athletic shoes. In 1949 he created the first modern running shoe, from which the present-day sneaker is derived. A year earlier the firm had split into two: Addas (later Adidas) and Puma (headed by Rudolf Dassler). Adidas achieved cult status in the 1980s when the hip-hop group Run DMC had a hit with their record 'My Adidas'.

Adolfo (Adolfo Sardiña, Adolfo of Emme). 1933–. Milliner/designer. US. Born Havana, Cuba. Adolfo emigrated to New York in 1948. He served an apprenticeship as a millinery designer at Bergdorf Goodman before spending time in Paris with Balenciaga. On his return to Bergdorf's he began to design hats under the name Adolfo of Emme. He opened his own house, as Adolfo, in 1962, offering clothes as well as hats. His many innovations in hat design included jersey visor caps, extra-large fur berets, a panama planter's hat of 1966 and a cossack hat of 1967. His house closed in 1993.

Agnès. Dates unknown. Milliner. France. After serving an apprenticeship in Levallois, a suburb of Paris, Agnès worked with Caroline *Reboux before opening her own house in Deauville in 1917. She was best known for her hats of the 1920s, which included stylish toques and cloches in strong Cubist designs, sometimes with appliqué – she collaborated with many well-known artists, including Léger, Mondrian, Robert Delaunay and the lacquer artist Jean Dunand. In the 1930s she moved to Paris and continued to produce charming, often slightly quirky hats until the closure of her house in 1949.

Jean Barthet. 1930–. Milliner. France. Born Nay. Barthet studied at the Ecole des Beaux-Arts in Toulouse before moving to Paris to work for a couturier. In 1960 he founded his own immensely successful house, whose clients have included Princess Grace of Monaco, Sophia Loren and Elizabeth Taylor – he also supplied Jackie Kennedy with her famous pillbox hats. Barthet has collaborated on the collections of Ungaro, *Chanel and others.

Bennis & Edwards. Shoe company. US. The partnership of the American Susan Bennis and the Englishman Warren Edwards, neither of whom had any formal design training, started in 1972. They showed their first collection, of ten shoe styles, the following year. Bennis & Edwards is known for handmade shoes of high quality, in classic designs, with a twist.

Manolo Blahnik. 1942–. Shoe designer. UK. Born Santa Cruz, Canary Islands. Blahnik studied literature at the University of Geneva before moving first to Paris, where he studied art, and then, in 1970, to London. His career began when he showed some theatrical sketches to various New York fashion editors and was encouraged by Diana Vreeland to concentrate on shoes. He opened his first shop, in London, in 1973. Blahnik is the world's best known contemporary shoe designer, with a devoted following among celebrities and fashion editors. He has contributed to the collections of many of fashion's foremost couturiers. Made in Italy, often in limited editions, his shoes combine the highest levels of handcraftsmanship with modern technical expertise. Constructed from a wide range of often exotic materials, in glowing, jewel-like colours, they are light, delicate, ethereal and feminine.

Borsalino. Hat company. Italy. Founded 1857 in Pecetto, Italy, by Giuseppe Borsalino (1834–?), who had trained as a hatter at Maison Berteil in Paris. By 1910 the company was producing two million hats a year. In the 1940s Borsalino gained an international reputation as a producer of high-quality classic felt hats, panamas and montecristos. In recent years it has expanded its range to include more contemporary styles .

Jean-Charles Brosseau. 1929–. Milliner. France. Born Cholet. After studying fashion at the Chambre Syndicale school in Paris, Brosseau went to Jean *Barthet as a trainee, later moving to Jacques Fath, where he remained until 1954. Then followed a brief period with *Paulette, before he finally opened his own house in 1960. He has collaborated with various designers on both haute-couture and ready-to-wear collections.

Camper. Shoe company. Spain. Founded 1975 by Lorenzo Fluxá (1947–), grandson of Antonio Fluxá (1853–1918), a Majorcan shoemaker who introduced mechanized shoemaking to Majorca in 1870. The first Camper shoe was an adaptation of a Majorcan country shoe, traditionally made from off-cuts of leather, strips of canvas and worn-out tyres. Known as the 'Camaleon', it is a rubber-soled, laced shoe with a toecap, made either in two-tone canvas and leather, or in single colour canvas. Other trendsetting designs include the 'Cartujano' boot (1986) – a handmade, knee-high boot in high-quality Cartujano leather; and the famous 'Twins' (1989) – non-matching, often asymmetrical, pairs of shoes.

Olivier Chanan. 1963–. Milliner. France. Born Paris. Chanan trained with various milliners, including Madame Ernestine Galanter, and opened his first shop in the French capital in 1981. His debut collection was shown in 1987. Chanan has an international clientele for whom he provides hats in fine, luxurious materials. His designs combine grace, femininity and fantasy.

Gabrielle ('Coco') Chanel. 1883–1971. Fashion designer. France. Born Saumur. In addition to being one of the century's greatest clothes designers, Chanel was responsible for two groundbreaking and hugely successful accessory designs: the two-tone slingback shoe of 1957 (*see* Massaro) and the quilted shoulder bag with gilt chain. The latter was first created in 1955 – the model is known as the '2.55'. Later versions, with subtle variations, have also proved enormously popular.

Jimmy Choo. Shoe company. UK. Jimmy Choo (1948–; Malaysia) began producing handmade shoes in 1988. The Jimmy Choo company, with Tamara Yeardye (1969–; London) as Managing Director, was founded in London in 1996. Yeardye, previously Accessories Director at *Vogue*, designs the Jimmy Choo ready-to-wear shoe range with Sandra Choi (1972; Isle of Wight). Jimmy Choo himself continues to produce a couture range of shoes. The signature Choo shoe is a high, elegant, sexy, strappy sandal.

Church's. Shoe company. UK. Founded in Northampton, England, in 1873 by Thomas, Alfred and William Church. Church's is best known for high-quality men's shoes, but also makes women's shoes. Its most successful men's styles are the Balmoral and the Consul (both plain, calf-leather oxfords) and the Westbury (a buckled monk shoe in high-shine leather).

Clarks. Shoe company. UK. Founded in 1825 by Cyrus Clark, as a firm producing sheepskin rugs. Cyrus's brother James joined in 1828 and began to make sheepskin slippers, known as 'brown peters', using offcuts. This led to the development of the company as a manufacturer of shoes, boots and slippers. The 1950s and 1960s saw Clarks rapidly expand with the creation of children's footwear – including the famous sandal – and the launch of the suede, crepe-soled desert boot, designed in 1950 by Nathan Clark.

Robert Clergerie. 1934–. Shoe designer. France. Born Paris. Clergerie started his career as manager of women's shoes for Xavier Danaud (a subsidiary of Charles *Jourdan) before buying a small shoe company in 1978 and launching his own label in 1981 with a line of mannish lace-up oxfords for women. Clergerie is a forward-looking shoemaker, known for his innovative heel designs and for elegant, architectural, unadorned footwear.

Kenneth Cole. 1954–. Shoe/menswear designer. US. Cole worked for his father's shoe company before starting his own women's shoe business in 1982 with inexpensive stone-washed canvas boots. He has subsequently branched out into handbags, men's shoes and men's clothing, and is known for up-to-the-minute looks at affordable prices, including sexy, high-heeled women's shoes and black, thick-soled styles for men.

Patrick Cox. 1963–. Shoe designer. UK. Born Alberta, Canada. Cox studied shoe design at Cordwainers College in London and while still a student created footwear for Vivienne Westwood's Autumn/Winter 1984–85 collection. On graduation in 1985, he set up his own company. The design for which he is best known is the Wannabe loafer, which took young, fashionable London by storm in Spring 1993. Cox has designed for Anna Sui, John Rocha, Jean Colonna and others.

Lilly Daché. c.1904–89. Milliner. US. Born Bègles, France. After an early apprenticeship with a milliner, Daché spent time in Paris with *Reboux and at Maison Talbot. In 1924 she moved to New York, where she began work as a saleswoman, first in the millinery department of Macy's department store and then in The Bonnet Shop, which she took over in the same year. The chic, flamboyant Daché was one of America's leading milliners from the 1920s to the 1950s. Alert to Parisian trends, she successfully adapted these to an American clientele. She was particularly known for draped turbans, half-hats, snoods and cloches, as well as for innovative designs for movie stars, including Carmen Miranda's flamboyant fruit-covered turbans.

Herman B. Delman. 1895–1955. Shoe manufacturer. US. Born Portersville, California, to parents who owned a small shoe shop. After the First World War Delman opened various shoe stores in Hollywood and New York and encouraged young designers to make shoes for his windows. In the late 1930s he began to manufacture shoes for *Vivier.

Dr. Martens. *See* R. Griggs Group Limited.

David Evins. c. 1915–. Shoe designer. US. Born England; emigrated to the US at the age of thirteen. After studying illustration at the Pratt Institute in New York, Evins began his career working for a footwear magazine. He eventually moved to the shoe company I. Miller, where he began designing shoes under his own name. He is often called 'shoemaker to the stars': his name first reached a wider public as a result of the alligator wedge clogs he created for Carmen Miranda; he also made both on- and offscreen shoes for Elizabeth Taylor and Lena Horne. He provided shoes for the collections of many of America's top designers but was also known for his stylish, comfortable pumps for the mass market.

Georgina von Etzdorf. Accessories company. UK. Founded 1981 by three design graduates: Georgina von Etzdorf (1955–; Lima, Peru), Martin Simcock (1954–; Widnes, Lancashire) and Jonathan Docherty (1955–; Stevenage, Hertfordshire). It produces a range of handprinted textiles and clothing, but the Georgina von Etzdorf name is particularly associated with the company's velvet (often combined with devoré), silk and chiffon scarves.

Fendi. Accessories/fashion house. Italy. Founded in Rome in 1918 by Adele Fendi (1897–1978); headed since 1954 by her five daughters. Well known for its soft leather handbags and canvas summer bags, Fendi also specializes in fur. Karl Lagerfeld was associated with the firm for a number of years and is responsible for the famous Fendi double-F logo. In 1997 Silvia Venturini (1960–), granddaughter of the founder, designed a short-strapped shoulder-bag known as a 'baguette', which was produced in a wide variety of colours and materials and became hugely popular.

Salvatore Ferragamo. 1898–1960. Shoe designer. Italy. Born Bonito, near Milan. At the age of nine Ferragamo was apprenticed to a local shoemaker and within five years was in charge of his own workshop. He moved to the US at fourteen, joining his brothers, with whom he opened a custom-made shoe and repair shop in Santa Barbara, California. A contract from the American Film Company brought him fame as a supplier of shoes to movie stars, including Mary Pickford and Douglas Fairbanks. Ferragamo moved his workshop to Hollywood in 1923. During his fifteen or so years in the US, he schooled himself in the techniques that would make his shoes the finest in the world. Returning to Italy in 1927, he set up a workshop in Florence. His designs during this period were highly inventive, and included patchwork uppers as well as the use of expensive skins such as kangaroo and crocodile, or more unusual materials such as fishskin and bark. Various factors, including the Wall Street Crash, forced the firm's closure in 1933, but it reopened in 1935. The late 1930s saw the launch of the first wedge sole, made of cork. In the 1940s wartime shortages brought even greater experimentation and some of Ferragamo's most beautiful shoes were created in pigskin, hemp, raffia and cellophane. Ferragamo is known as the designer of the 'invisible shoe', created in 1947, a sandal with a vamp formed of transparent nylon threads, and an F-shaped wedge heel.

Frederick Fox. 1931 –. Milliner. UK. Born New South Wales, Australia. Fox trained with various milliners in Sydney before moving to London in 1958. After working for the millinery entrepreneur Otto Lucas and for Langée, he took over the latter company in 1964. Fox has created hats for many designers, including Bill Gibb, John Bates and Hardy Amies, and is 'By Appointment' the Queen's milliner.

Maud Frizon. 1941–. Shoe designer. France. Born Paris. Frizon opened a boutique in 1969 and enjoyed immediate success with a pair of red, zipless, high-heeled Russian boots. Other equally popular designs followed: in 1970, a pair of canvas boots; in 1974 a flower sandal; in 1977 court shoes with stiletto heels. She has collaborated with Montana and Alaïa, among others.

R. Griggs Group Limited [Dr. Martens]. Shoe company. UK. R. Griggs and Co. Ltd, Wollaston, Northamptonshire, made the first pair of Dr. Martens boots on 1 April 1960. The company had been given the exclusive rights to the boots' manufacture by Dr Klaus Maertens (1915–88) and Dr Herbert Funck, the German inventors of the first heat-sealed air-cushioned sole. As of 1999, Dr. Martens footwear was being manufactured by Griggs at a rate of one million pairs per month. This growth in sales was the result of the

adoption of Dr. Martens footwear by members of various streetstyles, from the Mods of the 1960s, through the Skinheads of the 1970s, and the Punks, Indie Kids and Grunge followers of the 1980s and 1990s. In the late eighties, sales were further increased by the popularity of Dr. Martens among girls and young women. The company's very first design (first made on 1. 4. 1960) – the 1460 eight-eyelet boot – remains its most popular.

Gucci. Accessories/luxury goods company. Italy. Founded as a saddlery shop in Florence in 1906 by Guccio Gucci. The shortage of leather in the Second World War led to the introduction of its signature canvas, with red and green striped panel and double-G Gucci motif. Gucci produces luggage, shoes, scarves and other accessories. The firm's famous loafer with the gilt snaffle trim was introduced in the early 1930s and became an international status symbol. Gucci remained in family hands until the early 1990s, when it was bought by an investment company. The American designer Tom Ford was appointed design director in 1994.

Lulu Guinness. 1960–. Bag designer. UK. Born London. After studying at an art school in South Africa, Guinness started her business in London in 1989. She is best known for glamorous, hand-embroidered evening bags – her signature designs are her floral bags, including the 'Florist's Basket' and the 'Violet Hanging Basket' – but she has also produced the Lulu Case, an expensive, pigskin-suede-lined leather briefcase. Guinness has created bags for the collections of Collette Dinnegan and Mark Whitaker, among others.

Hermès. Luxury goods company. France. Founded 1837 by Thierry Hermès (1801–78) as a saddle- and harness-making business. After 1922, under the direction of Emile-Maurice Hermès (1871–1951), younger son of the founder, the company moved into the production of saddle-stitched leather goods (including belts and gloves), as well as couture, jewelry and wristwatches. By the 1930s it had launched such classics as the Kelly handbag (named in the 1950s after the actress Grace Kelly); the reporter's bag and the 'Chaine d'Ancre' bracelet. The famous Hermès scarf, employing the silk used for jockey's shirts and featuring equestrian motifs, was introduced in 1937, the company's centenary year.

Anya Hindmarch. 1968–. Bag designer. UK. Born Burnham-on-Crouch. Hindmarch started her own company in 1987. She produces approximately 45 handbag designs each season, each named after a London street, and is known for unfussy, practical day bags and quirky, feminine evening bags, often made in luxurious silk satin.

Akio Hirata. 1925–. Milliner. Japan. Akio Hirata studied at the Bunka College of Fashion while at the same time producing hats for Koorai. In 1955 he started his own business, but spent 1962 to 1965 training with Jean *Barthet in Paris. He opened his house, Haute Mode Hirata, in 1965. He designs hats for Yohji Yamamoto, Comme des Garçons and others.

Emma Hope. 1962–. Shoe designer. UK. Born Portsmouth. After graduating in 1984 from Cordwainers College, London, Hope established her shoe business the following year with a collection of brocade mules. In 1986 she opened her first shop. In addition to shoes, she also produces a handbag line. Hope has described her shoes as 'regalia for feet' and she is known for her use of exquisite materials, including nappa, suede, silk velvet, embroidered brocade and grosgrain. She has designed shoes for the collections of Anna Sui, Jean Muir, Betty Jackson, Paul Smith and others.

Jan Jansen. 1941–. Shoe designer. Netherlands. Born Netherlands. After two years in the shoe trade in Rome, Jansen began in 1964 to design for the Jeannot label, where his immensely successful designs included the quirky clog, 'Woody', which transformed the traditional Dutch design into a desirable fashion item. Jansen began to work under his own name in the early 1990s. He is known not only for his unconventional and often extreme shapes and styles, but also for his exuberant use of colour.

Eric Javits. 1956–. Milliner. US. Born New York. Javits graduated in painting and sculpture from the Rhode Island School of Design in 1978 and embarked on a career as a milliner – his first batch of hats was bought by Bonwit Teller. He is known for his restrained, sculptural designs. The success of his 'Derby' hat of the 1980s reached its peak in 1990 when it was worn by Mia Farrow in Woody Allen's film *Alice*. His packable 'Squishee' hat – made in rayon, nylon, cotton and viscose – and his 'Paysa' model – a lightweight, water-resistant, hand-sewn polyester hat – have proved similarly popular.

Joan and David. Shoe company. US. The husband-and-wife team Joan Helpern (b. New York) and David Helpern (b. Boston) founded their footwear company in Cambridge, Massachusetts, in 1968 and introduced the Joan and David label in 1977. Joan Helpern designs the company's shoes. Her popular modern classics are created with the working woman in mind. Stylish but comfortable, they include court shoes, brogued oxfords, loafers and boots. Joan and David trademarks are newness of line, proportion and silhouette combined with interesting texture and subtle colour. Extraneous elements are rare. The company also produces clothing, handbags and belts.

John P. John (born Hans Harberger?), also known as John-Frederics, John Pico John, Mr. John, John Piocelle. 1902–93. Milliner. US. Born Munich, Germany, the son of a milliner. John moved to New York in 1919 but returned to Europe to study medicine briefly at the University of Lucerne and art at the Sorbonne in Paris. Back in New York in the late 1920s, he opened a hat shop with Frederic Hirst (at which time John changed his name to John-Frederics). In 1948 he set up his own salon, 'Mr. John', and took the name John P. John. From the 1930s to the 1950s John was one of America's most celebrated and successful milliners, creating hats for more than 1000 films, including Greta Garbo's turban in *The Painted Veil* (1934) and Vivien Leigh's famous cartwheel hat in *Gone with the Wind* (1939). A colourful character as well as an astute businessman, John made both classically simple hats and vivid, exuberant creations, often employing ribbons and flowers to achieve a romantic effect. He closed his house in 1970.

Stephen Jones. 1957–. Milliner. UK. Born West Kirby, Liverpool. After graduating from St Martin's School of Art, London, in 1979, Jones achieved a high profile through his hat designs for various pop stars and pop groups and opened his first salon in London the following year. His witty, irreverent, often Surrealist designs have made him the milliner of choice for many couturiers, including Westwood, Ungaro and Galliano.

Charles Jourdan. Shoe company. France. Founded by Charles Jourdan (1883–1976; Romans) in 1919 in Romans. Jourdan's ambition was to create moderately expensive luxury shoes for the ready-to-wear market and in the 1930s he was the first shoe designer to place advertisements in fashion magazines. His sons – René, Charles Jr and Roland – joined the firm after World War II. In 1959 Charles Jourdan was contracted to create and distribute shoes for Christian Dior. A successful enterprise, with branches worldwide, Charles Jourdan produced popular, youthful styles from the late 1950s to the 1970s, including 'Maxime' (1958), a low-heeled, square-toed court shoe with a satin bow. The firm's profile was greatly enhanced in the 1960s by its use of surreal advertising photography by Guy Bourdin. Since the 1980s the Charles Jourdan image has been more conservative.

Kangol. Hat company. UK. Founded 1938 in Cleator, Cumbria, by Jacques Spreiregen (b. Jakob Henryk Spreiregen, 1893; Warsaw, Poland). Spreiregen was initially employed as an importer of basque berets, which he distinguished from other beret imports by devising the brandname Kangol. 'Kangol' is believed to be an amalgam of the 'k' from knitting, the 'ang' from angora and the 'ol' from wool. With the rising popularity of the beret in the 1930s, stocks became scarce and Spreiregen launched his own beret-making company. In 1942 Kangol became the official supplier of berets to the armed forces. In the 1950s it introduced a number of successful cap designs for men and in the 1960s commissioned Mary Quant to create women's designs. Kangol gained street credibility in the 1990s when the classic '504' design was worn by the singer Michael Jackson on his 1994 Far Eastern tour and by the actor Samuel L. Jackson in Quentin Tarantino's film *Jackie Brown*.

Stephane Kélian. Shoe company. France. Founded 1978 and run by three brothers: Georges (1929–), Gérard (1932–) and Stéphane (1942–) Kéloglanian. In 1960 Georges and Gérard set up a factory in Romans making men's shoes. In 1975 Stéphane joined the firm and two years later the brothers brought out their first, hugely successful, collection of shoes for women. Stephane Kélian has contributed to the collections of a number of designers, including Gaultier and Montana. The firm combines high fashion and fine craftsmanship. Its signature style is the much copied platform-soled 'Cape', made in a variety of materials, including ponyskin and crocodile.

K.Jacques. Shoe company. France. Founded in the 1920s in St Tropez by Jacques Kéklikian (1911–89), an Armenian refugee. The firm is best known for its greco-roman sandal, a design that had been initially created in the 1920s by a St Tropez shoemaker at the request of a visitor but which was reintroduced by K.Jacques in 1933. Known as the 'Trapézienne', it was taken up by a number of celebrities, including Colette. It enjoyed its widest popularity from 1952 on, when it was worn by both Brigitte Bardot and Queen Fabiola. The 'Trapézienne' was produced not only in the original

leather but also in gold and silver. In the 1980s the model was still being used by a number of couturiers to accessorize their collections.

Tokio Kumagaï. 1947–87. Shoe designer. France. Born Sendai, Japan. Kumagaï studied at the Bunka College of Fashion. In Paris in the 1970s he designed shoes for Castelbajac and Fiorucci, among others, before beginning in 1979 to produce under his own label the handpainted shoes for which he is best known. Kumagaï's shoe paintings mimicked the styles of many different artists, including Kandinsky, Pollock and Mondrian.

Sidonie Larizzi. Dates unknown. Shoe designer. France. Born Oran, Algeria. Larizzi studied at the Ecole des Beaux-Arts in Paris. In 1978, after spending eighteen years at Carvil, she opened her own salon, where she created made-to-measure shoes in fabric to match clients' dresses. She was soon producing shoes for Lacroix and Ungaro, among others. Larizzi focuses on high-heeled shoes, in unorthodox materials, such as straw, wood and cork, and in more traditional skins, such as crocodile, lizard and ostrich.

Launer London. Bag company. UK. Founded 1941, as S. Launer & Company, by the Czech-born refugee Sam Launer (?–1960s). Launer makes understated, elegant, classic bags in high-quality materials – calfskin, lizardskin and ostrich skin – with gold-plated fittings featuring its twisted rope emblem. The company is famous for supplying bags to Queen Elizabeth II and also counts Margaret Thatcher among its customers.

Legroux Soeurs. Milliners. France. Founded 1913 in Roubaix by two sisters, Germaine and Héloïse Legroux. They opened a principal branch in Paris in 1917 and achieved their greatest success in the 1920s. Their niece, Madame Serge Robert, succeeded them in the 1950s.

Judith Leiber (b. Judith Peto). 1921–. Bag designer. US. Born Budapest, Hungary. After an apprenticeship with the Hungarian Handbag Guild (in the 1940s she became the first woman Meister), Leiber moved in 1947 to New York, where she designed for Nettie Rosenstein, among others, before founding her own firm in 1963. Leiber's small-scale bags combine artistry and technique. She often uses exotic materials, such as reptile and ostrich skins, for her day bags; her tiny evening bags, for which she is famous, are usually jeweled or made with rich embroideries. Endlessly inventive, she has produced bags based on Fabergé eggs, sleeping cats and Chinese Foo dogs.

Beth and Herbert Levine. Shoe designers. US. Beth Levine (1914–; New York) began her career at I. Miller. In 1950 she married Herbert Levine, a shoe designer and salesman, and the couple formed the company Beth and Herbert Levine. Highly unconventional shoemakers, they produced a Spring-O-Lator mule with an elasticated sole, as well as high-heeled topless shoes in which the sole was stuck to the foot with spirit gum. They also created all-in-one boots-and-pants by attaching transparent acrylic heels and soles to pantyhose. In the 1960s their stretch boots were celebrated by Nancy Sinatra in the song 'These Boots Were Made for Walking'.

John Lobb. Shoe company. UK. Founded 1849 by John Lobb. Lobb's opened in 1866 in St James's Street, London. It makes what are reputed to be the finest handmade footwear in the world and is best known for its shoes for men, which include the plain oxford, the half-brogue oxford, the monk and the skin derby. Groucho Marx, Frank Sinatra and the Duke of Windsor are numbered among the company's many prestigious clients.

James Lock & Co. Hat company. UK. Founded 1676, James Lock & Co. is the oldest hatters in the UK. It has introduced a number of famous hat styles for men – including the bowler – and has had an illustrious list of clients, among them Lord Nelson (who commissioned a bicorne hat with a built-in eye shade), the Duke of Wellington, and the Prince of Wales (for whom it produced the tweed flat cap known as the turnberry). In 1993 the company began to produce hats for women.

Loewe. Accessories/fashion company. Spain. Founded 1846 in Madrid by Heinrich Loewe Rossberg (1829–1919; Germany) as a leather goods company producing supple leather bags. In 1939, at the end of the Spanish Civil War, the company diversified into scarves, umbrellas and costume jewelry. It has subsequently added both menswear and womenswear to its production, but is still strongly associated with leather goods.

Christian Louboutin. 1963–. Shoe designer. France. Born Paris. After studying dress design and drawing, Louboutin learned the craft of shoemaking by spending one year with Charles *Jourdan and two seasons with Roger *Vivier. In 1991 he launched his own label, offering shoes in stunningly original materials: guinea fowl, eel, mackerel, for example. He has also produced a line called 'Inséparable', in which the design runs across both shoes. In his famous 'Love' shoes, for instance, the 'L' and half of the 'o' are on the right foot; the remaining letters appear on the left foot.

Massaro. Shoe company. France. Founded 1894 in Paris. Massaro has a long history of providing shoes to couture houses, including, before the Second World War, Vionnet, and later, when the firm was headed by Raymond Massaro (1929–), *Chanel and Grès. Massaro was responsible for producing Chanel's famous two-tone low-heeled slingback pump in 1957.

Marie Mercié. 1942–. Milliner. France. Born Fontainebleau. Mercié studied history of art and archaeology at the Sorbonne before taking up journalism. She began her career in millinery in 1986, working from home with such success that after six months she was able to open her own salon. Among her best-known designs are her 'Zulu' hats, her eighteenth-century-inspired basket-weave collection, and her straw and raffia hats with plaited chignons and ponytails.

Simone Mirman (b. Simone Parmentier). c.1920–. Milliner. UK. Born Paris, the daughter of a dressmaker. In her early years Mirman worked for Rose *Valois and for Schiaparelli. After eloping to London in 1937, she was employed in Schiaparelli's London salon. Ten years later she set up on her own and came to public notice in 1952, when Princess Margaret became a customer and recommended Mirman to other members of the British royal family. Mirman's youthful styles were popular in the 1950s and 1960s.

Philippe Model. 1956–. Milliner/shoe designer. France. Born Sens. In 1978, with no formal fashion training, Model started a business making haute-couture hats and shoes. In the late 1970s and early 1980s he accessorized the collections of Gaultier, Montana and Mugler. Though best known for his hats, Model has also had success with his 'elasticated shoes'.

Mulberry. Accessories/fashion company. UK. Founded 1971 by Roger Saul (1950–; Lottisham, Somerset). Saul started his design career making leather chokers and belts which he sold to high fashion houses, including Biba. Mulberry began with belts but added a handbag collection in 1973 and in 1976 launched its signature accessories range, based on a huntin', shootin' and fishin' theme which epitomizes the company's rather nostalgic, quintessentially English image.

Sara Navarro. 1957–. Accessories/fashion designer. Spain. Born Elda, Alicante, into a family of shoemakers. After studying psychology at the University of Valencia, Navarro took a course in shoe styling at the Ars Sutoria Institute in Milan and was later taught fashion design by Gianfranco Ferre at Domus Academy, Milan. She joined the family firm, Kurhapies, in 1979 and launched the first Sara Navarro shop the same year. She has created both clogs and espadrilles based on traditional Mediterranean styles.

Nike. Sports shoe/sportswear company. US. Company originating in the BRS/Tiger partnership formed in 1964 by the coach Bill Bowerman and the athlete Phil Knight to manufacture sports shoes. The Nike brand was launched in 1972 and the company was officially named as Nike, Inc. in 1978. The famous Tailwind shoes, with Nike-Air cushioning, were introduced in 1979. Nike produces shoes for a wide variety of sports, including running, tennis, soccer and basketball.

Gilbert Orcel. Dates unknown. Milliner. France. Orcel studied music before opening a hat salon in Paris in 1938. His success was rapid. He gave a name to each of his collections: the best-known, 'Shell', was the source of his US nickname: 'Shellman'. Orcel's hats sold well in America – Jackie Kennedy was one of his clients. The house closed in 1972.

Paulette (b. Pauline Adam; Pauline Marchand, Madame Paulette). Dates unknown. Milliner. France. Born Normandy. After early years as a mannequin and saleswoman, Paulette opened her first hat shop in 1921. It was for her second establishment in 1929 that she took the name Paulette. A third salon, opened in 1939, coincided with the expansion and success of her business and in the war years she became famous for her draped wool turbans (created in response to wartime shortages). The turban became her signature design and from 1950 on she included a version of the style in each of her collections. Her hat designs often included scarves and draping. For many years Paulette was France's best known milliner. She not only made hats for a star-studded clientele, but also supplied the collections of many young couturiers in the 1960s and 1970s. She closed her house in 1984.

Michel Perry. 1949–. Shoe designer. France. Born Saint-Lô into a family which owned a chain of shoe shops. After studying at the Ecole des Beaux-

Arts, Perry worked at Bata and Bobb and with *Model before starting his own label in 1987. He is known for shoes with elongated lines and high heels. His clients include Madonna, Linda Evangelista and Naomi Campbell.

André Perugia. 1893–1977. Shoe designer. France. Born Nice. Apprenticed to his shoemaker father at an early age, Perugia opened a shop selling his own designs at the age of sixteen. His shoes eventually caught the eye of Paul Poiret, who invited Perugia to show his footwear in Poiret's couture house in Paris. The First World War interrupted this plan, but by 1920 Perugia was established in the French capital, where he provided shoes for *Chanel, Schiaparelli, Fath and Givenchy, among others. He made the fashion headlines with his eye-catching fantasy footwear, including a fish shoe inspired by Braque (1939), but was equally well known for his practical, finely balanced designs.

Andrea Pfister. 1942–. Shoe designer. Italy. Born Pesaro. Pfister studied languages and art at the University of Florence and in 1961 took a course in shoe design at the Ars Sutoria Institute of Footwear Design in Milan. Two years later he moved to Paris, where he designed shoes for Lanvin and Patou. In 1965 he showed his first collection under his own name and opened his first shop in Paris in 1967. Today Pfister produces shoes for the Krizia label. His designs are highly colourful and ornamented. He uses jewels and sequins for decorative effect and favours luxurious materials, including embroidery and silks. A famous design from the early 1980s was 'Mosaique', a white kidskin court shoe with a patchwork design of multicoloured snakeskin.

Jacques Pinturier. 1932–. Milliner. France. Born Auxerre. Pinturier served an apprenticeship with his uncle, Gilbert *Orcel, from 1949 to 1963, during which time he invented the half-hat (1950) and moulded veils (1955). In January 1964, he began work in Castillo's studio, where he remained until he opened his own salon in 1968. His innovations have been numerous: he has experimented with Rhodoid, copper and aluminium and has also created flower hats, made from a variety of materials. He has collaborated with many couturiers, including Molyneux, Scherrer, Balenciaga and Schiaparelli. His witty, Surrealist designs have won him a young, sophisticated clientele.

Prada. Accessories/fashion house. Italy. Founded 1913 by Mario Prada as Fratelli Prada, manufacturer of luxury leather goods, including luggage and handbags. In 1978 Miuccia Prada (1949–), granddaughter of the founder, took over and began producing strikingly plain, almost anti-fashion, accessories, chiefly in black. Among them, in the mid-1980s, was a light-weight black nylon backpack with leather straps – a bestselling design which spawned a host of imitations. Prada also produces footwear and clothing.

Edward Rayne (H. & M. Rayne). 1922–92. Shoe designer/ manufacturer. UK. Born London. Rayne was appointed managing director of the family firm H. & M. Rayne (founded 1889) in 1951. It became one of Britain's most successful footwear firms, producing quality shoes in classic styles. It was patronized by the British royal family, and both Hardy Amies and Norman Hartnell designed shoes for Rayne. In the 1960s more youthful designs were contributed by Mary Quant and Jean Muir, among others. H. & M. Rayne manufactured Roger *Vivier's shoes in 1963 and in the 1970s provided shoes for the collections of a number of French couturiers.

Caroline Reboux. c.1837–1927. Milliner. France. Born Paris. In the 1860s Reboux was discovered by Princess Metternich and was taken up as court milliner. By 1870 she had opened her own establishment in rue de la Paix. Reboux was Paris's most successful milliner up to and during the 1920s, when she retired. She collaborated with many couturiers, most notably with Vionnet. The firm continued under the direction of Lucienne Rebaté.

Red or Dead. Shoe/fashion house. UK. The first Red or Dead footwear was launched in 1986 by Wayne Hemingway (1961–; Morecombe, Lancashire) and Gerardine Hemingway (1961–; Padiham, Lancashire), who had founded the Red or Dead label with a range of clothing in 1983, the same year in which Red or Dead became the first retailer to sell Dr. Martens footwear as fashion items. A streetwise, youth-oriented company, Red or Dead had its first own-label footwear success with the 'Watch Shoe', a black lace-up with a watch mounted on top. Other inventive designs followed, including, in 1989, a plastic Union Jack slip-on and a camouflage slingback.

Reebok. Sports shoe/sportswear company. US. In the 1890s Joseph William Foster founded J. W. Foster & Sons in Bolton, Lancashire, making shoes for top runners. In 1958 two of his grandsons started a company that became known as Reebok (named after a South African antelope). North American distribution rights for Reebok shoes were acquired in 1979 by

Paul Fireman, who introduced three models into the US in the same year. In 1981 Reebok brought out 'Freestyle', the first athletic shoe for women. Designed for aerobics, it became the best-selling athletic shoe of all time.

Claude Saint-Cyr (b. Simone Naudet). 1911–. Milliner. France. Born Paris. At seventeen, Saint-Cyr was apprenticed to Gaby Mono, and then studied with Rose Descat and Patou, among others, before opening her own house in 1937. She became known for spare, refined millinery. During the war she opened branches in Biarritz, Marseilles and Lyons, and, in keeping with the wartime vogue, produced more extravagant hats. The hostilities over, she launched her famous and enormously successful 'oblique line'. In the 1950s Saint-Cyr became milliner to Queen Elizabeth II, working with the couturier Norman Hartnell. She closed her house in 1964; went to work for three years for *Barthet; reopened briefly, but finally shut her doors in 1972.

David Shilling. 1953–. Milliner. UK. Born London. Shilling designed his first hat (for his mother to wear at Ascot) at the age of twelve and opened his hat salon in 1976. He is known for eyecatching, often whimsical designs, including his disco hats of the 1970s.

Graham Smith. 1938–. Milliner. UK. Born Bexley, Kent. After studying at Bromley College of Art and the Royal College of Art, London, Smith worked for Lanvin-Castillo in Paris and for Michael of Carlos Place, London, before launching his own label in 1967. Since 1981 he has been associated with *Kangol. Smith's designs are relatively simple and restrained but their flattering lines make them popular with British hat buyers. In the 1980s Smith created hats for the Princess of Wales and the Duchess of York.

Kate Spade. Accessories company. US. Founded in 1993 by Katherine Noel Brosnahan (1964–; Kansas City) and Andy Spade (1961–; Birmingham, Michigan). Their first accessories were six handbags in simple shapes that emphasized utility, colour and fabric. These boxy, no-nonsense designs, based on the nylon tote bag, were followed by backpacks and knapsacks. The range expanded to include evening bags, wallets and a weekend travel collection. Kate Spade also produces clothes and footwear.

Walter Steiger. 1942–. Shoe designer. Switzerland. Born Geneva. After a three-year apprenticeship at St Gall, Steiger moved first to Paris to work for Bally and then, in the 1960s, to London, where he designed for both Bally and Mary Quant. He started his own label in 1968. Steiger is known for elegant, high-quality shoes for both men and women. He has collaborated with Karl Lagerfeld, *Chanel, Oscar de la Renta and Nina Ricci.

Svend (Svend Gravesen). Dates unknown. Milliner. France. Born Denmark. Gravesen worked with Fath from 1947 to 1951 before setting up his own house under the name Svend. He supplied hats to Pierre Balmain and Jacques Heim until 1957, when he moved to Heim as house milliner.

Suzanne Talbot (Juliette Suzanne Talbot). Dates unknown. Milliner. France. Talbot founded her millinery establishment in Paris in 1917. She was part of the avant-garde, artistic circle of the 1920s, and produced many designs along geometric, Art Deco lines. In 1924 she moved into clothes design. Her house closed in 1957.

Aage Thaarup. 1906–87. Milliner. UK. Born Copenhagen, Denmark. Thaarup began his career in the hat department of a Copenhagen fashion store. In the 1920s he travelled around Europe, before ending up in Delhi, where he supplied hats to British expatriate wives. By 1932 he was in London, where his witty, Surrealist creations met with much success. Thaarup made hats for the Duchess of York (later the Queen Mother) and for Marlene Dietrich and Vivien Leigh. He was an inventive designer, who caught the spirit of each decade with his charming, sometimes outré creations.

Timberland. Shoe/sportswear company. US. The Timberland brandname, created to market the first rugged waterproof boots, was launched in 1973 by Herman and Sidney Swartz, sons of Nathan Swartz (b. Russia), a shoe manufacturer who had taken over the Abington Shoe Company in Massachusetts in 1955. The first Timberland store opened in Newport, Rhode Island, in 1986.

Philip Treacy. 1967–. Milliner. UK. Born County Galway, Ireland. While a student of fashion and millinery at the Royal College of Art in London, Treacy worked for various British designers, including Rifat Ozbek and John Galliano. Treacy's degree show in 1990 brought him immediate financial backing and he opened his own house in the same year. His success was meteoric: initially invited to design hats for the collections of Lagerfeld at *Chanel and Bohan at Hartnell, by the late 1990s he was also supplying

Versace and Thierry Mugler, among others. In 1993 he began showing his own collections. Treacy is a master of technique. Though his hats are always bold, often oversize and sometimes idiosyncratic to the point of eccentricity – a two-foot-high sailing ship, for example – they always sit naturally on the head and display a perfect balance. He often works with feathers.

Patricia Underwood. 1947–. Milliner. US. Born Maidenhead, England; moved to the US in 1967. After an evening course in millinery at the Fashion Institute of Technology, Underwood founded her company in 1976. She is known for unadorned, handmade designs which rely for their effect on shape, colour and proportion. She has contributed to the collections of Blass, de la Renta, Karan, Mizrahi and others.

Mario Valentino. 1928–91. Shoe designer. Italy. Born Naples. Valentino started his shoemaking career around 1953 and became known both for his refinements to the court shoe – the chief woman's style of the period – and, though there is some dispute about this (see Vivier), for the introduction of the stiletto heel. In the 1960s he diversified into accessories and clothes.

Rose Valois. Dates unknown. Milliner. France. Valois founded her house in 1927, after an apprenticeship at *Reboux. Cubism and Surrealism were strong influences on her work. The house closed in 1970.

Sally Victor (b. Sally Josephs) 1905–77. Milliner. US. Born Scranton, Pennsylvania. After studying painting in Paris, Victor worked in the millinery department of Macy's and as head buyer in a New Jersey store. She then married Sergiv Victor, the head of Serge, a wholesale millinery company, and became its chief designer. Victor started her own millinery business in 1934, becoming one of the most respected milliners in the US. She introduced many innovative designs: a sailor hat, hats inspired by Chinese lanterns, and, in the 1940s, for working women, a denim hat with an adjustable snood.

François Villon. Dates unknown. Shoe designer. France. Villon worked with *Perugia before starting his own label in 1960. He achieved enormous success in the sixties, with a client list that included Princess Grace of Monaco, Maria Callas and Elizabeth Taylor. Among his best known styles are leather thigh boots, city cowboy boots and cut-out boots.

Roger Vivier. 1907–98. Shoe designer. France. Born Paris. Vivier enrolled as a student of sculpture at the Ecole des Beaux-Arts, but turned to shoemaking when various designs he had submitted to a shoe factory proved enormously successful. It was by working in factories that he learned his craft, eventually opening his own workshops in 1937 and designing shoes for some of the world's best-known manufacturers. In 1940 he moved to New York, where wartime shortages forced him to turn briefly to the craft of millinery (as half of the hatmaking partnership Suzanne and Roger). He returned to shoe design in 1945 and was back in Paris by 1947, at which time he was introduced to Christian Dior. In 1953 Dior took Vivier on as shoe designer and for the next ten years, until he set up his own business, Vivier designed all Dior's shoes. Vivier was one of shoemaking's great masters. His innovations were legion: the stiletto, comma and choc heels; the square-toed shoe, and the moon boot were among his many designs. Described as 'the Fabergé of footwear', he was also known for his jeweled and embroidered shoes, among them the gold kidskin sandals decorated with garnets which he created for the coronation of Queen Elizabeth II.

Louis Vuitton. Accessories/luxury goods company. France. Founded 1854 in Paris by Louis Vuitton (1821–92; Anchay, Jura). Initially the firm specialized in trunks: Vuitton designed the first ever flat-topped trunk (suitable for stacking) – made from poplar covered with waterproof grey Trianon varnished canvas. In 1896, in an attempt to prevent plagiarism, the founder's son Georges (1857–1936) devised the now internationally famous LV monogram design. It was not until 1958, however, that a process was discovered whereby the monogram canvas could be coated, a development which lay the groundwork for Louis Vuitton's entire range of soft bags. Louis Vuitton is the world's best known and most exclusive luggage maker. In 1985 the firm launched its Epi leather line – a range of bags and accessories in plain-coloured textured leather with a grain running through it.

Pietro Yantorny (Yanturni). 1890?–?. Shoemaker. France. Born Calabria, Italy. Yantorny was Curator of the Cluny Museum in Paris. He also worked as a shoemaker, creating exquisite shoes for a select group of clients (reputed to be no more than twenty). His shoes were constructed from pieces of antique materials and often took many years to complete. One of his most famous customers was the millionaire socialite Rita de Acosta Lydig, for whom he made shoes in medieval velvets and cloth of gold.

Sources for 20th-Century Fashion Accessories

The Bagot Collection, *Volume 1: Female Clothes and Accessories,* Stoke-on-Trent City Museum and Art Gallery, Stoke-on-Trent, 1983

Baudot, François, *A Century of Fashion,* London and New York, 1999

Baynes, Ken, and Kate Baynes, *The Shoe Show: British Shoes since 1790,* London, 1979

Becker, Vivienne, *Fabulous Fakes: The History of Fantasy and Fashion Jewellery,* London, 1988

Blum, Stella, *Everyday Fashions of the Twenties: As Pictured in Sears and Other Catalogues,* New York, 1981

Bradfield, Nancy, *Historical Costumes of England from the Eleventh to the Twentieth Century,* London, 1966

Bury, Shirley, *Jewellery,* London, 1972

Byrde, Penelope, *The Male Image: Men's Fashion in Britain 1300–1970,* London, 1979

Campione, Adele, *Women's Hats,* Milan, 1988

Chaille, François, *The Book of Ties,* Paris, 1994

Chenoune, Farid, *A History of Men's Fashion,* Paris, 1993

Cumming, Valerie, *Gloves,* London, 1982

—, *The Visual History of Costume Accessories,* London, 1998

Cunnington, C. Willett, *English Women's Clothing in the Present Century,* London, 1952

Daché, Lilly, *Talking Through My Hats,* London, 1946

De Courtais, Georgine, *Women's Headdress and Hairstyles in England from AD 600 to the Present Day,* London, 1973

De Greef, John, *L'Homme et la mode: Cravates et accessoires,* Paris, 1989

De Marly, Diana, *Fashion for Men: An Illustrated History,* London and New York, 1985

Doe, Tamasin, *Patrick Cox: Wit, Irony and Footwear,* London and New York, 1998

Double, W.C., *Design and Construction of Handbags,* London, 1960

Elestici, Letizia Bordignon, *Bags and Suitcases,* Milan, 1989

—, *Umbrellas,* Milan, 1990

Ewing, Elizabeth, *Fur in Dress,* London, 1981

Farrell, Jeremy, *Umbrellas and Parasols,* London, 1985

Ferragamo, Salvatore, *Shoemaker of Dreams,* London, 1957

Folledore, Giuliano, *Men's Hats,* Modena, 1989

Foster, Vanda, *Bags and Purses,* London, 1982

Gibbings, Sarah, *The Tie: Trends and Traditions,* London, 1990

Ginsburg, Madeleine, *The Hat: Trends and Traditions,* London, 1990

Girotti, Eugenia, *Footwear: Fifty Years History, 1945–1995,* Milan, 1995

Henzel, S. Sylvia, *Old Costume Jewellery: A Collector's Dream,* Des Moines, Iowa, 1978

Hinks, Peter, *Jewellery,* London, 1969

Howell, Georgina, *In Vogue: Six Decades of Fashion,* London, 1975

Kennett, Frances, *The Collector's Book of Twentieth Century Fashion,* London, 1983

Langbridge, R.H. (compiled and introduced by) *Edwardian Shopping: A Selection from The Army and Navy Stores Catalogues 1893–1913*, London, 1975

Leiber, Judith, *The Artful Handbag,* London and New York, 1995

McDowell, Colin, *Forties Fashion and The New Look,* London, 1997

—, *Shoes: Fashion and Fantasy,* London and New York, 1994

—, *Hats: Status, Style and Glamour,* London and New York, 1997

Mackrell, Alice, *Shawls, Stoles and Scarves,* London, 1986

Martin, Richard, and Harold Koda, *Jocks and Nerds: Men's Style in the Twentieth Century,* New York, 1989

Martin, Richard, *The St. James Fashion Encyclopedia,* Detroit, 1997

Mendes, Valerie, and Amy de la Haye, *20th Century Fashion,* London and New York, 1999

Mercié, Marie, *Voyages autour d'un chapeau,* Paris, 1990

O'Hara Callan, Georgina, *The Thames and Hudson Dictionary of Fashion and Fashion Designers,* London and New York, 1998

Probert, Christina, *Hats in Vogue since 1910,* London and New York, 1981

—, *Shoes in Vogue since 1910,* London and New York, 1981

Reilly, Maureen, and Mary Beth Detrich, *Women's Hats of the 20th Century: For Designers and Collectors, With a Price Guide,* Atglen, Penn., 1997

Richter, Madame Eve, *ABC of Millinery,* London, 1950

Robinson, Julian, *Fashion in the Thirties,* London, 1997

—, *Fashion in the Forties,* London, 1976

—, *The Fine Art of Fashion: An Illustrated History,* London, 1969

Smith, Desire, *Hats: With Values,* Atglen, Penn., 1996

Stevenson, Pauline, *Edwardian Fashion,* London, 1980

Swann, June, *Shoes,* London, 1982

Thaarup, Aage, *Heads and Tails,* London, 1956

Trasko, Mary, *Heavenly Soles,* New York, 1989

Wilcox, Claire, *Icons of Style in the 20th Century,* London, 1997

—, *A Century of Style: Bags,* London, 1998

Wilcox, R. Turner, *The Mode in Costume,* New York, 1942

—, *The Dictionary of Costume,* New York, 1969

—, *The Mode in Hats and Headdresses,* London and New York, 1959

Wilson, Eunice, *A History of Shoe Fashions,* New York, 1969

Worthington, Christa, *Chic Simple: Accessories,* London and New York, 1996

Yesterday's Headlines: The Hat Collection of Stoke-on-Trent City Museum and Art Gallery, Stoke-on-Trent, n.d.

Yusuf, Nilgin, *Georgina von Etzdorf: Sensuality, Art and Fabric,* London and New York, 1998